Alfred Buregeya
Kenyan English

Dialects of English

Editors
Joan C. Beal
Karen P. Corrigan
Bernd Kortmann

Volume 14

Alfred Buregeya
Kenyan English

DE GRUYTER
MOUTON

ISBN 978-1-5015-2572-8
e-ISBN (PDF) 978-1-61451-625-5
e-ISBN (EPUB) 978-1-5015-0097-8
ISSN 2164-7445

Library of Congress Control Number: 2019937539

Bibliographic information published by the Deutsche Nationalbibliothek
The Deutsche Nationalbibliothek lists this publication in the Deutsche Nationalbibliografie; detailed bibliographic data are available on the internet at http://dnb.dnb.de

© 2021 Walter de Gruyter, Inc., Boston/Berlin
This volume is text- and page-identical with the hardback published in 2019.
Typesetting: Integra Software Services Pvt. Ltd.
Printing and binding: CPI books GmbH, Leck
Cover image: CUHRIG/E+/getty images

www.degruyter.com

This book is dedicated to my daughter Lydia (especially for her assistance in adjusting the examples and tables used in it) and her siblings Clément, Modeste and Cassilde, and her mother Xavérine, all of whose love and support kept my morale high.

Preface

This book is published almost half a century after Hocking's (1974) highly prescriptive discussion of the grammatical "errors" in the English of East Africans in general and of Kenyans in particular. The present book is much wider in scope: it covers all the main areas of linguistic study, in addition to offering a historical and cultural background to this coverage. Moreover, and more importantly, it views Hocking's "really common errors", which, as stated in his own preface, are "made every day, by many people", as deep-rooted features of Kenyan English that need to be recognised as such.

The book is aimed first of all at the doubters (mostly from Kenya) of the existence of a language variety that can rightly be called Kenyan English. But it is also obviously aimed at the wide network of researchers on second language varieties, especially post-colonial ones, of English around the world. Since they are already "converted" and need not be "preached to", they will find a lot of detail in this book that is likely to inspire their own research.

Acknowledgements

My expression of gratitude first goes to the editors of the Dialects of English (DoE) series, namely Joan C. Beal, Karen P. Corrigan, and Bernd Kortmann, who, in October 2012, invited me to write a monograph on Kenyan English (KenE). It then goes to the publishers (De Gruyter Mouton) for offering me, in Feb. 2014, a contract to write it. It has been a most rewarding experience to contribute the first African English variety to the series.

I am also grateful to Martin Bygate, my former lecturer at the University of Reading (UK), who, in 1999, put me in touch with Anthea Fraser-Gupta (University of Leeds, UK), who in turn introduced me to the network of linguists researching KenE at a time when I quite naively thought I was the first person to be researching it.

From this network I am most grateful to Paul Skandera: not only did he, in those early days, make available to me a great deal of the existing literature on KenE, the most valuable of which being his own book on idiom in KenE, but also he later created an opportunity for me to join the wider world of writing about varieties of English around the world. From this wider world I received valuable support from Edgar Schneider (a former editor of *English World-Wide*), Thomas Hoffmann (with whom I wrote the proposal of this book at its project stage) and, notably, from Bernd Kortmann. In his capacity as my corresponding editor (for De Gruyter Mouton's DoE series), he meticulously went through the draft and revised versions of each chapter of this book to check every detail. His comments and corrections (and those he relayed to me from his two co-editors) are an immense contribution to the quality of this book. I am deeply indebted to Bernd. May he and his colleagues at the Freiburg Institute for Advanced Studies (FRIAS), who hosted me during the summer of 2018 for the final stage of the writing of the book, find in its publication the fruits of their own priceless contribution.

My deep gratitude further goes to James Rumford, my former teacher of English at the National University of Rwanda from 1978 to 1981, who has always kept faith in me, and who served as my main informant on the lexical and semantic aspects that KenE might have borrowed from American English.

Many thanks are due to three colleagues of mine: Joshua Itumo (Kenyatta University), Zipporah Otiso (University of Nairobi), and Jane Oduor (University of Nairobi). Joshua offered me invaluable assistance in recording sample KenE speech and analyzing it acoustically. Zipporah served as a key informant on all aspects of the book and read several of its draft chapters for very useful comments. Jane contributed a great deal to the chapter on the history of English in Kenya, which she co-authored.

The valuable input of the following informants needs to be acknowledged as well: Mohammed Akidah, Ngulamu Mwaviro, Everlyine Ongaga, Eunice Arungo, Purity Njimu, Dianah Nyabuto, Judith Mbwika, Kamau Ndoria, and Innocent Michael.

I am also grateful to Claudius Kihara, David Barasa, Patrick Kiliku, and Atichi Alati for their support in providing me with useful literature on KenE.

Finally, my family's contribution towards the successful completion of this book can only be acknowledged through the book being dedicated to them.

Contents

Preface —— VII

Acknowledgements —— IX

1 A brief history of English in multilingual Kenya —— 1
    1.1   The pre-independence period —— 1
    1.2   The post-independence period —— 5

2 Geography, demography, and cultural factors —— 11
    2.1   Geography —— 11
    2.2   Demography —— 13
    2.3   Cultural factors —— 16

3 Phonetics and phonology —— 29
    3.1   Vowel-related pronunciations in KenE —— 31
    3.2   Consonant-related pronunciations —— 40
    3.3   The pronunciation of miscellaneous words —— 46
    3.4   Word stress in KenE —— 46
    3.5   Aspects of connected speech —— 52
    3.6   Conclusion —— 60

4 Morphology and syntax —— 63
    4.1   Lack of number agreement —— 64
    4.2   Addition of inflections to and omission of them from words —— 67
    4.3   Aspects of the noun phrase —— 70
    4.4   Aspects of the verb phrase —— 81
    4.5   Aspects of the prepositional phrase —— 105
    4.6   *(As) compared to* used for *than* as the second element of the comparative —— 111
    4.7   Non-use of subject-auxiliary inversion in questions —— 113
    4.8   Use of resumptive pronouns —— 115
    4.9   Non-use of the relative determiner *whose* —— 115
    4.10   The pronoun (subj.) + pronoun (obj.) sequence used in subject position —— 117
    4.11   The plural pronoun *we* used instead of the singular *I* —— 119

- 4.12 *Isn't it* used as an invariant question tag —— **119**
- 4.13 *No/not/none ... nor* used instead of *no/not/none ... or* —— **120**
- 4.14 Non-use of *It is I who am* and *It is you who are* —— **121**
- 4.15 *Those ones* used instead of *those, these, they*, etc —— **122**
- 4.16 Miscellaneous structures —— **124**
- 4.17 Features which KenE shares with AmE rather than with BrE —— **128**
- 4.18 Parallels between KenE and other African L2 varieties of English —— **130**
- 4.19 Summary and conclusion —— **131**

5 Lexis and semantics —— 139
- 5.1 Loan expressions from indigenous languages of Kenya —— **139**
- 5.2 Coinages of Kenya English —— **149**
- 5.3 Additional meanings in Kenyan English —— **159**
- 5.4 To what extent do the various KenE lexical features coexist with their StdIntE variants? —— **168**
- 5.5 Formal vs. informal KenE vocabulary —— **171**
- 5.6 The influence of other varieties of English on KenE vocabulary —— **172**
- 5.7 Conclusion: the most visible features are *not* the most characteristic of KenE —— **176**

6 Discourse features —— 179
- 6.1 Anaphora phenomena —— **179**
- 6.2 Cultural appropriateness phenomena —— **185**
- 6.3 A rhetorical-force device: code-mixing Swahili words into English —— **199**
- 6.4 Written-English features in spoken KenE: contracted vs non-contracted forms —— **202**
- 6.5 Conclusion —— **207**

7 Survey of previous work and annotated bibliography —— 209
- 7.1 General overviews —— **209**
- 7.2 History of the development of language policy in Kenya and of KenE —— **212**
- 7.3 Geography and demography —— **215**
- 7.4 Phonetics and phonology —— **215**

7.5	Morphology and syntax —— **217**	
7.6	Lexis and semantics —— **222**	
7.7	Discourse features —— **224**	
7.8	Survey of previous work —— **225**	

8 Sample texts —— 227

8.1 An email (on 4 May 2018) from the Chairman of the CHUNA Board, University of Nairobi (ca. 735 words) —— **227**

8.2 An email (on 8 Aug 2018) from the CEO of CHUNA, University of Nairobi (ca. 140 words) —— **229**

8.3 From draft "Regulations and Syllabus for Master of Medicine in Urology", a University-of-Nairobi syllabus presented in Oct 2013 (ca. 150 words) —— **230**

8.4 From an article, by W.T. & M.M., on an election petition, in *The Standard* (25 Mar 2013, p. 1 & p. 4) (148 words) —— **231**

8.5 From "State to review public varsity fees", an article by A.O. in *The Standard* (12 Jun 2013, p. 7) (161 words) —— **231**

8.6 From "Fund Status Report as at 30th October 2009", a notice from the youth enterprise fund in *The Standard* (18 Nov 2009, p. 44) (ca. 150 words) —— **232**

8.7 From "Setting the record straight on school heads", an article by J.K. in *The Standard* (24 Apr 2015, p. 13) (222 words) —— **233**

8.8 From an advertised pre-publication blurb of a book called *Handbook for data analysis using SPSS*, by O.M.J. (2002) (164 words) —— **234**

8.9 From "Knut to call nationwide strike from September 1", an article by E.M. in the *Sunday Nation* (5 Aug 2018, p. 2) (170 words) —— **235**

8.10 From a questionnaire by a University-of-Nairobi MA student, W.W.B. (Apr 2001) (87 words) —— **235**

8.11 From a questionnaire by a University-of-Nairobi MA student, T.B. (May 2012) (80 words) —— **236**

8.12 From Daniel Nyaga's (1997) book *Customs and traditions of THE MERU* (304 words) —— **236**

8.13 From Meja Mwangi's (1974) novel *Carcase for hounds* (223 words) —— **237**

8.14 From Ngugi wa Thiong'o's (1982) novel *Devil on the cross* (353 words) —— **238**
8.15 Picture of the name of a furniture-selling shop on Koinange Street, Nairobi —— **239**
8.16 The audio samples —— **240**

9 Conclusion —— 241

References —— 245

Index —— 253

1 A brief history of English in multilingual Kenya

Good historical accounts of English in Kenya are already available, e.g. in Gorman (1974), Mazrui and Mazrui (1996), Skandera (2003: 8–15), Schmied (2004a), Schneider (2007: 189–197), Higgins (2009: 21–28), and Hoffmann (2010). Schneider's (2007) and Hoffmann's (2010) articles offer accounts which are structured similarly, and very clearly, along the lines of the Dynamic Model of how new Englishes have evolved, a model associated with Edgar W. Schneider and first propounded in Schneider (2003). In both Schneider (2007) and Hoffmann (2010), English in Kenya is said to have gone through a first phase, also referred to as the "foundation" phase (from the 1860s to 1920), during which Kenya had its first, and quite limited, contact with English; then through a second phase, referred to as the "exonormative stabilization" phase (from 1920 to the late 1940s), during which English was more widely spoken in Kenya by a "stable" community of British settlers, whose "written and spoken English as used by educated speakers" had to be, as an external norm, the "accepted [...] linguistic standard of reference" (Schneider 2003: 245); and, finally, through a third phase, referred to as the "nativization" phase, "the central phase of both cultural and linguistic transformation", one which, in the case of Kenya, has gone on from the late 1940s to the present, according to the two authors. Since it is beyond the scope of this chapter (and the whole book at large) to be an argument for or against the Dynamic Model, it will take into account the historical events that have shaped Kenyan English through the three phases, but refer to them in purely historical terms of "pre-independence" and "post-independence" periods.

1.1 The pre-independence period

Roughly, this is a period during which there was no enthusiasm from the British occupiers and colonizers for promoting English. This period can be divided into three sub-periods: 1) before Kenya's status as an official British colony, 2) from the official-colony status to just after World War II, and 3) between after World War II and Kenya's independence.

Note: This chapter was co-authored with Jane Akinyi Ngala Oduor.

https://doi.org/10.1515/9781614516255-001

1.1.1 Before Kenya's status as an official British colony

This sub-period runs from the time of the first contact of Kenya with English to 1920, when Kenya's status changed from that of East African Protectorate to that of official colony. It is a period during which Kenya came into contact with English, but limited contact. Schmied (2004a: 919) notes that "English came late to East Africa". All the historical accounts cited above mention the second half of the 19th century as the first real contact of Kenya with the English language. According to one account, "[u]ntil the end of the 19th century [...] British interest in eastern Africa was largely limited to trade and, since the 1850s, to the expeditions of such British explorers as Richard Burton, David Livingstone, and John Speke" (Skandera 2003: 10). We are also reminded by Higgins (2009: 24) that "[t]he Germans were the first Europeans to occupy East Africa in the form of a protectorate over the Sultan of Zanzibar's coastal possessions in 1885", while "[t]he British occupied Kenya from the late 19th century, transforming Kenya from a protectorate to a British Crown colony in 1920".[1]

Going by Schneider's (2007) account, it should be pointed out that well before the few years before the end of the 19th century, some amount of English had already been disseminated, even away from the coastal area, mainly by missionaries. Schneider (2007: 189) writes:

> In the nineteenth century, contact with English in the interior grew but slowly. The impact of explorers was restricted and not lasting. Missionaries brought English with them, and started teaching and spreading it systematically. However, they also, and in many cases primarily, used indigenous languages, chiefly Kiswahili, already an established lingua franca, for evangelization. In some cases soldiers, like the King's African Rifles, also disseminated English [...].

Schneider adds that "[...] for a long time, education was left to the missions, as the State did not want to spend money on it and the settlers were primarily interested in their profits" (2007: 189).

---

[1] Hoffmann (2010: 288) gives useful, specific information: "In 1895, when the IBEAC [the Imperial British East Africa Company, which, in 1888, replaced a commercial venture called the British East African Association] ran into problems, the British Government officially took over East Africa, which from then was known as the East African Protectorate".

1.1.2 From 1920 to just after World War II

This sub-period witnessed an influx of British settlers in Kenya, which increased the number of English speakers. Paradoxically, this greater number did not mean a greater dissemination of the English language beyond the settler community. This is what Schneider (2007: 191) says about this period: "British settlers kept immigrating in substantial numbers, and English became firmly established as the language of administration, business, law, and other higher domains in society". Since the colonial rulers needed the assistance of some locals, they "trained a small indigenous elite as administrators but essentially were not interested in disseminating the English language" (2007: 191). They were not because "[t]he settlers in particular are reported to have resisted the spread of English to Africans on a larger scale, deliberately using kiSettla, a reduced form of Kiswahili, instead. Many of them were aware that knowledge of the dominant language means access to power, and that they did not want to share" (191). Mazrui and Mazrui (1996: 272) use strong terms to refer to this apparently paradoxical situation: "In Kenya, the presence of a strong British settler community was initially a curse rather than a blessing to the spread of English".

But it was not just the colonial administration and the settler community at large that were not keen on disseminating English. "Even the three British mission societies [...] did not use English in their evangelization" (Schmied 2004a: 920). The author explains how this preference for Kiswahili and indigenous languages over English fitted into a broader language policy: "It is important to remember that colonial language policies did not favour English [...] wholesale, but established a 'trifocal' or trilingual system with (a) English as the elite and international language, (b) the regional lingua franca [i.e. Kiswahili in the case of East Africa, for 'intraterritorial' communication] and (c) the 'tribal' languages or 'vernaculars' for local communication" (2004a: 921).[2]

1.1.3 Between after World War II and Kenya's independence

As Hoffmann (2010: 290) puts it, "[a]fter the Second World War, the British Empire started to fall apart" after "[t]he role-model India became independent

---

[2] It is worth specifying in this chapter (and elsewhere in the book, where applicable) that the phrase *vernacular languages of Kenya* does not cover Swahili (despite it being a native language of Kenya), but all the other languages of the various ethnic groups of Kenya, including those of Asian origin like Gujarati, Hindi, and Punjabi.

[in 1947], and shortly afterwards the Africans started demanding political rights as well". In the particular case of Kenya this demand for political rights was most forcefully (and forcibly) expressed by the Mau Mau movement (composed mainly of people from the Kikuyu tribe) whose uprising, from 1952 to 1959, was about claiming back their land that had been taken by the white settlers.

Away from fighting for land, although still within the same broader context of, on the one hand, fighting for and, on the other hand, granting rights, the 1945–1963[3] sub-period is one during which, in Kenya, the interests of both the colonial administration and the African nationalists converged, to the extent that both parties wanted more English for the indigenous populations. Schneider (2007: 192) offers an explanation for this:

> The stable colonial status, with its clear separation of [settler] and [indigenous] strands, was concluded by the aftermath of World War II. Africans returning from the war demanded political rights, including language education [...]. The British were reasonable enough to understand that independence of their African colonies would come before too long. In a sharp turn of their policy, their goal now was to "modernize" these countries and prepare them for independence (amongst other things by teaching English on a broader scale) [...].

What was the "educational language policy and practice", to use Gorman's (1974) terms, is summarized in the following statement:

> In summarizing the state of the existing school system [,] the 1948 report [[4]] observed that in the past the language of instruction in sub-elementary schools was the vernacular, "but from standard 3 onwards Swahili is taught as the *lingua franca* of the Colony and has been the medium of instruction in junior secondary schools, although it is being rapidly replaced by English". (Gorman 1974: 428)

Although it transpires that already before the war the Beecher committee had, according to Gorman (1974: 427), recommended that "English should take the place of Swahili as the colony's lingua franca in as short a time as practicable" (while at the same time recommending that "more emphasis should be placed on the teaching of the vernacular languages"), it was not until after the war, in 1948, that the Advisory Council on African Education in Kenya "recommended the adoption of the report" (1974: 427). And it was only in

---

3 This is a period acknowledged by Gorman (1974: 427), who devotes a section to it under the heading "Educational language policy and practice, 1945–63".

4 This is the report "on the Teaching of Languages in African Schools which had been drawn up by a committee appointed in December 1942 under the chairmanship of the Venerable Archdeacon L. J. Beecher", a report discussed "after the war" by "the newly appointed local Advisory Council on African Education in Kenya" (Gorman 1974: 427).

1950 that the "*Proposals for the Implementation of the Recommendations of the Report on African Education in Kenya* [were] published as Sessional Paper No. 1 of 1950", during the debate on which "it was affirmed that the 'language policy in the schools is that English shall be adopted as soon as possible in the post-primary classes'" (1974: 430).

The suggestion that African nationalists wanted more English after the war can be illustrated by the position of one of them, Mr Ohanga, who sat on the Legislative Council that discussed the proposals mentioned above, and who is reported to have "stated in [the] debate [that took place in August 1950] that 'I should like to say that for a long time very many of us have pressed that the teaching of English should be at an early stage and the ... general policy of the country has not always been sympathetic to this view ... '" (Gorman 1974: 430). Gorman further reports that "[i]n the early 1950s the trend for English to be used as a medium of instruction in the primary schools in urban and rural areas increased, although it was admitted in the Education Department Report for 1952 that 'possibly the transition was premature in the more backward areas'" (1974: 431). And the author further notes that "[i]n 1953 English became the compulsory medium in the examination held at the end of the eighth year of primary education" and goes on to comment that "[t]his was of course a most significant development" (1974: 432). The significance of this lay in the fact that English, which until then had not even been the language of junior secondary schools, had so quickly become the language of even primary school, albeit the very end of it.

We are further informed by Gorman (1974: 435) that "[in 1958] many schools did in fact begin the teaching of English in the second year [of primary school] though the majority began it in the subsequent year; and in most schools it became the medium of instruction in the sixth year". Three years later, that is "[i]n 1961, the course [that had been decided upon in 1957 as a pilot course using English as the medium of education for Asian children in Nairobi] was adopted for general use in the schools and in the following year [i.e. 1962] all first year classes in Nairobi made the changeover" (Gorman 1974: 437). And "[t]he use of English as a medium of instruction continued to spread [...]" so quickly that "[t]he number of English medium classes in African primary schools rose from 14 in 1962 to 290 in 1963" (1974: 437).

1.2 The post-independence period

This is a period of language policies and constitutional amendments initiated by a government of Kenya composed of the local élite. To use Gorman's (1974) words, this is a period of "policy decisions made or accepted by the Government of Kenya since the attainment of independence in December 1963" (1974: 438). In the present book, it will be divided into three sub-periods: from 1964 to 1974, from 1974 to 2010, and from 2010 onwards.

1.2.1 From 1964 to 1974

This is a decade dominated by the effects of the strengthened status of English in the wake of the Ominde Commission's Report of December 1964[5] and the revision of the Constitution of Kenya in 1969. But, at the same time, it is also a period of strong lobbying for a greater role for Swahili and of the diminishing role of local vernaculars in education.

The Ominde Commission's findings were much heeded because, among other things, and as Gorman (1974: 441) puts it, "[i]n its membership and aims, [the commission] constituted 'an attempt to ascertain as accurately as possible the views of the people of Kenya as a whole'" and "the commission reported that 'the great majority of witnesses wished to see the universal use of English language as the medium of instruction from Primary [1]'", a view with which the Commission itself agreed.

For its part, the revision of the Constitution of Kenya in 1969 is quite relevant here because it made English the language of parliament in two major respects: on the one hand, "[...] clause 55 [...] states that 'the business of the National assembly shall be conducted in English,'" and, on the other hand, "Clause 40(1) (b) [...] provides that a person shall not be qualified for election to the House of Representatives 'unless he is able to speak and [...] to read the English language well enough to be able to take an active part in the proceedings of the National assembly'" (Gorman 1974: 438).

Regarding the advocacy of a greater role for Swahili, despite their views unequivocally strengthening the English language, the respondents to the Ominde Commission's survey are reported to have, at the same time, recommended more use for Swahili: "[The commission's report] stated that 'those giving evidence

---

[5] As Gorman (1974: 440–441) tells us, "[a]fter Kenya became an independent state, the Minister for Education appointed a commission under the chairmanship of Professor S. H. Ominde of University College, Nairobi, [...] to advise the government in the formulation and implementation of national policies for education" (1974: 440). The commission was to be known as the "Kenya Education Commission". "The first part of [its] report was submitted [...] in December 1964, and [its] recommendations established the guidelines for [...] language use in education".

were virtually unanimous in recommending a general spread of this language'" (Gorman 1974: 442). But the greatest advocate of an increased role for Swahili at the time seems to be the president of Kenya himself, Jomo Kenyatta: "On more than one occasion in Parliament, President Kenyatta, speaking in Swahili, has referred to the desirability of using Swahili in the House of Representatives" (Gorman 1974: 438). The president had the support of his ruling party, KANU (the Kenya African National Union), as the following statements suggest: "In August 1969, formal recognition of Swahili as the national language was given by the National Governing Council of KANU and in April 1970 detailed plans relating to an increasing use of Swahili were announced by the Acting Secretary General of the party"; later "[the Acting Secretary General of KANU] reiterated the party's decision to make Swahili the national language by 1974 on two further occasions in April 1970" (Gorman 1974: 446).

As for the vernaculars, which until independence had enjoyed the quasi-monopoly of being used as the media of instruction in early primary school, not everyone that gave evidence to the Ominde Commission supported them on this role anymore: "On the matter of use of vernacular languages in education, evidence was divided. [...] [I]t is of interest also that for the first time, the use of the vernacular languages in education was called into question by an advisory body not only on educational grounds but also in relation to the issue of national unity and integration" (Gorman 1974: 442).

In summary, during the first decade after independence, English became stronger than ever before, while Swahili, which had been weakened a decade earlier mainly through the influence of the Beecher Committee's recommendations, was given a new lease of life, as it were. And in this language policy realignment, the vernacular languages became the losers. All in all, and to borrow Gorman's (1974) own conclusion, "[a]t present [i.e. in the early 1970s] the educational role of Swahili as a subject of instruction is being emphasized and that of English as a medium of instruction maintained, while less emphasis is being laid than was previously the case on the educational roles of the vernacular languages" (1974: 447).

1.2.2 From 1974 to 2010

This sub-period corresponds to almost four decades of "fluctuating" fortunes for Swahili as a serious rival to English, and of the somewhat "reinstated" role of vernaculars in education in early primary school.

The first good fortune for Swahili during this period first came in 1974. Mazrui and Mazrui (1996: 293) put it this way: "After some ten years of recurrent debate, in and outside parliament, however, the nationalist position prevailed. In 1974, Kiswahili was declared the national language and, for the first time, English had to share the parliamentary forum with a local language". Skandera (2003: 14) gives further details: "[...] the constitution of [Kenya] 1963 stated competence in English as the only language requirement for election into parliament, and it specified English as the sole parliamentary language. [...] In 1974, an amendment to the constitution replaced English with Swahili as the sole language of parliament, and Swahili, by decree, was declared the national language".

However, just one year later, Swahili saw this sole-language-status in parliament reduced. Skandera (2003: 14) informs us that "[i]n 1975, another amendment to the constitution repealed the previous one, and instead required that Swahili be merely the language of debate in parliament whereas all legislation be written and all discussion thereof be quoted in English". Five years later, English was officially made Swahili's competitor in parliamentary debate. Skandera (2003) goes on to say: "And in 1979, barely one year after succeeding Kenyatta as president, Daniel arap Moi reintroduced English, by a third constitutional amendment, as a language of parliamentary debate along with Swahili [...]" (2003: 14). However, at the same time, the new president enhanced the role of Swahili, still regarding parliamentary matters: "[...] he added competence in Swahili to the qualifications for parliamentarians besides competence in English" (2003: 14–15). That was the second good fortune for Swahili after 1974.

The third one was to come a decade later, but this time concerning educational, not parliamentary matters: in 1984, Swahili was made a compulsory and examinable subject in both primary and secondary school (until then it was examinable, though not compulsory, only in secondary school), thus implementing, "with the advent of the 8-4-4 system of education" (Oduor 2010: 90), a recommendation first made by the Gachathi Commission's Report of 1976, and later taken up by the Mackay Commission's Report of 1981[6] (Oduor 2010: 90–91).

---

[6] It is the Mackay Commission that recommended the 8-4-4 system of education (i.e. 8 years of primary school, 4 of secondary school, and 4 of undergraduate university studies). In January 2016, the current government launched, at a "National Conference on Curriculum Reform", the process of replacing the 8-4-4 system with a new one of 2-6-3-3-3 (i.e. 2 years of pre-primary school, 6 of primary school, 3 of junior secondary school, 3 of senior secondary school, and 3 of undergraduate university studies). The new system is based on the recommendations of a 2012 report by a taskforce chaired by Prof. Douglas Odhiambo.

There was no other change in the relative statuses of English, on the one hand, and of Swahili and the other indigenous languages of Kenya, on the other, until the new constitution of Kenya enacted in August 2010. Until this date, English remained the only official language of Kenya and, with specific reference to language educational policy, it remained the language of instruction from class 4 of primary school in non-cosmopolitan areas, with the "catchment-area" languages (mainly the local vernaculars) being used for instruction up to class 3; in cosmopolitan areas, English was, and still is, used for instruction from even nursery school.

1.2.3 In the wake of the 2010 Constitution and of the analogue-to-digital broadcasting migration

This is a period during which English is still the most prestigious language in Kenya, but is at the same time facing a clearly greater competition than before, not only from Swahili, but also from the local vernaculars, following the digital migration and local-content policy and the creation of counties. Details of these potentially game-changing factors are given in Chapter 2, under the section on "cultural factors".

2 Geography, demography, and cultural factors

This chapter will first situate Kenya in Africa, describe its landscape, and offer a brief overview of its economic geography. It will then provide a short description of the country's overall population and of the breakdown of the latter into its ethnic groups, its religious composition, its age groups, and its school attendance ratios. But the bulk of the chapter will be devoted to the cultural factors that are reflected in a variety of phenomena that bring to light the relative dominance of the English language in the multilingual setting of Kenya.

2.1 Geography

Most of what will be written in this chapter regarding geography and demography was taken from the various publications by the Kenya National Bureau of Statistics (hereafter KNBS, for the purposes of referencing) related to the 2009 Kenya Population and Housing Census.

Kenya is an East African country that straddles the Equator: it lies between 4 degrees of latitude south and 4 degrees of latitude north. As for its longitude location, it lies between 34 and 41 degrees east. It is bordered by Uganda to the west, by South Sudan to its north-western tip, by Ethiopia to the north, by Somalia to the east, by the Indian Ocean to the south-east, and by Tanzania to the south. According to the KNBS (2012: 10) Kenya "covers an area of approximately 582,000 km^2".[1]

Kenya is a country of plains in its eastern part, all the way from its border with Ethiopia, along its long border with Somalia and a 536 km-long coastline on the Indian Ocean, to its border with Tanzania. The northern part of this long eastern stretch is commonly referred to as arid and semi-arid lands, and so is its northern strip along the country's border with Ethiopia, South Sudan, and Uganda. In fact, more or less half-way in this northern strip, on the eastern shore of Lake Turkana, lies an area called the Chalbi desert (but called "desert" more on maps than in reality by the general public).

---

[1] The term "*approximately*" is quite appropriate here to capture the different and potentially confusing figures given for Kenya's area. For example, two encyclopaedic dictionaries give differing figures: the *Collins English Dictionary*, 10th edn. (2009) gives 582,647 sq km (i.e. 224,960 sq miles), while the French dictionary le *Petit Larousse Illustré* (2017) rounds it up to 583,000 sq km. Several Internet sources (through Google Search) give other, and differing, figures as well.

As one moves from the country's eastern area (from the southern to the northern end of the latter) into its interior, the altitude gradually rises: for example, from Mombasa, the second largest city of Kenya and its main port town in the south-east on the Indian Ocean, the altitude rises from sea-level (just at 50 metres in Mombasa) to around 1,650 metres (5,500 feet) in Nairobi, the capital city, situated in the south-centre-west of the country, at a driving distance of a little under 500 km from Mombasa. (For example, the country's standard gauge railway line, inaugurated on 31 May 2017, is 472 km long from Mombasa to Nairobi.) However, the highest peak in Kenya, Mount Kenya, at 5,199 metres, is not situated further west, but at 138 kilometres (85.76 miles) to the north-east of Nairobi. Indeed, the (East African) Rift Valley, to the west of Nairobi, breaks the rise in altitude. The KNBS (2012: 14) states that "The Kenya [h]ighlands are found to the east and west of the Great Rift Valley. [...] The [h]ighlands to the east of the Rift Valley [vary] between altitudes 1,500 metres [and] 5,199 metres [...] The highlands to the west of the Rift Valley lie between altitude[s] 1800 [and] 2750 metres [...]". It adds that "the Rift Valley of Africa [,] which cuts Kenya from Lake Turkana [in] the north to [the] Tanzania [b]order [in] the south [at Lake Natron]", can reach an altitude of as low as "1,000 metres" in its eastern part (2012: 14). An altitude map of Kenya will show that the highlands of Kenya are concentrated in the west-centre of the country.

Kenya has very many tourist attractions, not only along its coastal line, but also in all other parts of the country. For example, along its long southern border with Tanzania can be found two of its famous game-park reserves, the Amboseli National Park and the Maasai Mara National Reserve. There are many other national parks in the country's eastern region (starting with the Tsavo National Park in the south), especially in its eastern-central part, to the east of Mount Kenya. The Rift Valley plains and valleys are another huge tourist attraction, not only because of the volcanic mountains that surround them, but also of the eight lakes along their path, from Lake Turkana (the biggest of them) on the Ethiopian border to Lake Natron (albeit just the northern tip of it) on the Tanzanian border, through Lakes Baringo, Bogoria, Nakuru, Elementaita, Naivasha, and Magadi. Tourist attractions in the western part of the country include Mount Elgon (about 4,300 metres in the Mount Elgon National Park), which straddles the border between Kenya and Uganda in the centre-west of Kenya, the Kakamega Forest to the south, and, further south, Lake Victoria (shared by Kenya, Uganda, and Tanzania). On the shores of its arm that goes deep into Kenya lies the city of Kisumu, the third largest town in the country.

Kenya is largely an agricultural and livestock farming country. The KNBS (2012: 10) points out that "Agriculture (including coffee and tea cultivation) is the main source of revenue for 70.0 per cent of the population". It adds that

"Major cash crops are tea, coffee, pyrethrum, wheat and maize". Both cash crops and other foodstuffs are mainly produced in the highlands on both sides of the Rift Valley. Livestock farming is practised mostly on the Rift Valley plains and in the semi-arid and arid lands of eastern and north-eastern Kenya, and the entire northern stretch of the country. But Kenya is also "one of the most industrially developed countries in East Africa and its manufacturing sector accounts for 14.0 per cent of the Gross Domestic Product" (KNBS 2012: 10). In fact, it is the most industrialized of the (now) six East African Community member countries (Kenya, Tanzania, Uganda, Rwanda, Burundi, and its newest member, South Sudan), which makes it "[the] regional hub for trade and finance in East Africa" (KNBS 2012: 10).

With regard to administrative units, at the time of the 2009 census Kenya was divided into 8 provinces and 158 districts. But in August 2010 a new constitution was enacted which scrapped the 8 provinces and replaced them with 47 counties as the "focal point for development" (KNBS, 2012a: 20). Figure 2.1 is the county map taken from the KNBS (2012a: 13).

2.2 Demography

The last population census in Kenya was conducted in the last week of August 2009. It produced a total of 38,610,097 people, of whom 19,417,639 (i.e. 50.3%) were female and 19,192,458 (i.e. 49.7%) were male. 67.7% of the entire 38.6-million population was rural, against 32.3% urban. (See Kenya National Bureau of Statistics [2012], *The 2009 Kenya Population and Census Highlights*). Nairobi, the capital city, had a population of 3,181,369. According to the KNBS (2012: 60), in its "Analytical report on population dynamics", "[...] Kenya's population by 2015 [was] expected to be 44.2 million [...] [and] 50.3 million by 2020 [...]". These projections were based on "[a] natural [population] growth rate [of] 3.0 percent per annum" (2012: xv). In line with these projections, at the time of writing this chapter (in 2017), Kenya's population should be somewhere between 47 and 48 million.[2]

A detailed breakdown of the 38.6-million population of Kenya by tribe (and ethnic) affiliation is given in Table 13 on pp. 397–398 of the KNBS (2010a). While it is generally said and accepted that there are 42 tribes in Kenya, it is not

---

[2] Note, however, that in his speech commemorating the 54th Madaraka Day ('Self-Rule' Day) on 1 June 2017, Kenya's president, Uhuru Kenyatta, mentioned the figure of 45 million as the country's population.

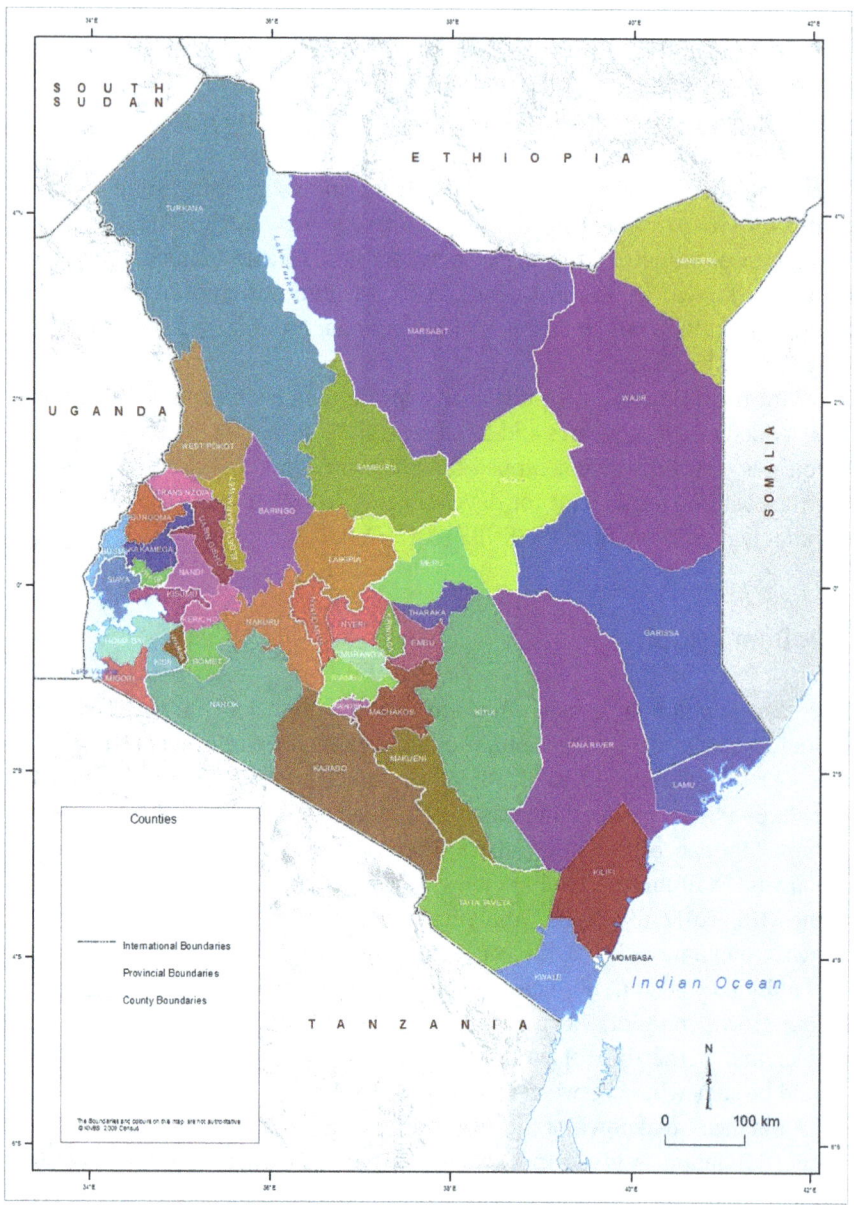

Figure 2.1: Map of the counties of Kenya (taken from the KNBS 2012a: 13).

easy to tell what exactly those are, especially the small ones.[3] The six largest tribes, those that number at least 5%, are the following – with their percentages of August 2009: Kikuyu: 17.15%; Luhya (which covers 17 ethnic groups): 13.83%; Kalenjin (which covers 19 ethnic groups): 12.86%; Luo: 10.48%; Kamba: 10.08%; Somali (which covers 6 ethnic groups): 6.17%. Put together, the non-African Kenyans, referred to as "Kenyan Arabs [40,760]", "Kenyan Asians [46,782]", "Kenyan Europeans [5,166]", and "Kenyan Americans [2,422]" (2010a: 398), represent 0.25%. (The different percentages given in this paragraph were computed by the present author; they are not indicated in the original source.)

While the statement that there are 42 tribes in Kenya is hardly disputed, and while it is also likely to be generally accepted that to each tribe of Kenya corresponds a different language, there is likely to be much controversy in limiting the number of languages in the country to just 42 or thereabouts. The controversy will arise from the expected difficulty in deciding whether certain ethnic groups that have been, primarily for political reasons, assigned to one tribe, do indeed speak different dialects of the same language or different autonomous languages instead. This difficulty applies most acutely to the 17 ethnic groups subsumed under a single Luhya tribe in the KNBS (2010a: 397). The specific question that arises is whether the 17 linguistic varieties spoken by the 17 ethnic groups are only dialects of the "Luhya language" or are autonomous languages in their own right. The answer to this question is beyond the scope of this book, bearing in mind the difficulty, described by sociolinguists (see e.g. Trudgill 2000: 4), in distinguishing between the notions of language and dialect. Because of this difficulty, some authors will avoid giving any precise figure at all about the number of languages of Kenya (see e.g. Whiteley 1974: 13–68), while some others are likely to simply mention 42, and others likely to give a much higher figure (see e.g. Ethnologue,[4] which talks of 67 "living" languages, of which "60 are indigenous and 7 are non-indigenous"). What is less controversial, though, is that the indigenous languages of Kenya belong to three language families[5]: Bantu, Nilotic, and Cushitic – in descending order of numerical importance. In addition to these

---

3 The Makonde of Kenya were officially recognized as the 43rd tribe of Kenya after they were granted Kenyan citizenship in December 2016. They number only about 5,000. They are descendants of the Makonde of northern Mozambique, "[...] who were recruited by the British during the colonial period to work in sisal farms and sugar plantations across Kenya's coastal province in Kwale, Kilifi and Taita Taveta", according to the United Nations High Commissioner for Refugees (UNHCR); see: http://www.unhcr.org/ke/wp-content/uploads/sites/2/2016/05/The-Makonde-of-Kenya-The-Struggle-To-Belong1.pdf, accessed: 11 June 2017.
4 At: https://www.ethnologue.com/country/KE.
5 An early (and most likely now outdated) different classification is that by Whiteley (1974: 13) who talks of "four major groups", by splitting the Nilotic group into "Nilotic" and "Para-Nilotic".

are Asian languages, from the Indian sub-continent, and, of course, the English language, which is already the first language of a sizable minority of Kenyans, among whom a number of African Kenyans, mostly from the affluent neighbourhoods of Nairobi.

In terms of the population distribution by age group, some interesting figures given in the KNBS (2012: xii) "Analytical report on population dynamics" are the following: children under 15 years: 42.9%; young people between 15–24: 20.6%; young people between 25–34: 14.8%; elderly people (60+): 5%. Concerning the figures for the "population, 3 years and above, attending school" at the time of the census (end of August 2009), they are given in the following table.

Table 2.1: Population aged 3 years and above attending school in Kenya in 2009.

	Pre-Primary	Primary	Secondary	University
Male	1,150,890	4,838,278	962,887	115,094
Female	1,096,181	4,587,112	833,580	83,025
Total	2,247,071	9,425,390	1,796,467	198,119
%	5.82	24.41	4.65	0.51

(Adapted, by adding the % row, from the KNBS 2010b, the *2009 Kenya Population and Housing Highlights*)

Regarding religious affiliation, Table 12 in the KNBS (2010a: 396), or Table A in the KNBS (2012a: 22), shows that the five major groups are: the Protestants (47.4%), the Catholics (23.3%), the other Christians (11.8%), the Muslims (11.1%), and those who said they had "no religion" (2.4%).

2.3 Cultural factors

This section somehow picks up from the end of Chapter 1, as it presents elements that offer a detailed picture of what the present status of English within the current sociolinguistic situation of Kenya is. Indeed, the cultural factors that are discussed in this section are the various phenomena that link Kenyan culture with the use, or non-use, of the English language.

In the process of identifying those phenomena, an interesting concise conceptual framework within which one may want to discuss them is three observations made by Kramsch (1998: 3), namely that "[...] *language expresses cultural reality*", that "[...] *language embodies cultural reality*", and that "[...]

language symbolizes cultural reality". The *expresses*-aspect refers to the author's suggestion that "[w]ords [...] reflect their authors' attitudes and beliefs, their point of view, that are also those of others"; the *embodies*-aspect refers to her suggestion that "[t]he way in which people use the spoken, written, or visual medium itself creates meanings that are understandable to the group they belong to [...]"; the *symbolizes*-aspect refers to her suggestion that "[s]peakers identify themselves and others through their use of language; they view their language as a symbol of their social identity" (1998: 3).

The main phenomena which a keen observer of Kenyan English is likely to notice are the following: (i) the use, in English, of loanwords from Swahili and other indigenous languages of Kenya; (ii) the codemixing of Swahili words into English; (iii) the transposition of local language idioms into English idioms and English idioms into local languages; (iv) the use of English as almost the sole language of reading both fiction and non-fiction; (vi) the stiff competition between English and Swahili in writing fiction; (vi) the dominant use of English in producing cinema; (vii) the use of English as almost the sole language of the print media; (viii) the dominant use of English in social media communication; (ix) the stiff competition between English and Swahili and other indigenous languages of Kenya on radio and television; (x) the preference of the indigenous languages to English in producing music; (xi) the dominant use of English in religious preaching by evangelical churches, but not by the other religious organizations, and (xii) the use of an English-based mixed-language variety (called *Engsh*) by the youth from affluent urban neighbourhoods. There are also two additional phenomena which, although rather fringe ones, are still likely to be noticed by an observer of Kenyan culture: (xiii) the use of high-flown English by members of the Luo community, and (xiv) the adoption of English names as family names by members of the Kamba community.

Loan words from Kiswahili and other indigenous languages of Kenya are often used in English to express local realities. Such loanwords are borrowed not only for notions which do not have a direct translation into English (as is the case of *ugali*, 'a kind of maize meal that is a staple food in Kenya and in eastern and southern Africa'), but also for those that do (as is the case of *mwananchi*, 'common man/citizen'). More on such loan words will be said in Chapter 5.

A somewhat related phenomenon, but a more widespread one in Kenyan English usage, is the codemixing of Swahili words into English. (More will be said about this in Chapter 6.) This type of codemixing is currently fashionable in commercial advertising, especially by mobile telephony companies, the largest of which is Safaricom, with its now world-famous money transfer service, *M-Pesa*, for Mobile-*Pesa*, in which *pesa* is the Swahili word for 'money'. But this type of codemixing has been made use of for decades, particularly in the naming of national holidays (e.g. *Jamhuri* Day, 'Independence Day') and buildings (e.g. *Afya* House 'Health House', i.e. the Health Ministry building). Speakers who introduce, into English, Swahili words which have direct equivalents in English must be of the view that the English language is not adequate enough to bring out the Kenyan nature of the entity being named. So, because of this assumed inadequacy, recourse should be made to Swahili, as the sole national language of Kenya.

Kenyan English speakers also sometimes literally translate and then transpose certain idioms from local languages into English. One frequent example is the use of the phrase *clean heart* in a sentence like *He said it with a clean heart*, which is a direct translation from the Swahili *Alisema hivyo kwa roho safi* ('He said it with no ill intention'), where *roho safi* literally corresponds to 'heart clean'. Even though this is a direct translation, it could be argued that those who use *clean heart* are not necessarily aware that they are transposing it into English in the first place. However, there are instances where such a transposition must have been a conscious process, as a way of showing that the author/speaker has appropriated the English language. Abundant evidence of this feeling of "appropriation of the English language" will be found in Kenyan (and African) creative writing, as illustrated by the following passage, which is the opening paragraph of a novel entitled *The River and the Source*, written by Margaret A. Ogolla[6]:

> ONE NIGHT, IN THE MORNING OF THE SMOKY HUT OF AKETCH, the second wife of the great chief Odero Gogni of Yimbo, a baby was born. It was about thirty seasons before that great snaking metal road of *Jorochere*, the white people, reached the bartering market of Kisuma. The baby yelled so lustily on its first gulp of acrid air, that the chief strolling around unconcernedly as befitted his station and manhood, thought with satisfaction, "Another rock for my sling", by which he meant another son. Actually he had already covered himself in considerable glory by siring seven sons. However, this time he was wrong because for the first time he was the father of a daughter. Later he would say wisely, with something of a turnabout, that a home without daughters is like a spring without a source; for it was his right as a great chief not only to lead but to utter wisdom as well, change of heart notwithstanding.

There are several phrases in this passage that sound African and Kenyan, namely *thirty seasons* (possibly 'fifteen years'), *great snaking metal road* ('the railway line'), and *another rock for my sling*. In this latter phrase, a baby boy is compared to a rock used e.g. to hunt, from which comparison one can say that

---

[6] It was published in 1994 by Focus Publishers Ltd, Nairobi; its school edition was published in 2012. The novel is currently a set book for teaching English literature in the final year of high school in Kenya.

he is (or at least was, then) seen as a guarantee for the survival and physical protection of his father's family.

However, while some Kenyan-language idioms are imposed on English, at the same time some English-language idioms are equally imposed on local languages. For example, a football commentator on one Kenyan radio station, while commenting on the UEFA Champions League semi-final match between Real Madrid and Atlético de Madrid on Tuesday 2 May 2017, said that "Cristiano Ronaldo *amekuwa akiuliza maswali mbele ya mlango wa* Atlético Madrid" ('Cristiano Ronaldo had been asking questions in front of Atlético Madrid's goal [before he scored]'). The phrase *amekuwa akiuliza maswali* ('had been asking questions') is Swahili, linguistically speaking, but is purely a literal translation of an idiom which does not mean anything in Swahili in the context of playing football. This paragraph and the preceding one show that when it comes to the use of idioms, the English language is deemed to be both adequate (i.e. has enough structures) and inadequate at the same time.

In relation to reading culture, the prevailing tendency in Kenya is to read the traditional literature (i.e. novels, short stories, poems, and plays) that is in English, not that in local languages. This must have to do with the fact that from early on (from as early as nursery school), the literature that is made available to pupils and students for reading is in English, a language in which all the school subjects (except for Swahili) are taught. This means that Kenyans are trained to read practically only in English. Swahili is taught as a school subject as well, and as part of this students are required to read some literature in Swahili. Nonetheless, there is much less exposure to it than there is to English. Hardly is there any formal exposure to written forms of the other indigenous languages of Kenya. So, against this background, English enjoys a highly privileged position in relation to reading culture.

That English is *the* language of reading culture in Kenya is also manifested in the fact that it is almost the only language of the print media. While quite a number of newspapers (at least five of which are dailies) and magazines will be seen on sale by the roadside on the streets of Nairobi, only one is in Swahili, namely *Taifa Leo* (literally 'the country today'), published by the Nation Media Group, which also publishes a much more voluminous English counterpart of it, the *Daily Nation*. *Taifa Leo* must have been meant for people who do not know enough English. In support of this is the fact that it is customary for offices in public administration to buy newspapers (usually the *Daily Nation* and *The Standard*) for the staff to read, but hardly, if at all, is *Taifa Leo* one of those bought.

Despite the visible tendency to read more in English than in Swahili, when it comes to writing fiction (novels, short stories, poems, and plays), English is in stiff competition with Swahili, even though it probably has a slight edge over the latter. Arguably, the best-known Kenyan fiction writer is the world-renowned Ngugi wa Thiong'o. He has written novels, plays, short stories, and even children's books. From his (1962) play *The Black Hermit* to the mid-1970s he wrote in English, before deciding to make a case for the promotion of indigenous languages by writing in his native Gikuyu, starting with his (1977) play *Ngaahika Ndeenda* ('I Will Marry When I Want'). Since then, he wrote his fiction works first in Gikuyu before they were translated into English. However, his plea to write in Kenyan languages (other than Swahili) has definitely not been heeded by his compatriots. There are, though, quite a number of them who have written and are writing their fiction in Swahili. Among them are the playwright and poet Kithaka wa Mberia (who published e.g. *Kifo Kisimani*, 2001) and the novelist John Habwe (who published e.g. *Pendo la Karaha*, 2016).

Away from fiction writing, English is the dominant language for social media communication, for an obvious reason: social networking services such as Facebook and Twitter have a world-wide audience. So, it naturally follows that the users of these services must turn to English first if they too are to be part of the global social-media community. But there are also closed groups (e.g. WhatsApp and Telegram groups) that occasionally chat in local vernaculars on social media, which can be interpreted as a move on their part to signal their identity as a specific sub-group of social-media users among a multitude of others around the world.

In relation to the audio-visual media, English loses a considerable amount of its lion's share as the language of use: it competes for space with Swahili and many other indigenous languages. Starting with television stations,[7] the five biggest of them, namely the KBC (Kenya Broadcasting Corporation), NTV (formerly Nation TV), KTN (Kenya Television Network), Citizen TV, and K24, all run their programmes in the only two official languages of Kenya, English and Swahili. This is manifested in news broadcasting: for example, on all the five TV stations news is in Swahili at 7 pm (local time) and in English at 9 pm. However, overall, even the five devote more airtime to English than to Swahili, because of foreign programmes, such as films and other forms of entertainment.

On the other hand, there are TV stations whose visible aim is to promote local vernaculars, especially in the wake of the (new) Constitution of Kenya 2010, which provides a solid foundation for this promotion. In its article 44 (on "Language and culture"), it stipulates that

---

[7] An Internet source lists 86 TV stations operating in Kenya, but some of those on the list (Al Jazeera, EWTN, DW, and France 24 TV) are not Kenyan, while at least one Kenyan one, QTV, is no longer in service. See: www.superbox.co.ke/tv-channels-list, accessed: 4 May 2017.

(1) Every person has the right to use the language, and to participate in the cultural life, of the person's choice.
(2) A person belonging to a cultural or linguistic community has the right, with other members of that community—
   (a) to enjoy the person's culture and use the person's language; or
   (b) to form, join and maintain cultural and linguistic associations and other organs of civil society.

Examples of TV stations broadcasting only in local vernaculars are *Inooro* TV and *Kameme* TV, which broadcast in Kikuyu (a Bantu language), and *Kass* TV, which broadcasts in Kalenjin (a Nilotic language). Viewers of these stations will hear English and Swahili only in commercials and in interviews with people who do not speak Kikuyu or Kalenjin. An example of TV stations broadcasting almost only in local vernaculars is STN (Star Television Network) TV, which broadcasts mainly in Somali and Borana (two Cushitic languages) and, occasionally, in Swahili (e.g. for news).

For their part, radio stations in Kenya[8] are less "flexible" than televisions in terms of which languages they broadcast in: very many of them broadcast in just one language, except when they are airing commercials. Radio stations in Kenya can be grouped into five categories: first, there are those that broadcast only in English, especially those that target the residents of Nairobi and its environs. Among them are Nation FM, Capital FM, Kiss 100 FM, and Hot 96, in addition to the government-run KBC English Radio, which broadcasts nationally and "has the second largest coverage after the KBC Radio Taifa [its sister radio broadcasting in Kiswahili]".[9] Second, there are those that broadcast only in Swahili, among which are Radio Citizen, Milele FM, Radio Jambo, Radio Maisha, Qwetu Radio, in addition to the government-run KBC Radio Taifa.[10] These first two categories are the largest.

---

8 An Internet source lists 118 radio stations in Kenya, at least half a dozen of which are not Kenyan (Radio Tanzania, Radio Ethiopia, Radio Djibouti, BBC, China Radio International, and Deutsche Welle). See: buzzkenya.com/radio-stations-in-kenya, accessed: 4 May 2017. However, the list is not up to date: for example, the Kenya Broadcasting Corporation (KBC) has more than ten regional branches, not just the four listed there, namely KBC Eastern, KBC Central, KBC Western, and KBC North Eastern – names which are no longer used.
9 According to Ngulamu Mwaviro, a news editor with the Kenya Broadcasting Corporation (KBC), in personal communication, 4 May 2017.
10 There is one radio, Ghetto FM, which broadcasts only in a Swahili-based youth language called Sheng (about which more will be said in Chapter 6), though e.g. its 9 pm news is read in standard Swahili.

The third category is that of those (very few) radios that broadcast in both English and Swahili, but with more airtime being allocated to the latter, especially regarding news bulletins. Interestingly, those which the author of this book is aware of are all owned by religious organizations: Radio Waumini (owned by the Catholic Church), Biblia Husema Broadcasting (owned by the Africa Inland Church) and IQRA FM (an Islamic radio). This latter also broadcasts for at least one hour daily in Somali and runs shorter "counselling" programmes in Kikuyu and Dholuo.[11]

The fourth category is that of radios that broadcast both in English and in other non-Kenyan languages (and, for some of them, occasionally in Swahili as well). This category is essentially comprised of radios that broadcast worldwide on short waves and also in FM in Kenya. The best known of them are the BBC (broadcasting in English and Swahili), the Voice of America (broadcasting in English and Swahili), Radio France International (broadcasting in French, English, and Swahili), and China Radio International (broadcasting in Chinese, Swahili, and English). Among the less known radio stations in this category is Sound Asia FM (broadcasting in English and Hindi).

The fifth category is that of radios, very many of them, that broadcast only in local vernaculars. The bulk of them are run by two companies: the government-owned Kenya Broadcasting Corporation (KBC) and the Royal Media Services. The KBC operates 19 radio stations (10 of which run for 24 hours and 9 on alternate hours) spread throughout the country to cater for the various regions and ethnic groups. Examples are: Coro FM (in Kikuyu), meant for Nairobi and the central Kenya region; Pwani FM (in Swahili), for the coastal region; and Radio Ingo (in Luhya), for the Western region. The Royal Media Services operate about 10 vernacular radio stations, also geographically spread. Examples are: Ramogi FM, meant for Dholuo speakers; Musyi FM, for Kikamba speakers; and Egesa FM, for Ekegusii speakers. Although the initiative of the government of Kenya and that of the Royal Media Services (and some other similar initiatives on a lesser scale) to promote the use of vernacular languages through radio (and television) predate the Constitution of Kenya 2010, they too are a clear operationalization of its article 44 referred to above.

Turning now to the realm of music, while (at the time of writing this chapter) there are no survey data available on which to base any observation about which language is the dominant one in relation to Kenyan artists' music production, impressionistically it can be claimed that English is *not* their language

---

11 According to Mohammed Akidah, a lecturer in Arabic at the University of Nairobi (p.c., 4 May 2017), it even used to broadcast in Urdu.

of choice. There seem to be very few Kenyan songs sung purely in English compared to those sung in Swahili and local vernaculars. The music of the young generation (people in their twenties and thirties, e.g. the band *Camp Mulla* and solo singers such as Khaligraph Jones and Muthoni the Drummer Queen[12]) typically mixes English and Swahili; in fact, it would not be an exaggeration to say that the language of Kenyan hip-hop music is Sheng. Songs that are intended to have a patriotic overtone tend to be in Swahili (e.g. Eric Wainaina's *Daima Mkenya* 'Forever Kenyan') and in local vernaculars (e.g. Susan Owiyo's *Kisumu 100/Kisumu Ber* 'Beautiful Kisumu'). It was brought to the attention of the present author[13] that there were at least two "patriotic" songs in English that were worth mentioning: Roger Whittaker's *My Land is Kenya* and David Amunga's *Going Back to Africa*. Gospel music, which is a thriving genre in Kenya, is typically in Swahili (e.g. Esther Wahome's *Kuna Dawa* 'There is medicine [for one's sins]') and in local vernaculars (e.g. Emmy Kosgei's *Taunet Nelel* 'New Beginning' in Kalenjin). One gospel musician known to sing *also* in English is Paul Mwai (e.g. with his songs *I Need You* and *Only Jesus*).

The language of Kenyan cinema, unlike that of its music is, so far, typically English, at least for feature films. A major reason for this is that, according to Nyutho (2015: 102), these films are Kenyan to the extent that they tell stories about Kenya and were shot in Kenya, but are otherwise Hollywood films. The author notes that "[i]n terms of Hollywood movies shot in Kenya, the 1980s stand out as by far the most successful period for Kenya cinema made by foreign crews. Among the successes, *Sheena, Queen of the Jungle* won great acclaim in the 1980s and was one of the first foreign movies to be shot entirely on location in Kenya" (2015: 102). He goes on to also mention the following titles: *Flame Trees of Thika (1981), Out of Africa (1985), In the Shadow of Kilimanjaro (1986), White Mischief (1987),* and *The Happy Valley (1987)*, "among a galaxy of highly profitable movies shot in Kenya" (2015: 102).

Nyutho's (2015) use of "galaxy" is an exaggeration.[14] A Wikipedia page ("last edited [in] June 2016") lists only 57 "Kenyan films" (with *In the Shadow of*

---

12 Information obtained from Kamau Ndoria, a 3rd year Law student, Strathmore University, Nairobi (p.c., 6 May 2017).
13 By Zipporah Otiso, a University-of-Nairobi lecturer (p.c., 8 May 2017).
14 From the history of the Kenyan film industry presented in Nyutho (2015), the rather confused picture of it looks like this, in outline: firstly, Nyutho (2015: 84) reports that as early as the mid-1930s, the colonial Kenyan government had already "established a mobile cinema", which was still attracting "the highest audiences in the 1980s"; secondly, the author devotes an entire section (4.1.5) to the "Lack of films to market Kenya internationally after independence" (see pp. 86–90), in which he argues that the films which had been produced until then portrayed a negative image of Kenya and Africa, and, as a consequence, the country was not keen on publicizing them; thirdly,

Kilimanjaro being the only film among the six mentioned above appearing on that list). But, once again, those are more of films *about* Kenya than *Kenyan* films proper. A good illustration of this is *The First Grader*, a film about the real life of a Kenyan, Kimani Maruge, who decided to go to school, in 2003, at the age of 84, but a film directed and produced by non-Kenyans. The Wikipedia list contains four titles in Swahili,[15] but despite this the films themselves are in English, a fact explicitly acknowledged for at least one of them, *Pumzi* (2010). Nyutho (2015: 97) informs us that the "first local Kiswahili film [,] *Mlevi* [the drunkard]", was produced "in 1968, [by] a Kenyan of Indian extraction, Ragbir Singh". However, the author does not mention other films that may have later been produced in Swahili.

Yet, there must have been a number of them, especially if one broadens the definition of film to cover the comedy series aired on local televisions (e.g. *Papa Shirandula*, on Citizen TV), a good number of which are in Swahili. In fact, it cannot be an exaggeration to say that the production of films in Swahili and local vernaculars has been burgeoning since the analogue-to-digital-television-migration broadcasting process, which was completed in Kenya in the first half of 2015. As part of this process, in 2012 the government of Kenya produced a policy termed the "Communication Authority of Kenya Programming Code for Free-to-Air TV and Radio Broadcasting", which required all Kenyan TV and radio stations to have at least 40% of broadcasts in "local content". (The policy came into force on 1 July 2016.) It is obviously those TV stations that broadcast only in local vernaculars that seem to have complied with the policy most. One of them, *Inooro* TV, airs films in Kikuyu. (It also airs Nigerian[16] and Indian films voiced over in Kikuyu, as does the KBC TV, with Chinese films voiced over in Swahili).

Another aspect of Kenyan culture in relation to which the choice of language seems to matter a great deal is religious preaching. English is *the* language of preaching for the (new) evangelical churches, most of which have

---

for a real beginning of Kenyan film industry, Nyutho (2015) refers us to the 1980–90 decade (see section 4.1.10, pp. 99–104). This industry has been given the name "Riverwood" (see Nyutho 2015, passim, esp. Chap. 5), to parallel Hollywood (in the USA), Bollywood (in India), and Nollywood (in Nigeria). Riverwood was named after River Road, a famous street in the centre of Nairobi.

15 The four are: *Chokora* ['Street boy'], *Gari Letu Manyanga* ['Our hip bus'], *Haba na Haba* ['Little by little'], and *Pumzi* ['Breath'].

16 Perhaps in a bid to publicise itself as a big promoter of films in the Kikuyu language, it refers to the series of films it airs as *Centrosinema*, to mirror the Nigerian term *Afrosinema*. While the prefix *Afro-* is supposed to reflect the whole of Africa, the prefix *centro-* reflects the fact that the Kikuyu language is predominantly spoken in what used to be officially called the "Central Province" (of Kenya).

parent churches in the USA. One of them is Christ Is the Answer Ministries (CITAM), all of whose services in cosmopolitan areas like Nairobi are in English. At the other extreme of language choice, hardly any English is used by the "African Independent Churches" (also called "African 'Separatist' Churches"), which "were formed by African Christians breaking away from the established mother churches or Western Christian Churches" (Aoko 1974: 253). A hallmark of those churches is that their membership typically comes from the same tribe, even in cosmopolitan areas like Nairobi. Because of this, the language of preaching is that of their ethnic affiliation. One such church is the Legio Maria Church of western Kenya (which broke away from the Roman Catholic Church) whose language of preaching is Dholuo.

For the older churches (such as the Catholic Church and the mainstream Protestant churches), English and Swahili share airtime (more or less equally for the Catholic Church) in cosmopolitan areas, but allocate greater airtime to Swahili and, especially, to the local vernaculars the further one moves away from urban areas. For Islam, no English is used in preaching in mosques (according to Mohammed Akidah of the Arabic section at the University of Nairobi, p.c., 8 May 2017): in most of the country, only Swahili is used, and only the three sermons (the one on Fridays and the two on the two Eid's, i.e. Eid ul Fitr and Eid ul Hajj/Eid ul Adha) must be delivered in Arabic. In the north-eastern region of Kenya, inhabited mainly by Somali-speaking populations, Somali is used as well.

A further cultural phenomenon worth describing is the use of Engsh by the youth of affluent urban areas, typically in Nairobi. Engsh is a mixed language variety based on English. Sheng, its counterpart based on Swahili and some other languages of Kenya, is much more known, and indeed in most publications both are simply referred to as Sheng.[17] An example of Engsh is *They kujad dem late wid jamaaz who were chekaing visilly* ('They came late with guys who were laughing in a silly manner'). Swahili words and a bound morpheme can be recognized in this example: *kuja* ('to come'), *jamaa* ('people/guys'), *cheka*

---

[17] While so much has already been written about Sheng, that is from an undergraduate degree paper (Nyauncho 1986, the first known academic paper on Sheng), to PhD dissertations (e.g. by Samper 2002, Githinji 2006, and Bosire 2008), through a number of scholarly articles (e.g. Githiora 2002, 2016, Mazrui 1995, and Ogechi 2005), little has been written about Engsh: perhaps only Abdulaziz and Osinde (1997) and Muthiora (2004), so far. Locally, there is a magazine, *The Insyder*, devoted to promoting Engsh (see: www.theinsyder.com). The two main dailies, the *Daily Nation* and *The Standard*, sometimes also contain pull-out magazines written in Engsh and/or Sheng. For Sheng, there is even (at least) one online Sheng-Swahili-English dictionary, at: www.sheng.co.ke/kamusi However, no grammar of Sheng has been written yet.

(from the verb *kucheka* 'to laugh'), and *vi-*, a prefix indicating 'manner'. The English suffixes marking the past tense, the plural, and the progressive aspect can also be seen (or guessed) in *kujad, jamaaz*, and *chekaing*, respectively. An example of Sheng is *Wakitutrick kwa hii game tutawashow si pia si wastupid* ('If they trick us in this game we also will show them we are not stupid', corresponding to *Wakitudanganya kwa mchezo huu, tutawaonyesha pia sisi si wapumbafu* in Standard Swahili. (Both examples were taken from Buregeya 2009.)

Finally, there are another two cultural phenomena, although rather fringe ones, which need some highlighting because they are, at least on the face of it, a reflection of the "fascination" for the English language by members (admittedly a minority, but nonetheless a conspicuous one) of two tribes of Kenya. The first phenomenon concerns the use, by members of the Luo community of Kenya (who mainly inhabit the south-western part of the country to the north-east of Lake Victoria), of high-flown English marked by rare and/or very formal vocabulary and convoluted phrases and sentences. Some people have even given this type of speech a name: "Luopean English". (There are already Internet links to this English.) In the *Sunday Standard* (28 Oct 2012, p. 39) there is an article entitled "The 'Luopean' in the making", in which the author says that "Luo speakers are fascinated with big words". To illustrate this, he quotes the extract below (which is part of a longer one in the same article), which he took from "A piece [that] was doing the rounds on the Internet with [a] clear difference between normal understandable English and 'Luo English'":

[A] Ordinary English: *Dead men tell no tales.*
   Luo English: *Male cadavers are incapable of rendering any testimony.*
[B] Ordinary English: *People who live in glass houses should not throw stones.*
   Luo English: *Individuals who make their abodes in vitreous edifices would be advised to refrain from catapulting perilous projectiles.*

It might be that nobody from anywhere in the world has ever said things in this "Luo-English" way, and indeed one will come across many invented jokes of this type in the media. However, it is also true that some *real* Luo speakers of English, among whom politicians, will be heard on radio and seen on TV saying things like "We will deal with you perpendicularly", most likely to simply mean 'We will deal with you ruthlessly'.

The second, and less noticeable, phenomenon is the adoption of English names, by native African Kenyans, as *family names*. While there is nothing unusual in native African Kenyans having European names as their Christian names, having them as their last (and, hence, family) names sounds rather unusual. But this is not an uncommon practice among the Akamba community (who mainly inhabit the land to the east of Nairobi), whose first language is Kikamba. A former postgraduate student (Innocent Kyama Michael) of the present author and who is a member of this community said (p.c., 1 May 2017) that he "knew quite a number" of the Akamba, both men and women, whose last names were English names (such as his, *Michael*). He added that some of them had just two names, that is without a single Kamba name at all.[18] Innocent was not able to give the exact reasons why a number of Kamba parents preferred British names to Kamba ones as their children's last names, and (by his own admission) he had not bothered to ask his own father. However, whatever those reasons may be, they have led to the parents in question being impressed by the English language.

Now, to go back to Kramsch's (1998) definitional conceptual framework and relate the more than a dozen cultural phenomena discussed in the preceding paragraphs to it, three conclusions can be made: first, each one of those phenomena can be argued to reflect a certain point of view, or a belief, on the part of the users of English in Kenya, about whether the English language is adequate to be used alone in specific culture-bound situations or whether it is not. In the latter case it needs to be either complemented by the indigenous languages of Kenya, through borrowing from them or in competition with them, or needs to be replaced by them altogether. Whatever the case may be, each one of those phenomena is a reflection of the language-*expresses*-cultural reality aspect. Second, most of the same phenomena are also a reflection of the language-*symbolizes*-cultural-reality aspect in the sense that when the users of English in Kenya allow it to borrow words and idioms, and when they decide not to use it but instead use Swahili or local vernaculars, they deliberately want to mark their identity as Kenyans, nationally through Swahili, and locally through the respective vernaculars. Third, in relation to the language-*embodies*-cultural-reality aspect, it is only one phenomenon, namely the use of Engsh (as a youth dialect of English) that, in addition to being an expression of identity, is a clear reflection of how English is used in a way that its meanings are understandable by only those who use it.

---

18 Innocent's Kamba (and middle) name is *Kyama*. He added that *Michael* was his father's name, but, interestingly, not his grandfather's. The grandfather chose, for reasons unknown to his grandson, Innocent, to give the latter's father a British name instead of his own Kamba name. That was in the late 1950s.

3 Phonetics and phonology

The KenE pronunciation described in this chapter will be compared to the British English RP pronunciation as the historical reference from which it evolved. But it must be acknowledged, from the outset, that there is more than one account of RP: for three different lists of RP phonemes, see Cruttenden (2014: 960), who has replaced *RP* with *GB* – for *General British*; Upton (2008: 241–242), and Roach (2009: x). Roach's list, which is the same as that given in e.g. Wells (1982: 119, for the vowels), represents the "traditional RP" – a term borrowed from Upton (2008: 239). It is this traditional RP that will serve as the reference in the present study simply because it is the one that has so far been recommended as the reference for teaching pronunciation in Kenyan schools.[1] The twenty traditional RP vowels are for example listed in Kenya Institute of Education (1987: xi), not as RP sounds, but simply as "Sounds of English". It should be pointed out that Roach (2004: 240), who mentions "an alternative set of transcriptions [...] used in the *Oxford Dictionary of Pronunciation* [by Upton et al. (2001)]", defends the use of the traditional RP symbols on the grounds that they are already widely used around the world, in connection with English language teaching (ELT). That is the same line of argumentation taken by Wells (2014: 60), who writes: "But when I came to be a phonetics teacher myself, and to publish books, it seemed better to stick with the same transcription that other people use."

To come to KenE pronunciation proper, Schmied's (1991b) paper was the first publication on the sound aspects of KenE. The author set out to "investigate which features in the pronunciation of Kenyan English (KenE) may be interpreted as sociolinguistic signals of national (all-Kenyan) or subnational (ethnic) identities" (1991b: 420–421). He went on to say:

---

[1] Except for /i/ of *happy* and /u/ of *actual*, which Roach (2009: xi) says are non-phonemic, the traditional RP symbols are the very ones used both in the *Oxford Primary Dictionary for Eastern Africa* and the *Oxford Advanced Learner's Dictionary of English (OALD)*, the two dictionaries recommended for use in Kenyan schools. It is worth adding that the *OALD*, 9th edn, 2015, still uses this traditional list despite the fact that it clearly states that "The British pronunciations given are those of younger speakers of General British. This includes RP (Received Pronunciation) and a range of similar accents which are not strongly regional" (2015: R30). Upton (2008: 239) informs us that it is "the larger native-speaker dictionaries of Oxford University Press" that use transcriptions which reflect the current pronunciations of BrE. One such dictionary is the *Oxford Dictionary of English (ODE)*, 3rd edn, 2010, whose list (on p. xviii) of RP symbols is indeed different from that in the (smaller) *OALD*, 2015.

> The basic hypothesis of this study was that the pronunciation of vowels (levelling of quantitative distinctions between vowels, monophthongising diphthongs and avoiding central vowels) systematically differentiates KenE from "Standard English", that is, southern British standard English (including RP), whereas the pronunciation of consonants [...] expresses differentiations within KenE. (Schmied 1991b: 421)

The most conspicuous of these "within KenE" differentiations (i.e. the "subnational" features) are the following:

a) adding a nasal sound before plosives, especially word-initially, so that the words *boss, good,* and *day* get pronounced as if they were *mboss, ngood,* and *nday*; this phenomenon characterizes the regional English of people whose first language is Kikamba or Kimeru and the closely-related neighbouring languages, spoken in what is referred to in Kenya as the Lower-Eastern region (of the former Eastern Province), which is an expansive area to the east of Nairobi;

b) dropping /h/ before vowels, so that the word *harm* is pronounced as *arm*, and, paradoxically, adding the same /h/ where it does not occur in general English, so that *arm* in turn becomes *harm*, and, hence, *it harmed my arm* gets pronounced as if it were *it armed my harm*, and *my head is aching* gets pronounced as /maɪ ed iz ˈhekiŋ/; this is a feature of Kikamba-influenced English, spoken to the east of Nairobi;

c) interchanging /r/ and /l/, so that *rice* and *lice*, on the one hand, and *literary* and *literally*, on the other, are pronounced the same way in the Kikuyu-influenced English spoken mainly to the north and north-west of Nairobi, in what is referred to as the Central region of Kenya;

d) dropping the nasal sound before consonants, so that *conjunction* gets pronounced as if it were *cojuction* (although the related misspelling, common in KenE, usually retains the first <n>, to produce *conjuction*); this is a Kikuyu-influenced feature;

e) voicing the dental fricative /θ/, from the influence of Kikuyu and neighbouring languages to the east (e.g. Kimeru), so that *three* is pronounced as /ðri/ and *Ruth* as /ruð/;

f) substituting the voiceless plosives for their voiced counterparts, so that *book, madam* and *glue* get pronounced as if they were *pook, matam,* and *clue*; this is a feature that characterises the English influenced by several languages in western Kenya, starting with languages such as Nandi and Kipsigis spoken in the Rift Valley region, spreading to Ekegusii in the Nyanza region (in the south-west) and Lubukhusu in the centre-west of Kenya; and

g) substituting the alveolar /s/ for the palatal /ʃ/, so that *sugar* and *English* get pronounced as /ˈsuga/ and /ˈiŋglis/, respectively, in Dholuo-influenced English spoken chiefly in the Nyanza region.

The focus in this chapter will be on the "national" features of spoken KenE, that is on those that appear in the English of people from all the regions of Kenya, i.e. regardless of their first indigenous (African) language, and including those (especially from Nairobi) whose L1 is the very KenE being described. The aim is to show how both the segmental features (vowels and consonants), the suprasegmental ones (stress, rhythm, and intonation), and even some aspects of connected speech (little assimilation, elision, and r-linking, but no r-intrusion) differentiate KenE pronunciation from RP.

3.1 Vowel-related pronunciations in KenE

The vowels constitute the centrepiece of the differences between KenE pronunciation and RP. Schmied (2004a: 927) observes that "the vowel system of EAfE deviates systematically [e.g.] vowels tend to merge [...]". A little further he is more specific:

> On the whole three basic generalisations may be made for English vowels:
> a) Length differences in vowels are levelled [...] [U]sually short vowels in EAfE are longer and more peripheral than in RP [...]
> b) The central vowels of STRUT, NURSE and lettER, are avoided and tend towards half-open or open positions of BATH and, less often, DRESS. [...] [Moreover,] whereas vowels in full syllables tend to be underdifferentiated, those in unstressed ones may be overdifferentiated.
> c) Diphthongs tend to have only marginal status and tend to be monophtongized. (Schmied 2004a: 927).

The following subsections pick up and expound on these features and others not mentioned in the quotation above.

3.1.1 The avoidance of central RP vowels in KenE

The first, and most prominent, aspect of this phenomenon consists in substituting /a/ for RP /ə/ and /ɜː/. This systematically[2] affects the following letter sequences <er>, <ir>, <or>, and <ur>, in words such as *per, perk, perfect, stir,*

---

[2] And it applies to the speakers of all indigenous languages of Kenya, and not just "[...] Bantu speakers", who are said by Cruttenden (2014: 139) "to equate final /ə/ with /ɑː/"; note, though, that the author does not make any explicit reference to Kenya.

bird, girl, word, worse, spur, and *burden.* (The /a/ pronunciation is even extended to the verb *bury* and the related noun *burial,* in which the <ur> spelling is pronounced with /e/ in RP but with /a/ in KenE, i.e. as /ˈbari/.) A notable exception to the pattern involves words of French origin ending in *-eur,* the most frequent of which being *saboteur, rapporteur,* and *entrepreneur*: while the *-eur* letter sequence is pronounced as /ɜː/ in RP, it is realized as /ua/ or /jua/ in KenE, giving /saboˈtua/, /rapoˈtua/, and /ˌentepronˈjua/.³

The second aspect consists in substituting /a/ for the RP schwa /ə/ for some of the same sequences of letters as in the previous paragraph, as in *pressure* and *soccer,* or with a sound that graphemically looks like the letter it represents. Thus, the schwa in *comfort* and *oppose* tends to be replaced with /o/, that in *about* and the suffixes *-ance (significance)* and *-man (policeman)* with /a/, that in *support* with /a/, and that representing the <e> in the noun *moment* and the first <e> of the suffix *-ence (competence)* with /e/. To borrow words from Schmied (2004a: 927) quoted above, replacing the schwa with those "longer" and "more peripheral" vowel sounds is a case of the "unstressed" central vowel being "overdifferentiated".

In the light of what is said in the preceding paragraph, a relevant question to ask is whether the schwa occurs at all in KenE. Based on the acoustic measurements he obtained from his informants' reading of the *Boy Who Cried Wolf* passage, Itumo (2018) concludes that "[...] RP's schwa, [ə], is not realised in KenE. Instead, this commA vowel has four lexical splits. These are [a], [e], [o] and [ʉ]; which are, in this study, labelled *commA-a; commA-e; commA-o; and commA-u,* respectively" (2018: 189). However, the present author would claim that there is at least one specific context where the schwa *does* occur in KenE: at the end of words, and most frequently after the complementiser *that* and the conjunctions *but* and *and,* when speakers are hesitating, as in *I think that uh uh uh . . .* , which tends to be pronounced as /ai θiŋk ˈðatəəə. . ./.⁴ The schwa *seems* also to occur when the definite article *the* occurs before a consonant (see below in 3.1.3) and between the /ʃ/ (or /ʒ/) and /n/ sounds in the pronunciation of the *-tion* /ʃən/ (or /ʒən/) segment of words like *pronunciation* and *conclusion.* In the

---

3 Regarding the /ente/ segment of /ˌentepronˈjua/, the expected, more or less French-like pronunciation of the first two syllables of *entrepreneur,* namely /ɒntrə-/ or /ɑntrə-/, is hardly (if at all) used in KenE pronunciation.
4 Some linguists might argue that a hesitation sound is not a word. However, Cruttenden (2014) thinks it is. He writes: "In GB [i.e. General British accent] pauses are generally filled with [ə] or [m] or a combination of the two [...]." He adds that "Scottish English uses [eː] [...]" (2014: 302).

latter case, /o/ is used in /ʃon/ and /ʒon/ as a variant of the schwa in KenE, but which of the two occurs more frequently is still to be established.⁵

3.1.2 The shortening of long RP vowels and monophthongisation of two diphthongs

All the five long RP vowels (/iː, ɑː, ɜː, uː, ɔː/) tend to be shortened in KenE, as part of the phenomenon of levelling differences between vowels pointed out by Schmied (2004a: 927). Schmied's observations were largely confirmed by the two acoustic studies (known to the present author) that have so far focused on the pronunciation of KenE, namely Hoffmann (2011a: 164) and Itumo (2018).⁶ Hoffmann (2011a) points out, among other conclusions, that "[...] the edges of the high area are occupied by only a single vowel ([i] at the front and [u] at the back) and most low vowels have merged in [a]". But he straightaway cautions that "Nevertheless, the resulting system is not necessarily a five vowel one" (2011a: 164). However, his study does not say clearly how many monophthongs there are in KenE. Itumo's study is more specific: it concludes that "KenE has eight monophthongs" (2011a: 189), namely /i/ (for both *kit* and *fleece*), /e/ (for *dress*), /a/ (for both *trap* and *start*), /aː/ (for *strut* and *nurse*), /o/ (for *lot*), /oː/ (for *thought*), /u/ (for *foot*), and /uː/(for *goose*). Thus, Itumo's study observed duration with three of the traditional five vowels.

The present author's view is that the long /iː/, not reported in any of the three studies, is likely to occur as well, particularly in words ending in <ee>, such as *fee* and *nominee*, especially in isolation or if they occur utterance-finally. This

---

5 In a recent (informal) study, Itumo (June 2018) had two KenE speakers read, both in a list and in sentences, sets of words, one of which contained words ending in *–tion* (e.g. *selection*). After an acoustic analysis of their reading, he reports (in an email communication, 4 Jul 2018) that the relevant spectrograms for the pronunciation of the *–tion* segment show a vowel sound "closer to /o/ than [to] the schwa". It thus appears that the debate about what exactly the "KenE schwa", the existence of which is claimed on the one hand and discounted on the other, looks like, will continue. After all, even the RP schwa can take five different positions according to the phonetic context around it (see "Figure 24 Variants of /ə/", in Cruttenden 2014: 138), a reality which Cruttenden expresses otherwise by pointing out that "The acoustic formants of /ə/ are, therefore, likely to be similar to those for /ɜː/ or /ʌ/ according to the situation" (2014: 138).
6 Hoffmann (2011a) studied the pronunciation of 9 male University-of-Nairobi students, while Itumo studied that of 14 lecturers (7 male and 7 female) from five different universities in Kenya. Hoffmann had his informants read the passage *The North Wind and the Sun*, while Itumo had his read *The Boy Who Cried Wolf*. Both researchers analysed their data using the PRAAT software.

is indeed what Itumo (June 2018) found in the informal acoustic study referred to above (see footnote 5): he reported (in an e-mail sent to the present author, 4 Jul 2018) that "There is a tendency to pronounce the *-ee* words as [iː]".

All in all, while there is total agreement between Schmied (2004a), Hoffmann (2011a) and Itumo (2018) on the *qualitative* mergers[7] in the KenE vowel system, there is none on the *quantitative* ones. It seems that the subtle differences related to duration depend on the token words used for the same lexical set. Indeed, even Hoffmann (2011a: 162) found duration after the /u/ (but specifically in the pronunciation of *blew*) of the GOOSE lexical set, which tends to be pronounced in KenE as /bljuː/, i.e. with an inserted glide. And if we go back to the long vs. short /o/ contrast, the very frequent phrase (in Kenyan speech) *form four* is pronounced in three ways: some speakers, possibly a minority, pronounce it as /ˌfoːm ˈfoː/, others as /ˌfom ˈfo/, and still others, possibly the majority, as /ˌfom ˈfoː/.

With regard to the eight diphthongs in traditional accounts of RP,[8] there is agreement between Schmied (2004a), Hoffmann (2011a) and Itumo (2018) that KenE has six of them: the two that are reported to be absent from it are /eɪ/ and /əʊ/. In concluding his acoustic phonetic analysis, Hoffmann (2011a) observed that "As the statistical analysis showed, both FACE and GOAT are produced without any significant glide movement and can therefore be considered monophthongs in [Black Kenyan English] BlKE" (2011a: 164). So, *face* tends to be pronounced as /fes/ and *goat* as /got/. Itumo (2018) also concluded his own acoustic phonetic analysis by stating that "Data presented in Chapter Five shows a tendency towards six diphthongs in KenE. These are: /aɪ/, /ɔɪ/, /ua/, /ɪa/, /ea/ and /aʊ / [...]. The FACE and GOAT diphthongs [were] observed to monophthongize to /e/ and /o/, respectively [...]" (2018: 358).

However, while /əʊ/ seems indeed to be absent from KenE, it can still be claimed that /eɪ/ can be clearly heard, at least in some words, most likely because of their spelling. What both Hoffmann's (2011a) and Itumo's (2018) acoustic studies did not take into account in their measurement of the FACE diphthong is the pronunciation of the letters <ay>, <ai>, <ey> in words such as *say, said, pay, paid, play, stay, pray*, and *survey;* those letters tend to be pronounced as /eɪ/ by the majority of KenE speakers.[9]

---

[7] The qualitative mergers mean, for example, that in KenE there is basically one pronunciation, /hat/, for the following four words: *hat, hut, hurt,* and *heart.*
[8] Notice that both Cruttenden (2014: 96) and the *Oxford Dictionary of English (ODE)*, 3rd edn (2010: xviii) list only 7 diphthongs, that is without the traditional /eə/ in *hair*. In both sources, this diphthong has been replaced by the long monophthong /ɛː/. Note in passing that in this edition of the *ODE* the symbol for the diphthong in *my* is /ʌɪ/, instead of the traditional /aɪ/.
[9] The /eɪ/ sound is also more or less audible in the pronunciation of <ate> in verbs like *graduate.*

It can even be argued that it is from the overgeneralization of the pronunciation of *say* that KenE speakers pronounce the verb forms *says* and *said* as /seɪz/ and /seɪd/, compared to /sez/ and /sed/ in (traditional) RP. Thus, spelling seems to be a determinant of the monophthongization or otherwise of the FACE diphthong.

In connection to this, in his (June 2018) informal study, Itumo had the two informants (who had both been part of the sample he used in his doctoral research) read a list comprising the words *today, say, said, pay, paid,* and *survey*. He reported (in his e-mail communication of 4 Jul 2018) that their last two (or three) letters were pronounced as the diphthong /eɪ/, while in the words *days, they, escaped,* and *gave*, which the same informants read as part of connected speech in the *Boy Who Cried Wolf* passage, the /eɪ/ occurred only in *they* and was monophthongised to /e/ in the remaining three words. He argued that the informants were able to produce the diphthong /eɪ/ because of the careful style associated with word-list reading. But even if one concludes that this diphthong exists in KenE only in a word citation form, the point is that it *does* exist in the first place.

Furthermore, the consensus that the diphthong /eə/ is present in KenE (corresponding to RP /eə/) needs to be qualified: while /eə/ is indeed clearly audible word-finally in words such as *pair* and *share*, it seldom, if at all, appears in words such as *Mary, Sarah, vary, variable,* and *parent*, where the letter <a> in bold type is realized as /eə/ in (traditional) RP, but as /a/ in these other words in KenE, except for *Mary,* in which it is pronounced as /e/ – or perhaps as /ɛː/, the way it is pronounced in (modern) RP according to Cruttenden (2014) and the *ODE* (2010). (For its part, *Sarah* has a variant in KenE, spelt as *Serah* and pronounced with an /e/.)

Table 3.1 displays all the vowels which the present author claims do appear in KenE pronunciation.

Seven of the eight RP diphthongs in Table 3.1 appear in KenE pronunciation as well; the only one "missing" is the /əʊ/ of GOAT. Six of the seven were also reported by Schmied (2004a), Hoffmann (2011a), and Itumo (2018); the only one which was not is /eɪ/. With regard to the monophthongs, the table suggests that the present author's observations are not exactly the same as those reported by the other three authors either: in addition to the five vowels /i e a o u/, around which there is total agreement among all the four authors, the table adds the schwa (even if this were to be considered a "marginal schwa", because of "its [much lower] frequency" of occurrence than in RP, like that reported by Bobda 2008: 124 in Ghanaian English) and four long vowels, namely: /aː, oː, uː, iː,/, the last three of which were reported by Itumo (2018) as well. In a nutshell, ten monophthongs have been identified in the present study, against five in Schmied (2004a), five to seven in Hoffmann (2011a), and eight in Itumo (2018).

36 — 3 Phonetics and phonology

Table 3.1: The vowels of KenE (appearing against Wells's [1982] lexical sets).

FLEECE	ɪ, iː	FOOT	u	MOUTH	aʊ
KIT	i	GOOSE	u / uː	NEAR	ɪa
DRESS	e	LOT	o	SQUARE	ea
FACE	e, eɪ	CLOTH	o	CURE	ua
TRAP	a	THOUGHT	o, oː	lettER	a, ə
NURSE	a	NORTH	o, oː	commA	a
STRUT	a	FORCE	o, oː	About	a
START	a, aː	GOAT	o, oː	happY	i
BATH	a	PRICE	aɪ	horsES	i
PALM	a	CHOICE	oɪ		

3.1.3 Vowel-letter-related spelling pronunciations

The most conspicuous (to the present author at least) of such pronunciations is that of the letter sequence <*au*>, which is widely pronounced as /aʊ/ in *applaud, applause, clause, fraud, laud, launch,* and *laundry*. So, for example, *clause* and *fraud* are usually pronounced as /klaʊz/ and /fraʊd/ in KenE. However, there are exceptions: the first one is *pause*, pronounced as /poz/, not /paʊz/. Why *pause* should be an exception seems a mystery. The other exception consists of words such as *laugh* and *gauge*, whose pronunciation in KenE is close to that in RP, and not /laʊf/ and /gaʊdʒ/. This latter exception might be explained by the fact that *laugh* and *gauge* are, unlike the other words in the list, not pronounced with /ɔː/ in RP.

Less noticeable, despite the fact that it concerns a lot more words, is the pronunciation of the unstressed letter <*e*> as /e/ in KenE, which is realized as /ɪ/ or /ə/ in RP. That is the case of the <*e*> in bold type in the following (and very many other) words: *college, decision, deliver, destroy, develop, elect (v), electricity, electronic, element, employ, estate, example, excuse, executive, record (v), religion,* and *television*. In a number of words, though, two pronunciations, /i/ and /e/, can be heard (but not from the same person) in more or less equal frequencies. That is the case of the words *effect, elect* (adj.), *enjoy, enable, enjoin, engage, even,* and *eleven*. Further, the /e/ pronunciation is also widely used for the *-ed* suffix (for the past tense, the passive voice, and the past participle), as in *it connected/was connected*. It is also largely heard for the *-ed* adjectival ending, as in *beloved* and *blessed*, where RP has /ɪd/. In addition, /e/ replaces the RP /ə/ as the pronunciation of the *-en* participial suffix, in *broken* and *taken*, or indeed any other <en> ending, as in *happen* and *token*. However, there are cases that are exceptions to the tendencies pointed out in the preceding lines: first, the bold-faced <e> is typically pronounced as an /i/ sound in KenE, as it is in RP, in the following words: *sys-tem, frequent, English, event,* and *evil*. Second, the bold-faced <e> in *engineer* and *preposition* tends to be realised as /i/ in KenE.

A different case of spelling pronunciation still involving the letter <e> is that of the definite article *the*, which tends to be pronounced as /ðe/ in KenE in several phonological contexts where RP will have /ði/ or /ðiː/: a) in citation form; b) in utterance-final position, as in the phrase *the definite article "the"*; c) before a vowel sound, thus pronouncing *the event* as /ðe iˈvent/; d) where *the* is stressed for emphasis, as in *She's not a queen, she's **the** queen*. As regards the pronunciation of *the* before a consonant, as in *the teacher*, both the /ðe/ and /ðə/ can be heard.

The vowel-related spelling pronunciations in KenE involve other vowel letters as well. To start with the letter <a>, it tends to be pronounced as /a/ in words such as *particular* and *parenthesis*, where the schwa is expected in RP; in *parent, vary*, and *scarce*, where the diphthong /eə/ is expected in (traditional) RP (but it is realised as /e/ in *area* in KenE); in *matriarchy* and *patriarchy*, where /eɪ/ is expected in RP; and in *paltry*, where /ɔː/ is expected in RP. Quite understandably, for non-native speakers the pronunciation of the letter <a> is bound to be confusing, because of cases such as *participate, participant,* and *partake*, where it is not stressed but is realized, in RP, not as the schwa, but as /aː/. So, the "regularization" of its pronunciation as /a/ in KenE should be expected. However, to confuse the picture even more, this regularization does not affect the letter <a> in e.g. *care* and *fare*, where it is pronounced as /ea/, not as /a/, or in e.g. *all, ball,* and *stall*, where it is pronounced with an /o/ sound.

Regarding the letter <o>, it is pronounced as /o/ in the very many words in which the RP schwa is expected (in unstressed syllables, e.g. in *correct, effort,* and *police*) and in the following cases where /ʌ/ is expected in RP: *comfort, covenant, front, onion, sponge, stomach, shove, warmonger, won,* and *worry*. Interestingly, though, an /a/ sound is used for *brother, money, mother, none, other, power, shower,* and *son*. And there are at least two other cases where the same letter <o> tends to be pronounced as /a/ in KenE: first, in the words *committee* and *compulsory*, where the bold-faced <o> is realized with a schwa in RP, and in the prefix *non-* /nan/ (where <o> is realized as /ɒ/ in RP), as in *non-issue*.[10]

The letter <i> does not seem to have led to many conspicuous spelling pronunciations in KenE, even though the pronunciation of the word *divisive* as /di'visiv/ could be argued to be one such pronunciation. One can also add the case, but one really hard to notice for non-native speakers of English, of the <i> in *admirable* and *admiral*, pronounced as /ə/ in RP, but clearly pronounced as /i/ in KenE, although the <i> in *admirable* is also pronounced by many Kenyans as /aɪ/. However, in the sequence <ia> (e.g. in *facial, judicial, official,* and *parliament*), where the letters <ia> are realized simply as a schwa (or no vowel sound at all) in RP, <i> alone appears in full force in KenE, causing <ial> to be pronounced as /io(l)/ – as in /o'fiʃio(l)/ for *official*, and <ia> to be pronounced as /ia/ – as in /'paliament/ for *parliament*. (Note that in West-African varieties, in both cases the letter sequence <ia> tends to be /ia/, so that even *official* is pronounced more or less as /o'fiʃial/ – for e.g. Ghanaian English, see Huber 2008: 88.) In KenE, the same letter <i> in the sequence <ious>, as in *gracious, precious* and, *ambitious*, and even the sequence <ous>, as in *mountainous* and *mischievous*, also tend to be pronounced as /i/, thus giving /'greʃias/, /'preʃias/, /am'biʃias/, /maʊn'tenias/ and /mis'tʃivias/. The vowel sequence <ei> in *either* and *neither* also tends to be pronounced as /ei/.

It seems that the only vowel letter that is little associated with spelling pronunciations in KenE is <u>. The present author is (so far) aware of only two cases where it is involved: first, in the suffix *-ful*, e.g. in *careful* and *hopeful*, where, in KenE an /u/ sound replaces the RP schwa; second, in the individual word *jumbo*, which tends to be pronounced as /'dʒumbo/ in KenE.

Finally, a case that is only partially that of a vowel-letter-spelling pronunciation concerns the dichotomy created between the past tense and present tense forms of some verbs: while one would have expected KenE speakers to pronounce *ran* and *run, had* and *have* (and *has)* in the same way, they actually have a past tense pronunciation, namely /ren/ and /hed/, and a present tense one, /ran/ and /hav/ (and /haz/). Anecdotally, postgraduate students at the University of Nairobi, most of whom are also secondary-school teachers of English, have suggested that the distinction between present tense and past tense pronunciations is explicitly taught to students so that these are able to distinguish between

---

10 While the idiosyncratic /a/ pronunciation in *committee* and *compulsory* might have to do with the avoidance of the schwa, that of *non-* as /nan/ could be attributed to the influence of American English, which has also affected another two prefixes, *semi-* (as in *semi-final*) and *anti-* (as in *anti-corruption*): where they are specifically followed by a hyphen (in British English spelling), the two prefixes tend to be pronounced as /'semai/ and /'antai/ in KenE.

the two verb forms. Notice, though, that the past tense forms *sang* and *sprang* are pronounced with /a/, not with /e/, most likely because their present-tense forms, *sing* and *spring*, would have not caused any confusion in pronunciation, with their vowel sound /i/ not being close to /a/ at all. To return to /ren/ and /hed/, the former seems to be more pervasive than the latter.

3.1.4 Vowel-related overgeneralised pronunciations

There are many cases of, arguably, overgeneralised pronunciations in KenE. The first one concerns the nouns *admiration, aspiration* (and *aspirant*), *combination, derivation, immigration,* and *invitation,* in which the bold-faced letter <i> is pronounced as /ai/ by a substantial number of KenE speakers, on the analogy of how it is pronounced (both in RP and KenE) in the verbs from which they were derived, namely *admire, aspire, combine, derive, migrate,* and *invite*.

The second case concerns the verbs *include, conclude, exclude,* and *preclude,* in which the vowel letter <u> in the ending <ude> tends to be pronounced as /jud/ in KenE, compared to /uːd/ in RP, perhaps on the analogy of *compute, refute, confuse, amuse, consume,* etc., in which the letter <u> in the final syllable is indeed pronounced as /juː/ in both KenE and RP. And in the nouns *absolute* and the adjective *voluntary,* the letter <u> tends to be pronounced as /juː/ in KenE. We can call this KenE phenomenon "yod addition", to contrast it with the "yod deletion" discussed e.g. by Upton (2008: 249) and by Cruttenden (2014: 83) as one of the changes which traditional RP has undergone.

The third case concerns the past tense form <ew> in *blew, grew* and *flew,* which, in KenE, seems to attract the yod as well, hence the pronunciations /blju/, /grju/ and /flju/, most likely on the analogy of *knew*. Note that the noun *crew* is not pronounced with the /j/ sound, which confirms the suggestion that this is a past-tense pronunciation feature in KenE. However, even the non-past tense verb form *sew* is pronounced as /sju/, reportedly as a deliberate effort on the part of teachers to distinguish it from the verb *sow* (according to secondary school English teachers Everlyine Ongaga, p.c., 31 May 2016, and Eunice Arungo, p.c., 20 Dec 2016).

The fourth case concerns the verbs *determine* and *examine,* in which the ending <mine> is pronounced by a large number of KenE speakers as /maɪn/, most likely on the analogy of the word *mine*. By the same token, it could be argued that the KenE pronunciation of *premise* as /'premaɪs/ and that of *expertise* as /'ekspataɪz/ were copied on that of *compromise* and *demise,* while that of *intestine* as /'ɪntestaɪn/ was plausibly modelled on that of *Palestine* and *Philistine* (and maybe on that of *canine* and *concubine* as well).

The fifth case concerns the words *cowardice* and *prejudice*, whose <ice> ending is pronounced as /aɪs/, to give /ˈpredʒʊdaɪs/ and /ˈkawadaɪs/, most likely based on the pronunciation of words like *ice*, *lice*, and *rice*.

The sixth case is that of the words *executive* and *consecutive* on the one hand, and *curriculum* on the other. In the former two, the letter <*u*> tends to be pronounced in KenE as /**a**/ (compared to /jʊ/ or /jə/ in RP), so that *executive* is /egˈzek**a**tiv/, most likely on the analogy of the word *cut*. For its part, *curriculum* tends to be pronounced as /kaˈrik**a**lam/ in KenE (compared to /kəˈrɪkjʊləm, kəˈrɪkjələm/ in RP).

The seventh case is that of *national* and *rationing*, pronounced by most KenE speakers as /ˈneʃon(o)l/ and /ˈreʃonin/ (compared to RP /ˈnæʃənəl/ and /ˈræʃənɪŋ/), most likely on the influence of *nation* and *ration*, in which the vowel in the first syllable is some /eɪ/ sound both in RP and KenE pronunciation.

A further case of overgeneralised pronunciation concerns the word *peasant* (and its derivative *peasantry*), which is generally pronounced as /ˈpizent/ in KenE (compared to /ˈpezənt/ in RP). Considering that there are very many words (e.g. *peace*, *peach*, and *peat*) in which the letter sequence <*pea*> is pronounced as /pi:/ in RP, it is only "logical" that a non-native speaker of English pronounces the same sequence in *peasant* with an /i/ sound. (Even in RP, it is apparently only when the <*pea*> sequence is followed by an <*r*> or <*l*>, as in *pear* and *pearl*, that it is *not* pronounced with an /i/ sound.)

3.2 Consonant-related pronunciations

The consonant phonemes of KenE are exactly the same as those of RP. The KenE "changes" to the RP consonantal system that will be discussed in the following subsections have neither led to the addition of a new phoneme nor to the disappearance of one. As Schmied (2004: 926) puts it, "[...] even though phoneme mergers are clearly noticeable, they do not endanger the consonant system as a whole". The mergers referred to here consist in substituting some sounds for those close to them in terms of place of articulation. The other changes (to the RP system) consist in two opposite phenomena: the non-realization of RP sounds on the one hand, and the sounding of letters that are not realized in RP, on the other. But we will first look at a feature that is neither a merger nor a change, but a confirmation of what one would expect to see in KenE pronunciation as an inheritance of RP: the absence of a non-prevocalic /r/.

3.2.1 The non-rhotic nature of KenE /r/

This is what Schmied (2004: 926–927) says about the (non-) pronunciation of /r/ in East African English:

> At the subphonemic level, which is not important for differences in meaning but gives the English spoken a particular colouring, an interesting consonant is /r/. As in most English varieties, /r/ is usually only articulated in pre-vocalic positions (i.e. EAfE is non-rhotic) and its pronunciation varies considerably (whether it is rolled or flapped).[11]

If there is one feature of KenE pronunciation that does not seem to have an exception, it is the absence of /r/ in non-prevocalic positions. And while, in words ending in <er>, "Linking /r/ [...] is a normal feature of Received Pronunciation" (Upton 2008: 249), as in *soccer is soccer* /ˈsɒkər ɪz ˈsɒkə/, it is quite rare in such cases in KenE, where we should expect to hear /ˈsoka ɪz ˈsoka/. However, from the author's impressions, its (non-) frequency seems to depend on the nature of the preceding vowel: the rate of linking seems to be higher after an /o/ sound, as in *for it*, than after the schwa, as in *soccer*. The social variable gender may be a factor as well: from his acoustic study, Itumo (2018: 360) reports that in the minority instances where the linking /r/ appeared in his data (in the phrases *for a short while, for a change, fear of,* and *bother us*), it did so more in the speech of his female informants than in that of the male ones: in 43% of the cases for the female informants against only 14.3% for the male ones.

The intrusive /r/ (as in /aɪˈsɔːrɪt/ in RP, for *I saw it*, where it occurs at the end of the word *saw*) cannot be ruled out completely in KenE, but the present author has not observed it yet, neither has it been reported in any study yet. But intrusive /r/ would sound even more strange in KenE word-internally, while it is "the RP norm word-internally where the need to avoid the hiatus, thus [ˈdrɔːrɪŋ] *drawing*" (Upton 2008: 249). KenE, which will definitely have /dro/ for *draw*, will avoid the hiatus by simply pronouncing the letter <w> as a glide, thus /ˈdrowiŋ/.

3.2.2 Substituting the voiceless /ʃ/ and /s/ for the voiced /ʒ/ and /z/

Words like *occasion, pleasure* and *vision* are typically pronounced as /oˈkeʃon, oˈkeʃən/, /ˈpleʃa/ and /ˈviʃon, ˈviʃən/, compared to the RP pronunciations /əˈkeɪʒən/,

---

[11] From the present author's observation, where it occurs, the /r/ in KenE is predominantly rolled.

/ˈpleʒə/, and /ˈvɪʒən/.[12] (The substitution of /ʃ/ for /ʒ/ has also been reported in Cameroon English, cf. Bobda 2008: 131.) Similarly, the RP /z/ tends to be replaced with /s/ in KenE, mostly, but not only, in word-final positions, so that *peas, fleas,* and *disease* tend to be homophones of *peace, fleece,* and *decease*. Intriguingly, this devoicing seems to affect the third person singular present tense morpheme *-s* much less than it does the plural *-s*. And it does not affect at all the sound /z/ representing the letter <z>, as in *jazz* and *buzz*, with the latter being audibly different from *bus* (even) in KenE. (A reverse phenomenon can be observed in the nouns *use* and *abuse*: the substitution of the voiced /z/ for the voiceless /s/. Thus, they tend to be pronounced in KenE as their corresponding verbs.)

3.2.3 Substituting /dʒ/ for /ʒ/ in words of French origin

The letter <g> in *barrage, garage, massage, mirage, prestige,* and *regime* is widely pronounced as /dʒ/ in KenE, compared to just /ʒ/ in RP (except for *garage*, in which, according to the *Oxford Advanced Learner's Dictionary*, 9th edn, 2015, /dʒ/ is also used). All those words have in common the fact that they etymologically come from French. However, this etymology cannot, in itself, explain the substitution of /ʒ/ by /dʒ/, since it is /ʒ/, not /dʒ/, that is used in the pronunciation of similar words in French. A more likely explanation for the use of /dʒ/[13] in KenE seems to have to do with the fact that, according to Cruttenden (2014), this sound was used in "early RP" for the <g> words imported from other languages and, hence, must be the one that has persisted in KenE. He writes: "/ʒ/ is increasingly used in imports where formerly they were anglicised to /dʒ/, e.g. *beige, rouge, adagio, management, gigolo, genre*" (2014: 84). So, the substitution of /ʒ/ by /dʒ/ could be an inheritance from early RP, one that must have been strengthened through the process of overgeneralisation, as a result of which for KenE speakers all the words ending in <age> should be pronounced with /dʒ/. This is after all the case, even in "modern RP", of words such as *age, baggage, cabbage, carriage, courage, luggage, marriage, message,* and *rampage*. This overgeneralisation-based

---

[12] The reverse "unexpected" phenomenon, whereby it is /ʒ/ that has replaced the RP /ʃ/, occurs in (at least) one word, *coalition*, pronounced by a number of KenE speakers as /ˌkoaˈliʒon, ˌkoaˈliʒən/.
[13] Its voiceless counterpart /tʃ/ is also substituted for /ʃ/ seemingly always in *chassis* (pronounced as /tʃesis/ in KenE) and sometimes (i.e. for some people) in *champagne, chauffeur,* and *chef*. All four words are of French origin as well.

explanation leaves out *prestige* and *regime,* the pronunciation of which could in turn have been modelled on that of words like *region* and *regimen.*

3.2.4 Substituting /gz/ for /ks/

Substituting /gz/ for its voiceless counterpart /ks/ occurs extensively in the verbs *accept, excel, execute,* and *excite* (pronounced in KenE as /agˈzept/, /egˈzel/, /egˈzekjut/, and /egˈzait/), but seemingly less so in the related nouns *acceptance, excellence, excellency, execution,* and *excitement*. (A wide-ranging replacement of /ks/ with /gz/ has been reported in Cameroon English by Bobda 2008: 126; among the examples he gives are *"fle[gz]ible, ma[gz]imum, e[gz]odus",* the voicing of which is not a feature of KenE, though.) This voicing of the voiceless sequence /ks/ in KenE is an intriguing phenomenon in a variety which is at the same time characterized by the reverse phenomenon of devoicing fricative sounds, as seen in 3.2.2.

3.2.5 Inserting a vowel to split a consonant cluster

In KenE this phenomenon, discussed under "phonotactic patterns" in Schmied (2004a), seems to concern in a significant way only the words *uncertainty, certainty* and *sovereignty,* in which the vowel /i/ is inserted into the consonant sequence /nt/ to give e.g. /ˌansaˈtaniti/. Much less frequently the vowel /e/ gets inserted into the sequence /nst/ of *against* to give /ˈagenest/. So, the phenomenon is not a frequent one in KenE, contrary to what is implied in Schmied's (2004a: 929) suggestion that "[c]onsonant clusters are a major phonotactic problem in EAfE [...]"[14].

3.2.6 The non-realisation of the sound /l/ in the last syllable

A large number of KenE speakers do not pronounce the sound /l/ in two phonetic contexts, both in the last syllable of the words concerned: first, in words such as *hospital, parastatal, uncle,* and *angle,* in which the final *-al* or *-le* is realised either

---

[14] It is interesting to note that Cruttenden (2014: 258) discusses epenthesis in RP, but all the cases he points out involve adding consonants, e.g. /t/ before /θ/ in *anthem*; not a single one of them involves inserting a vowel.

as a syllabic consonant or as /əl/ in RP; second, in words such as *consult, result, solve* (but, surprisingly, not *resolve*), *twelve,* and *wolf,* in which the letter <l> is followed by another consonant. In both groups of words the vowel sound /o/ replaces both /əl/ or /l/, whether the latter is syllabic (as in *hospital*) or not. So, for example, *hospital* tends to be pronounced as /ˈhospito/,[15] *uncle* as /ˈaŋko/, *twelve* as /twov/, *wolf* as /wuf, wof/, *solved* as /sovd/, *consult* as /konˈsot/, and *result* as /riˈzot/ – although for the latter two words /konˈsalt/ and /riˈzalt/ are not uncommon.

One might be tempted to relate this non-pronunciation of the letter of <l> to an observation made by Cruttenden (2014: 257) that "[ɫ] is apt to be lost when preceded by /ɔː/ (which has a resonance similar to that of [ɫ]), e.g. *always* /ɔːwɪz/ [...]". However, he is talking of a case of "elision" that occurs in rapid casual speech, but not necessarily in careful speech, while in the case of KenE pronunciation those speakers who drop the <l> will drop it in all phonological styles. Besides, the same speakers do not drop it in words such as *always*.

3.2.7 Little (or no) aspiration after voiceless plosives in KenE

Little or no aspiration at all after the voiceless plosives /p, t, k/ is typical of KenE. In RP, these plosives are expected to be followed by aspiration "when initial in an accented syllable" (Cuttenden 2014: 164). In KenE pronunciation, *time* tends to be realised as /taim/, not as /tʰaim/. From an acoustic analysis perspective, Itumo (2018) measured the VOT values for the three plosives and concluded that they were "marginally aspirated", tending towards being unaspirated. For each one of them (for /p/ see p. 280; for /t/, see p. 287; for /k/, see p. 294) he reported a VOT mean value for both the male and the female informants to be around 30 milliseconds, which, in Itumo's own words, means "that there is a short voicing lag" (2018: 294). To put things in perspective, here is what Gut (2009: 159) reports about VOT duration for voiceless plosives in RP: "For voiceless plosives in English, the typical VOT ranges between +40 and +80 ms. Aspirated plosives can have a VOT of up to +120 ms, which means that there can be a 120 ms interval filled with friction between the release of the airstream obstruction and the vowel in words like *pat, tack*, and *cap*" (2009: 159). Thus it is obvious that the 30 ms reported by Itumo (2018) for the voiceless plosives in KenE makes them almost as unaspirated as the RP voiced plosives. About these latter Gut (2009: 159) writes: "For English voiced plosives, the burst typically occurs between 20 ms before and 20 ms after voicing begins. [...] The corresponding VOT values are thus -20 ms to +20 ms".

---

[15] Not as /ˈhosɪpɪtalɪ/, as suggested by Schmied (2004: 929).

Itumo made another, not unrelated, interesting finding, namely that the voiced plosives in KenE tend to be fully voiced, while their RP counterparts are only little voiced. For example, Itumo reports "a mean negative value of -0.07 for /d/", which "indicates that the segment was generally fully voiced" (2018: 287). In relation to RP, Roach (2009: 27) points out that the voiced plosives are "fully voiced" only "if the speaker pronounces [them] very slowly and carefully", but otherwise "in **b, d, g** there is normally very little voicing" and "in rapid speech there may be no voicing at all" (2009: 34).

3.2.8 Consonant-related spelling pronunciations

3.2.8.1 Pronouncing the silent letter <b>
In KenE, the silent <b> is sounded not only in words such as *bomb, climb, lamb, limb,* and *plumb,* where the letter appears both word-finally and after the letter <m>, but also in their derivatives such as *bomber, bombed, bombing, climber, climbed, climbing, plumber* and *plumbing*.[16] However, the <b> in *subtle, subtlety,* and *doubt* seems to be always silent in KenE (as it is in RP), while that in *debt* and its derivative *indebted* is occasionally sounded. (Note that "almost regular spelling pronunciations" of also the silent <g> in *sing/song* have been reported in Ghanaian English by Huber 2008: 84; the pronunciation of this <g> is, however, not a feature of KenE.)

3.2.8.2 Harmonising the pronunciation of the letter <h>
In the words *honest* and *honour,* and their derivatives *honesty, honestly, honorific, honorary, honourable,* etc., the letter <h> (aitch) is sounded in KenE, the way it is (both in KenE and RP) in very many other words beginning with it, such as *humble, here, hobby,* and *house*. There is, however, one exception, for which no explanation seems to be readily available: in the word *hour* (and *hourly*) the same aitch is not pronounced (except, as part of a *regional* dialect of KenE, by speakers whose L1 is Kikamba, as pointed out at the beginning of this chapter).

---

16 Note, though, that the <l> in *psalm, folk, balm,* and *palm* (and their derivatives such as *folklore* and *embalm*), as well as in the modal verbs *should, would,* and *could,* which is silent in RP, is equally silent for the vast majority of KenE speakers. However, the letter <l> tends to be sounded in the much less frequent words *salmon* and *almond*.

An interesting detail to note about the pronunciation of aitch is the fact that while naming it as a letter of the alphabet, it is always pronounced as /hetʃ/, not /etʃ/, in KenE.¹⁷

3.3 The pronunciation of miscellaneous words

There are individual words the pronunciation of which does not fit into the patterns described in the preceding paragraphs and, thus, which should be specified separately. In the following list, the KenE pronunciation under focus is that corresponding to the letters in bold type; the stress is indicated where it is placed in KenE as well: *bass* (as in *bass guitar*) /be**i**z/, *base* /be(i)**z**/, *cap* /k**e**p/, *cache* /ka'**ʃe**/, *cattle* /ˈk**e**tl/, *close* (adj.) /kl**o**z/, *conscientious* /konˈse**nʃ**i**a**s/, *corps* /ko**ps**/ (in *Peace Corps*), *dais* /d**ai**s/, *decision* /deˈz**i**ʃən/, *dose* /d**o**z/ (and *overdose*), *dossier* /ˈd**o**zia/, *e.t.c.* /ˌ**i**ti ˈ**si**/ (evidently because of this very spelling of *etc.* in KenE), *favourite* /ˈfevor**ai**t/, *flour* /fl**a**/, *heinous* /ˈh**i**njas/, *irate* /**ai**ˈret/, *jeopardy* /ˈdʒ**i**opadi/, *liaise* /ˈl**ai**as/ (and *liaison* /ˈl**ai**ason/), *maisonette* /ˈm**a(n)ʃ**onet/, *of* /**o**f/, *pronunciation* /proˌn**au**nsiˈeʃən/, *release* /riˈl**i**z/, *requisite* /ˈrekw**i**z**ai**t/, *sev**er*** /seˈv**ia**/, *shepherd* /ˈʃ**e**fad/, *sincerity* /ˌsinsiˈ**a**riti/ *stipend* /ˈst**i**pend/, *suitability* /ˈsw**i**tabiliti/, *sword* /sw**o**d/, *sycophant* /ˈs**ai**kofant/, *twitter*¹⁸ /ˈtw**i**da/ (and even /ˈtw**i**ɾa/), *tyranny* /ˈt**ai**rani/, *weapon* /ˈw**i**pon/, and *whopping* /ˈw**u**pɪŋ/.¹⁹ It is likely that there are more words than the present author is aware of at the moment.

3.4 Word stress in KenE

Stress placement in English is governed by rules with many exceptions in native speaker pronunciation (in the present case RP), especially regarding compound nouns. This section looks at how KenE has in fact reduced these exceptions by "regularising" some of them.

---

17 One of the reviewers of this chapter (Joan Beal, March 2018) wrote this: "This pronunciation of 'aitch' as 'haitch' is common in British English".
18 The un-Kenyan pronunciation of *twitter*, clearly copied on AmE pronunciation is obviously a recent phenomenon. That pronunciation is today so fashionable in Kenya that it has even crept into Swahili.
19 This KenE pronunciation of *whopping* with an /u/ sound must have arisen from confusing the word with *whooping* (in *whooping cough*), which is pronounced by the majority of KenE speakers in the same "strange" way it is pronounced in RP, namely as /ˈhuːpɪŋ/; few pronounce it as /ˈwupɪŋ/.

3.4.1 Words in which KenE stress placement is predictable

The first subset of such words concerns verbs ending in <*ate*>. In relation to them, Okombo (1987: 44) writes: "Perhaps the most conspicuous difference between EngEng and KenEng in word stress is in the pronunciation of words of more than two syllables in which the last syllable is spelt as -ate, [as in] 'educate, reiterate, congratulate' etc.". The "rule" in KenE pronunciation is simple: put the stress on the last (i.e. <*ate*>) syllable, irrespective of the number of syllables, that is, whether it is *inflate* (2 syllables), *educate* (3 syllables), or *congratulate* (4 syllables). Apparently, this rule applies in many other African English varieties (see Gut 2008: 48 for Nigerian English; Huber 2008: 89 for Ghanaian English, and Bobda 2008: 128 for Cameroon English – although this latter refers to "words of four syllables" only). By contrast, the rule in British (and American) English pronunciation is that when such verbs have two syllables, the stress falls on the last (<*ate*>) one, but when they have more than two the stress falls on the antepenultimate syllable (i.e. the third from the end).

The same KenE stress pattern, although in a less systematic way,[20] is also applied to verbs ending in <*ise*>/<*ize*> and <*ify*>. All the following verbs tend to be stressed on the last syllable: *advertise, analyse, compromise, sensitize, capitalize, apologize, characterize, regularize, liberalize, nationalize, beautify, pacify, intensify, justify, pacify, satisfy,* etc. This tendency seems to be greater with the <*ise*>/<*ize*>verbs than with the <*ify*> ones. In BrE (and AmE), except for *apologize*, they are all stressed on the first syllable, which is the antepenultimate one for those of them that have only three syllables.

There is another case where Kenyan English tends, though to a lesser degree, to place the stress on a different syllable in a predictable way: this has to do with the names of months. A non-negligible number of KenE speakers put the stress on the first syllable of *July, September, October, November,* and *December,* most likely in harmony with *January, February, April,* and *August,* which carry the stress on the first syllable in BrE (and AmE).

Yet another case is that of the adjective suffix *–able*, about which Cruttenden (2014: 247) says that "in most cases" it is "accent-neutral", since it does not lead to a shift in the stress (which Cruttenden refers to as "accent") in the stem to

---

20 Schmied (2004a: 929) treats both the <*ize*> and <*ate*> suffixes equally and says that the "tendency [to place the stress on them] is not systematic, since in most cases the frequency and familiarity of words supports the 'correct' British English pronunciation". However, from the present author's own observations, while frequency and familiarity may be relevant to the <*ise*>/<*ize*>and <*ify*> verbs, they are not to the <*ate*> ones: placing the stress on these latter is a pervasive, systematic, feature of KenE.

which it is attached. Cruttenden gives the examples of *adorable, companionable, questionable, realisable,* and *reconcilable*, where the affixation of *–able* has maintained the stress in the stems *adore, companion, question, realise,* and *reconcile*. But the author also notes that "in a number of dissyllabic stems with accent on the final syllable the accent may be shifted to the first syllable of the stem [as in]: ˈadmirable, ˈapplicable, ˈcomparable, ˈdespicable, ˈdisputable, ˈlamentable, ˈpreferable, ˈreputable, [and] *(ir-)*ˈreparable" (2014: 247). He then adds this caution: "But the general pressure from the accent-neutrality of *–able* often leads to alternative pronunciations of these words with the accent on the final syllable of the stem, e.g. adˈmirable, aˈpplicable, comˈparable, deˈspicable, diˈsputable, laˈmentable, preˈferable, reˈputable, [and] reˈparable" (2014: 247–248). In KenE pronunciation, the rule is much simpler: there are no alternative pronunciations; it is the latter pronunciation – with the stress on the final syllable of the stem – that obtains in all those cases, expect for *preferable*, in which the stress tends to be placed on the first syllable in KenE (ˈ*preferable).*

Staying with adjective suffixes, *-ative* is presented by Cruttenden (2014: 247) as "generally" accent-neutral. However, KenE has turned it into an "accent-attracting" suffix, that is one which itself takes the accent (Cruttenden 2014: 246). Thus, KenE puts the stress on the penultimate syllable in adjectives such as *argumentative, authoritative, qualitative, quantitative, speculative,* and *substantive*; that is, on the first syllable of the suffix itself, while RP places it on an earlier syllable (i.e. the 3rd or 4th from the end; see Cruttenden 2014: 247 for the relevant complex details). Note that the same phenomenon has been reported for Cameroon English (see Bobda 2008: 128, 130) and Nigerian English (see Gut 2008: 48). For these two varieties, it has also been reported that even the adjectives ending in <itive>, e.g. *competitive,* behave in the same way, but this does not seem to be the case in KenE pronunciation, where they tend to be stressed as in RP.

A further case of predictable stress placement in KenE is that of nouns which end in *-ism.* This suffix seems to be (partially) "accent-fixing" in KenE; that is, it has "the effect of fixing the accent on a particular syllable of the stem" (Cruttenden 2014: 246). In the present case it is the last syllable of the stem, i.e. the one just before *–ism* itself. Thus, for a good number (perhaps the majority) of the *–ism* nouns, among which *albinism, mechanism, nationalism, pragmatism,* and *professionalism,* KenE stresses the syllable *before* the *-ism*, as in mechˈanism and professionˈalism. However, for unclear reasons, another set of *-ism* nouns, among which *journalism, capitalism, communism, pessimism,* and *optimism,* tend to be stressed the way they are in RP, that is on the first syllable. (Note that in Cameroon English the two sets of words are reported, by Bobda 2008: 128, to behave in exactly the same way in terms of stress placement, with the stress placed on the syllable preceding *-ism.*)

The last case where stress placement is predictable in KenE is the complex one of compound words,[21] especially "compounds functioning as nouns", which, according to Cruttenden (2014: 249), are "by far the most frequent type of compound (and accounting for approximately 90 per cent)". A general rule for stressing compound nouns, "the so-called compound stress rule", was "formalized in Chomsky and Halle [1968: 17]"; it says that "stress is on the left-hand member of a compound" (Plag 2003: 137). But Plag acknowledged that "While the compound stress rule makes correct predictions for the vast majority of nominal compounds, it has been pointed out [...] that there are numerous exceptions to the rule" (2003: 138). However, he concluded that these exceptions seemed "in their majority [...] to be systematic exceptions that correlate with certain types of semantic interpretation or that are based on the analogy to existing compounds" (2003: 139). Two decades earlier, Bauer (1983: 104–109) had discussed the same Chomsky-Halle rule put forward through a "generative phonological approach" and had shown that whatever pattern emerged had indeed its own exceptions, including the one that emerged to account for specific exceptions to the general rule.

There is little wonder, therefore, that, as would be expected of any L2 variety, KenE has reduced the very many exceptions to the compound-noun stress: except for very few compounds (e.g. *chapter 'three* pointed out in the next paragraph) the general rule for stressing compound nouns in KenE is to put the stress on the first element. RP, on the other hand, follows a number of rules, each of which has many exceptions (see the detailed rules and exceptions to them in Cruttenden 2014: 248–251). Some examples of the many exceptions where RP places the stress on the second element, rather than the first, of the compound are: *apple 'pie, brick 'wall, cotton 'wool, paper 'bag, ice 'cream* ("where the second item is 'made' of the first item"); *London 'Road,*[22] *Manchester U'nited* ("where N1 is a name"); *banner 'headline, junk 'food* ("where both N1 and N2 are equally referential"); *100% 'effort, dollar 'bill* ("where N1 is a value"); *county 'council, daylight 'robbery,*

---

21 Only two-member compounds will be dealt with here; the question of "how to stress compounds [...] that have more than two members [e.g. *student feedback system*]" is raised and discussed in Plag (2003: 140).

22 Cruttenden (2014: 250) adds that "*Road* always induces this pattern whereas *Street* induces 'N+N, e.g. *'Oxford Street*". And, according to Plag (2003: 139), *avenue* behaves like *street*. This distinction does not hold in KenE. It should be added, though, that most roads, streets, and avenues in Kenya are named after Kenyan (and African) people, places, and, occasionally, even practices, whose names are not English and, hence, not necessarily stressed the English way. Examples are: *Mombasa Road, Nyerere Road, Kimathi Street, Kaunda Street, Kenyatta Avenue,* and *Harambee Avenue.*

kitchen 'sink, morning 'paper,[23] trade 'union[24]; living 'memory, black 'economy, compact 'disc, and inside 'dealing. In all these words (and many more others listed in Cruttenden 2014), KenE tends to stress the first element, thus: 'paper bag, 'junk food, 'Manchester United, 'county council, 'trade union, 'black economy, etc. It does the same in practically all the compound adjectives in the long list in Cruttenden (2014: 251). Here are some of them, stressed the way they are in KenE: 'deep-seated, 'faint-hearted, 'good-natured, 'long-suffering, 'long-winded, 'tax free, 'tight-'knit, and 'user-friendly. One (rare) exception, stressed in KenE the way it is in RP, is sky-'blue (and navy-'blue). In all these compound adjectives the stress is placed on the second element in RP: deep-'seated, faint-'heated, etc. In fact, it is only about the "compounds functioning as verbs (if we exclude phrasal and prepositional verbs)" (2014: 251) that KenE "concurs" with RP in stressing the second element of the compound, e.g. back'fire, out'number, out'wit, over'sleep, and under'go, all of which belong to the "sequence ADV or PREP + V" (2014: 251).

But there is a subset of compounds, all functioning as nouns, whose stress pattern in KenE itself seems to go *against* the general trend of stressing the first element of the compound. The following compounds tend to be stressed, in KenE, on the second element: chapter 'three, plan 'B, Whats'App, term 'paper. While the latter two could be mere exceptions to the general tendency, the former two represent a recognisable pattern: when the second element is the thing (i.e. figure, letter) being named, it tends to carry the stress in KenE.[25] This pattern was not pointed out by the authors referred to in this section (Bauer 1983, Plag 2003, Roach 2009, Cruttenden 2014, and Wells 2014).

The last word about the stress in compound words should be reserved for the question of whether there is stress shift in compounds in KenE, as in after'noon vs. afternoon 'tea. This shift is meant "to avoid adjacent accented syllables", which is the "tendency in English" (Cruttenden 2014: 307). The answer to the question should be "hardly is there any such flexibility in KenE". Even where "many [compounds] may vary in their accentual pattern between [British English]

---

[23] About the "rather large number of exceptions" which English has to its "general principle of putting primary lexical stress on the first element of a compound", Wells (2014: 122–123) proposes the following kind of rule: "These include cases where the first element names a material, ingredient, time or place. English usually stresses the second element [as in] ham 'sandwich, evening 'paper, summer 'holidays, kitchen 'table, and leather 'jacket".
[24] Notice that Bauer (1983) puts a double stress on 'trade-'union and a number of other compounds, e.g. 'bank 'holiday (p. 104), 'world 'war (p. 107) and 'return 'ticket (p. 109). He is indeed of the view that not "all compounds might be expected to have single stress (rather than merely the majority)" (1983: 107).
[25] One of the reviewers of this chapter (Bernd Kortmann, March 2018) suggests that regarding such compounds, even RP is variable.

and [American English]" (Cruttenden 2014: 252), KenE has aligned itself with just one variety, AmE, on all of them, except for one, ˈseason ticket, where the stress is on the first element in both BrE and KenE. All the others are stressed, in both AmE and KenE, on the first element: ˈAdam's apple, ˈpeanut butter, ˈshop steward, ˈstage manager, and ˈvocal cords.

3.4.2 The noun vs. verb stress-based contrasts

It has been suggested by Schmied (2004a: 929) that "[i]n EAfE the distinction between the verbs proˈtest [and] atˈtribute and the nouns ˈprotest [and] ˈattribute through stress is not always maintained". In KenE it seems to be always maintained, starting with the two contrasts involving protest and attribute and many common others such as ˈconduct (n) vs. conˈduct (v), ˈexport (n) vs. exˈport (v), and ˈperfect (adj.) vs. perˈfect (v). Two RP contrasts not maintained in KenE pronunciation involve ˈrecord, which is typically stressed on the first syllable both as a noun and as a verb, and transˈfer, which is typically stressed on the last syllable both as a noun and as a verb.

Notably, KenE has even created its own contrasts in the following pairs: ˈabuse (n) vs. aˈbuse (v), ˈaccess (n) vs. acˈcess (v), ˈaddress (n) vs. adˈdress (v), ˈadvance (n) vs. adˈvance (v), ˈadvice (n) vs. adˈvise (v), ˈalarm (n) vs. aˈlarm (v), ˈapproach (n) vs. apˈproach (v), ˈassault (n) vs. asˈsault (v), ˈassist (n) vs. asˈsist (v), ˈcement (n) vs. ceˈment (v), ˈcomment (n) vs. comˈment (v), ˈconsent (n) vs. conˈsent (v), ˈdeposit (n) vs. deˈposit (v), ˈeffect (n) vs. efˈfect (v), ˈexcuse (n) vs. exˈcuse (v), ˈimplement (n) vs. imˈplement (v), ˈmanifest (n) vs. manˈifest (v), ˈmistake (n) vs. misˈtake (v), ˈneglect (n) vs. neˈglect (v), ˈperfume (n) vs. perˈfume (v), ˈrequest (n) vs. reˈquest (v), ˈrespect (n) vs. reˈspect (v), ˈreview (n) vs. reˈview (v), ˈsupply (n) vs. supˈply (v), ˈsupport (n) vs. supˈport (v), ˈsurprise (n) vs. surˈprise (v), and ˈwitness (n) vs. witˈness (v). All these more than two dozen noun-verb pairs are stressed on the same syllable in RP: on the first syllable for (only) six of them (ˈaccess, ˈcomment, ˈimplement, ˈmanifest, ˈperfume, and ˈwitness), and on the second one for all the others.

3.4.3 Miscellaneous cases of word-stress placement

The words in the following list are not part of a recognisable pattern. They tend to be stressed in KenE as indicated: aˈdolescence, ˈagreement, agriˈculture, anˈcestor, aˈpostolic, arˈchitecture, ˈascertain, ˈastute, athˈlete, barˈgain (n & v), burˈsar, catˈegory, chalˈlenge (n & v), colˈleague, comˈmerce, ˈcomponent, ˈconstraint, ˈcontempt, con'valescence, coope'rative (n), 'decorum, 'develop, 'diploma, elec'toral, 'estate, 'extent, high'light, hi'jack, hy'giene, 'incumbent, infra'structure, 'intact, 'intestines, ma'dam (but note also 'madam discussed in section 6.2.2), mainte'nance, man'age, man'agement, 'mechanic, mis'chievous, mor'pheme, moun'tainous, offi'cer, 'opponent, oppor'tune, or'chestra pas'senger, pas'toral, pe'dagogy, 'phonetics, proof'read, prose'cute, pur'chase, rec'ognize, 'record (v), rec'tangle re'gister (v), rhe'toric, 'respondent, 'response, 'semester, sover'eignty, 'throughout trans'fer (n), 'umbrella, uncer'tainty, and 'verbatim.

There is variation, though, in the frequency of the stress placement suggested in the list above: while it will almost always obtain for e.g. *bursar, category, colleague, estate,* and *hygiene,* it is less pervasive in the case of e.g. *agreement, electoral, phonetics, respondent,* and *umbrella,* words for which the RP stress is not uncommon.

It is worth adding that the following words, with their stressed syllables as indicated in the list above, have also been reported in other African varieties of English (indicated in brackets): *a'dolescence* (CamE), *'agreement* (CamE), *an'cestor* (NigE), *a'postolic* (CamE), *cat'egory* (GhE), *con'valescence* (CamE), *coope'rative* (CamE), *'deposit* (CamE), *'diploma* (CamE), *hy'giene* (NigE), *moun'tainous* (CamE), *'opponent* (CamE), *or'chestra* (CamE), *pas'toral* (CamE), *pe'dagogy* (CamE), *'phonetics* (CamE), *proof'read* (NigE), *'record (v)* (CamE), *'semester* (CamE), and *'umbrella* (CamE). ,

3.5 Aspects of connected speech

Wells (1982: 88) has long observed that "[...] in particular in [African and South Asian English] stress and intonation constitute an area where native-speaker-like patterns are only rarely achieved". Therefore, in addition to the above word-stress-placement differences between KenE pronunciation and RP, more differences are naturally expected relating to intonation and other aspects of connected speech, such as rhythm, phonological assimilation, etc.

3.5.1 Rhythm

Discussion about rhythm here will focus on just this question: is the rhythm of KenE really syllable-timed? From Schmied's (2004a) point of view, the answer to it is obvious: *yes.* He writes:

> The most striking feature of African Englishes is the tendency towards a syllable-timed rather than a stress-timed rhythm. Thus an EAfE speaker tends to give all the syllables more or less equal stress and does not "cram" up to three unstressed syllables together into one stress unit to form so-called "weak" forms as speakers of British English do. (Schmied 2004a: 930)

While it is a fact that KenE "tends to give all the syllables more or less equal stress", because it indeed uses few weak forms,[26] syllables that carry word stress can still be easily heard as stronger and louder than the unstressed ones. It is not really accurate to say that KenE is "syllable-timed", the way a language like French or Swahili is. Based on Roach's (2009: 116) comment that "The 'stress-timed/syllable-time' dichotomy is generally agreed in modern work to be an oversimplification [and that] a more widely accepted view is that all languages display characteristics of both types of rhythm, but each may be closer to one or the other [...]", it could be argued that KenE is still closer to the stress-timed type of language than the syllable-timed one. It may be illuminating to refer to the case of Indian English, which has also been discussed in terms of whether it is syllable-timed or stress-timed. Here is what Sailaja (2009: 34) writes about the issue:

> The implication of syllable-timed rhythm suggested for IE [Indian English] is that there are no weak syllables or weak forms, which is certainly not the case. There is in fact a case for maintaining that IE rhythm is not syllable-timed. Prabhakar Babu (1971a, 1971b), in an experiment done to establish this, found that IE rhythm is neither stress-timed nor syllable-timed.

A deeper study of the issue than can be offered here is necessary for KenE before definitive statements can be made about its rhythm.

3.5.2 Intonation

Many intonation patterns in KenE pronunciation must be similar to those of RP, if we go by Cruttenden's (2014: 277) words that "[...] the variation in intonation between languages (and between dialects of English) is not as great as that involved in segments [even though] it is sufficient to cause a strong foreign accent and in some cases lead to misunderstanding". Three (of the) phenomena that are likely to distinguish between a KenE accent and an RP one are: the misplacement of the tonic stress in some cases, the frequent use of the level tone in some others, and the infrequent use of the rising tone.

---

26 In Chapter 6 we will see in detail how KenE uses fewer contracted forms than BrE.

3.5.2.1 Misplacement of the tonic stress in KenE

"Tonic stress" is used here for the commonly used "sentence stress", a term traditionally used to refer to the change in intonation for emphasis or contrast, but a term which Roach (2009: 153) says is "not an appropriate name". The best example to illustrate the misplacement of this type of stress in KenE occurs in the phrase *must go*, which is a very frequent one in the speech of Kenyan demonstrators when calling for some authority to be sacked: they will march along the streets chanting "*So-and-so must 'GO!*" They will clearly put the stress on the lexical verb *go*, while one would have expected them to stress the modal verb *must* (and, hence, chant "*So-and-so 'MUST go!*"), if one considers the kind of message they want to convey. It appears that KenE has "stuck" to the rule that "The most common position for [the tonic syllable] is on the last lexical word (e.g. noun, adjective, verb, adverb as distinct from the function words [...]) of the tone unit" (Roach 2009: 153), in spite of the fact that "[f]or contrastive purposes, however, any word may become the bearer of the tonic syllable" (2009: 153).

3.5.2.2 The frequent use of the level tone in KenE

In relation to how speakers of (British) English use intonation on one-syllable utterances, typically represented by the two answers *yes* and *no*, Roach (2009: 121) writes:

> [...] English speakers do not use level tones on one-syllable utterances very frequently. Moving tones are more common. If English speakers want to say "yes" or "no" in a definite, final manner they will probably use a **falling** tone – one which descends from a higher to a lower pitch. If they want to say "yes?" or "no?" in a questioning manner they may say it with a **rising** tone – a movement from a lower pitch to a higher one.

Of course situations arise when KenE speakers have "to say 'yes' or 'no' in a definite, final manner" or "in a questioning manner", and many of them do definitely use a falling tone or a rising tone. But the level tone is equally used by many others by way of definite answer, especially in the case of a negative answer. To a question like *Have you done your homework already?*, a *no* answer with just a level tone is quite common in KenE and, apparently, more in the speech of female speakers than in that of male ones.[27] Intriguingly, from the present author's observations, no similar level tone is used with the answer *yes*. The claim being made here is that the use of the level tone goes beyond the "rather restricted context" where, in British English, "it almost always conveys

---

[27] Jane Oduor, a phonology lecturer at the University of Nairobi, added (p.c., 4 Jan 2017) that it was common in the speech of *young* female speakers (perhaps before their thirties).

(on single-syllable utterances) a feeling of saying something routine, uninteresting or boring" (Roach 2009: 125).

The same level tone is also often used in KenE, instead of a falling tone, at the end of tone units within a (continuing) utterance, as on the word *arrived* in the following possible utterance: *He had just arrived and thus could not join the party.* Further, the level tone tends to replace a rising tone, particularly in typical KenE *yes-no* questions lacking subject-auxiliary inversion. One frequent such question is: *You get*? ('Do you get my point?'), typically pronounced with a level tone.[28]

3.5.2.3 The infrequent use of the rising tone in KenE

On the face of it, the relative infrequent use of rising tones should not be surprising because Cruttenden (2014: 291) informs us that "[...] in all styles of English speech, simple falls in pitch (whether from a high or mid starting-point) account for the majority of nuclear tones [...]". What is of more interest, instead, is that there seems to be some negative correlation between the frequent use of the level tone talked about in the preceding section and the infrequent use of the rising tone, as if the former had replaced the latter. This "replacement" would be a reasonable assumption to make in the light of the observation made about RP by Cruttenden (2014: 292) that "Level tones (most common among these being the mid level) belong with the rising tones in the sorts of meanings they convey".

To return to the infrequent use proper, of the five basic tones (the rise, the fall, the rise-fall, the fall-rise, and the level tone) discussed by Roach (2009), it is the rise tone that stands out as not being used in KenE where it would be expected in RP. One situation in which the rising tone tends not to be used is that where, in RP, the speaker uses it to ask for more information, as the following description from Roach (2009: 123–124) illustrates:

> [*Yes / No* said with a rising tone]
> In a variety of ways, this tone conveys an impression that something more is to follow. A typical occurrence in a dialogue between [A and B] might be the following:
>> A *(wishing to attract B's attention):* Excuse me.
>> B: yes [with a rising tone]

---

28 Jane Oduor drew the present author's attention to the fact that even the typical KenE question *Are you getting me?*, though involving subject-auxiliary inversion, is uttered with a level, not rising, tone. However, her own opinion about *You get?* is that this is usually uttered with a falling tone.

(B's reply is, perhaps, equivalent to "what do you want?") Another quite common occurrence would be:
> A: *Do you know John Smith?*

One possible reply from B would be *yes* [with a rising tone], inviting A to continue with what she intends to say about John Smith after establishing that B knows him.
[...]
With "*no*", a similar function can be seen. For example:
> A: *Have you seen Ann?*

[...]
[B's reply of] *no* [with a rising tone] would be an invitation to A to explain why she is looking for Ann, or why she does not know where she is.

KenE speakers are likely to react to the *Excuse me* above by turning to look at A without saying anything at all. They are likely to react to the question *Do you know John Smith?* by simply asking *Who?* or *Which One?* – if indeed they are interested in knowing more about him. Further, by way of answer to the question *Have you seen Ann?*, a reply of *no* with a rising tone to ask for more information is not used in KenE. A *no* reply expected in KenE will be one said with a level tone, and it will be a *no* of definiteness, not of request for more information. As for a *yes* with a rising tone, it simply sounds unlikely in KenE.

A rising intonation is also avoided in KenE after tag questions that request information from the interlocutor, as in the following example (slightly adapted from Roach 2009: 156): *They ′are ′coming on ↘Tuesday, ↗aren't they?*, in which intonation is marked as it appears in RP. In KenE pronunciation, we should expect the same utterance to be said like this: *They are ′coming on ↘Tuesday, ↘aren't they?* (that is, without even the primary stress on *are*). It should be noted, though, that question tags in general are very rarely used in KenE (see section 4.12).

At this juncture, it is interesting to compare intonation in KenE with that in Nigerian English. About the latter, Gut (2008: 51) informs us that "Compared to native varieties of English, NigE intonation seems simplified. Most utterances, both in read and spontaneous speech, have a falling tone. Rising tones are relatively rare and occur mostly in *yes-no* questions and tag questions. Complex tones such as fall-rises and rise-falls are even rarer [...]". While NigE intonation thus seems to be similar to KenE intonation to the extent that they both use rising tones rather rarely, they seem to go in opposite directions in terms of when these very tones are used: indeed, as already claimed in the preceding paragraphs, it is precisely in *yes-no* questions and question tags that rising tones tend to be avoided in KenE. As for complex tones, they must be very rare in KenE as well, as their use has not caught the present author's attention yet.

3.5.3 Are there phonological styles in KenE?

This question amounts to asking whether there are, in KenE, phonological styles of the kind of those established by Labov's (1966) New York City study and discussed e.g. by Trudgill (2000: 85–89), and which correlated with situational context and social class.[29] In other words, the question is whether or not we can point to specific pronunciations of the same segment(s), whether segmental or suprasegmental, which differ according to whether the speaker is being careful in his/her pronunciation, as when reading a word list or a passage (corresponding to Labov's "word-list style" and "reading-passage style", respectively), or speaking carefully in a formal style (e.g. while giving a lecture, thus corresponding to a "formal speech style"), or rather in a conversational manner (corresponding to a "casual style").

This question is worth asking for two reasons: first, Labov and other sociolinguists such as Peter Trudgill in his (1974) Norwich study (referred to in Trudgill 2000, chapters 2 & 5) studied English as a native variety, which, unlike KenE, was *not* acquired through a careful, formal style. So, it would be interesting to see if an L2 can behave like an L1 in terms of phonological styles. Second, the distinction between a careful, formal style and a colloquial one has indeed been claimed to exist in some L2 varieties. For example, here is what Sailaja (2009) says about Indian English (IE):

> Thus what are identified as non-standard [accents] above would surface in the speech of a speaker of SIEP [Standard Indian English Pronunciation] if the situation is one of informality or if the other interlocutor speaks a non-standard variety. A non-rhotic accent can and does become a rhotic accent if one is talking to a shopkeeper whose accent is non-standard and rhotic. (2009: 37).

And although Huber (2008), writing about Ghanaian English, does not put it so directly, he too suggests that that distinction exists. Referring to the phonetic realization of the final <b> in e.g. *bomb* and of <g> in e.g. *sing*, he writes: "Spelling pronunciations are not restricted to the colloquial level but are common in

---

29 In the case of KenE, at this point in time it can only be prudent not to venture into a discussion of linguistic variation along the variable "social class". While social classes must exist in Kenya, economically speaking, the present author is not aware of any social-stratification publication that can serve as a commonly accepted reference for a sociolinguistic study.

very formal and conservative GhE" (2008: 84). Further, referring to the pronunciation of <wh> in e.g. *what*, he writes: "As with many other features, there is again variability, with when speakers alternating between [hw-] and [w-]" (2008: 87).

While what has been suggested for both Indian English and Ghanaian English is well noted, the present author maintains that the answer to the question of whether KenE speakers can be said to adjust their pronunciations, of any sound, to the formality of the situation or to the interlocutor's own pronunciation or his/her (apparent) social status or level of education, is *no*, simply because he has not observed (yet) any such adjustment. It might be that some KenE speakers have two pronunciations for one word, but if they do they use them in the same sociolinguistic context. The only exception might occur in a classroom situation while teaching pronunciation: a teacher in Kenya is likely to tell his/her students that the word *girl* is supposed (according to the textbooks used, all of which, up to now, exclusively propose the RP model) to be pronounced as /gɜːl/. But no sooner would he/she have uttered this – if at all he/she would be able to pronounce the /ɜː/ in the first place! – than he/she would revert to /gal/. All in all, the present author is not aware of any discernible phonological styles in KenE.

3.5.4 How much of RP assimilation, elision, and r-linking is there in KenE?

The connection between assimilation and (possible) phonological styles is evident from the following statement by Roach (2009: 110): "Assimilation is something which varies in extent according to speaking rate and style: it is more likely to be found in rapid, casual speech and less likely in slow, careful speech. Sometimes the difference caused by assimilation is very noticeable, and sometimes it is very slight". The assimilation which Roach is talking about here, and which is the concern of this section, involves sound segments from (usually) adjacent words. (Some people have called it "non-obligatory" assimilation.) It is not the inevitable (hence, "obligatory") phonotactic assimilation that occurs within a word, as when "a vowel becomes [+nasal] when followed by [+nasal] consonant" (Fromkin, Rodman and Hyams 2011: 571).

One of the most frequent cases of assimilation we will expect to hear in colloquial speech in native English involves the palatalization of the preceding alveolar sound (/t, d, s, z/). The phrase *this year*, for example, is expected to sound, in colloquial style, as something like /ðɪʃɪə/ in RP pronunciation, where the /s/ of *this* has been assimilated to /ʃ/ because of the following palatal /j/.

3.5 Aspects of connected speech

But, hardly, if at all, does a pronunciation such as /ðiʃɪə/ occur in KenE. Neither do several examples of assimilation frequently given in the literature, such as /wʊdʒuː/ for *would you*, /gʊg gɜːl/ for *good girl*, and /gʊb bɔɪ/ for *good boy*. But there is some variation: both /gun naɪt/, for *good night*, and /lemmi/, for *let me*, are occasionally heard. It is worth pointing out that Itumo (2018) did not report any assimilation between words. Of course, from the kind of task he had his informants do (i.e. a formal reading of a text rather than an informal conversation) we should not have expected to see much assimilation. Nonetheless, since reading a text definitely involves connected speech, some was expected, e.g. between /d/ and /p/ and /d/ and /t/ in *good plan* and *third time*, two phrases which appear in the text read.

With regard to elision, Roach (2009: 113) points out that "As with assimilation, elision is typical of rapid, casual speech". This usually happens at the end of words, a phenomenon which is not common at all in KenE. But there are individual words from which certain sounds are typically not pronounced even in KenE, in particular those where the sound /θ/ appears with other consonants. Thus, for example, the word *eighth*, expected to be pronounced as /eɪtθ/ in RP, seems to be always pronounced as /eɪθ/ in KenE. And, for most KenE speakers, the cluster /stʃ/ in the RP pronunciation of *question*, /kwestʃən/, gets replaced by the single sound /ʃ/, giving /kweʃən/. The "avoidance of complex consonant clusters" is, however, not specific to KenE: Roach (2009: 114) tells us that "It has been said that no normal English speaker would ever pronounce all the consonants between the last two words of [the phrase] 'George the Sixth's throne'". For his part, Huber (2008: 88) reports that "[Consonant] cluster reduction is a phenomenon that GhE shares with other West African Englishes"[30] and that "[...] elision of one or more consonants [is] the most common strategy in acrolectal speech". He gives the example of "Syllable-final /t/ [which] may be dropped altogether in word-final position" (2008: 84), as in *got*. However, although the /t/ in *good night* may occasionally be dropped in KenE, this type of elision in not characteristic of KenE.

In relation to linking, since KenE is non-rhotic, a reasonable working hypothesis would be that it does not "allow" r-linking either. In this connection, Huber (2008: 88) seems to be categorical about this type of linking in Ghanaian English: "GhE is non-rhotic [...] However, in contrast to RP, GhE

---

30 Bobda (2008: 126), talking about Cameroon English, writes: "Although cluster simplification occurs in onset position, the most frequent cases of simplification are found in coda position".

does not have linking or intrusive R's". But the situation seems to be somewhat different in KenE because (as already shown in sub-section 3.2.1) Itumo's (2018) acoustic analysis suggests that r-linking does appear in KenE, albeit in a minority of cases, apparently more in the speech of female speakers than that of males, and possibly more after the vowel sound /o/ than any other. (For example, it is definitely audible in *for ever* /foreva/.) Regarding the intrusive /r/, Itumo observed its occurrence in the speech of only one individual (from his sample of 14) and concluded that it was just an idiosyncratic occurrence. And, since the present author has not observed any occurrence of intrusive /r/ either, it can still be maintained that this is not a feature of KenE pronunciation.

3.6 Conclusion

Sections 3.1 to 3.3 of this chapter have discussed the segmental aspects of the phonetics and phonology of KenE and sections 3.4 and 3.5 its suprasegmental ones. The vowel-related segmental differences between RP and KenE pronunciation centre around three phenomena: the pervasive use of /a/ to replace the RP central vowels /ə, ɜː, ʌ/, the shortening of all the long vowels, and the monophthongization of RP /eɪ/ to /e/ and of /əʊ/ to /o/. However, in relation to the latter two phenomena, the present study did not agree with earlier studies which concluded that there was no long vowel, no occurrence of the diphthong /eɪ/, and no occurrence of the schwa at all in KenE. It argued that such occurrences do happen and gave evidence of the words in which they are most likely to happen, because of the particular spellings of these words and the phonological context in which they are pronounced. Spelling as an even bigger determining factor in the pronunciation of vowels in KenE was also invoked to account for a large number of KenE pronunciations which can hardly be controversial, since their occurrence can be easily predicted from the patterns formed by the vowel letters associated with them. Spelling was also called upon to account for some consonant-related KenE pronunciations, in particular in the sounding of consonant letters that are silent (e.g. the <b> in *lamb* and the <h> in *honourable*). The other consonant-related pronunciations in KenE mainly involve the phenomenon of voicing or not voicing: some voiced sounds get substituted for voiceless ones, while some voiceless sounds get substituted for their voiced counterparts. And there is practically no aspiration after voiceless plosives. Finally, in relation to the segmental features of KenE, there must be dozens of words (thirty-odd were identified in this chapter) with a typical KenE pronunciation but which do not follow in any identifiable pattern.

3.6 Conclusion

Turning to its suprasegmental aspects, the easiest of these to notice and to describe are those related to word-stress placement. While there must be a non-negligible list of words stressed differently in KenE and in RP (sixty-odd have been listed in this chapter) but which do not fall under an identifiable category, many more are classifiable into groups marked by specific endings, whether these are identifiable morphemes (such as -*ise* in *apologise*) or not (such as <ate> in *congratulate*). KenE seems to have even simplified the otherwise complex rules (for having very many exceptions) governing the stress on compound nouns in RP: the general rule in KenE seems to be "stress the first element of the compound". Equally relatively easy to "notice", but largely because they are absent from KenE pronunciation, are the phenomena of assimilation, elision, and r-linking. Much more difficult to pinpoint are the aspects of connected speech that have to do with rhythm and intonation. For example, the question of whether, or to what extent, KenE rhythm is syllable-timed needs deeper investigation, as do questions related to which types of tones are used in KenE and for what functions exactly. One particularly pertinent one is the extent to which the frequent use of the level tone, claimed in this study, negatively correlates with the infrequent use of the rising tone, equally claimed in this study. Another relevant issue to investigate would be to identify what intonational, or lexical, devices KenE uses to express the meanings assigned to "tag-interrogatives" by Cruttenden (2014: 295–296), since it was asserted earlier (in 3.5.2.3) that "question tags in general are very rarely used in KenE".

Beyond the segmental-suprasegmental dichotomy, and from a wider sociolinguistic perspective, the so-called KenE features described in this chapter fall into three categories:

a) those that are shared by other African varieties which developed from the RP model (e.g. the absence of a non-prevocalic /r/ due to the non-rhotic nature of RP, the stress placement on the last syllable in the verbs ending in <ate>, and the "avoidance" of complex tones);

b) those that seem to be shared by only other East African varieties of English (i.e. Ugandan and Tanzanian English), in particular the replacement of the RP schwa by an /a/ sound in the pronunciation of the letter sequences <er>, <ir>, <or>, and <ur>;

c) those that (for the time being at least) seem to be exclusive to KenE, namely some of the pronunciations of specific individual words (e.g. /ren/ for *ran* and /sju/ for *sew*) and, possibly, the "additional" (to those in RP) stress-based contrasts between verbs and nouns (e.g. *a 'witness* vs. *to wit'ness*).

4 Morphology and syntax

The grammatical features of East African English (EAfE), and by inclusion KenE, have been reported in the existing literature to be less visible than its phonological and lexical and semantic aspects. Hancock and Angogo (1982: 306) note that "[...] East African English differs from international English mainly in phonology, lexicon and idiom [...]". For their part, Hudson-Ettle and Schmied (1991: 6) point out that "On the grammatical level an evaluation is even more difficult because it is not quite clear to what extent the deviations are part of a new regular sub-system that is rule-governed and consistently applied". Schmied (2004b: 929) is even more specific. This is how he opens his paper:

> An outline of grammatical features of East African English (EAfE) is even more difficult to produce than its phonology, because deviations in grammar occur in much lower frequencies. One reason for this lower frequency is perhaps that grammatical deviations are more stigmatised. Thus, an independent EAfE grammar is even less distinguishable than an independent phonology or lexicon.

Three phrases are of particular interest in this quotation: *much lower frequencies*, *more stigmatized*, and *less distinguishable*.

This chapter will show that grammatical features characteristic of KenE are not as "less visible", as implied in the suggestion that they occur in low frequencies. It will also show that while they may not be easily distinguishable by the ordinary KenE speaker, they are for grammarians and linguists. Further, it will argue that they are hardly stigmatised, simply because people are not aware that they are "deviations" in the first place.

Some of the morphological and syntactic features that will be called KenE in this chapter have also been identified in other African varieties of English, and even in South and Southeast Asian ones (see Mesthrie 2008b: 624–635). That is especially the case of features related to number agreement, omission of articles, and misuse and/or non-use of prepositions. But there are also quite a number of features – those that have gone unnoticed so far – which are characteristically KenE. Due to geographical proximity, they must feature in Ugandan English as well,[1] and, to a lesser extent, in Tanzanian English, too – allowing for Schmied's

---

[1] Ssempuuma's (2012: 479) conclusion that "[...] Ugandan English ought to be treated different[ly] from other East African varieties such as Kenyan and Tanzanian English which are mainly influenced by Kiswahili" cannot be convincing. For example, at least seven of the nine categories of "linguistic features of Ugandan English" identified by Fischer (2000: 60) under the heading "Syntax and morphology" can also be said to characterize KenE. Interestingly,

(2012: 462) strong reservations about an identifiable "grammar system" of TzE, which he calls "[u]nstable and fuzzy". The features described in this chapter belong to major categories (such as number agreement, inflections, the noun phrase, the verb phrase, and the prepositional phrase) which cover many aspects, and smaller categories (like the comparative), and even miscellaneous aspects that are hard to group together.

4.1 Lack of number agreement

The lack of number agreement between the verb and its subject, on the one hand, and between the noun and its determiners and pronouns, on the other hand, is one of those features of KenE (and EAfE and African English in general) that have by and large gone unreported in the literature. Isolated examples of number agreement may have been mentioned in some publications, but they have been accorded a heading of their own only in Buregeya (2001, 2008). Yet, there is evidence from the vast amounts of data collected by the present author (since 1998) from postgraduate students' academic papers and the main Kenyan newspapers, that agreement "errors" are frequent in KenE, and systematic enough beyond just random occurrences. The data show that the lack of agreement consisting in the use of a singular verb for a plural subject is more widespread than that consisting in the use of a plural verb for a singular subject, both of which are more widespread than the lack of agreement between a noun and its determiners or pronouns.

4.1.1 A singular verb used for a plural subject

About this type of lack of agreement, Kallen (2013: 112) writes that "The use of –s with plural subjects is common in vernacular English" and attributes it to the "invariant present tense forms due to generalization of third person –s to all persons" as a widespread phenomenon in World Englishes. This phenomenon was indeed investigated as feature F171 in the eWAVE survey (see Kortmann and Lunkenheimer 2013). However, two points of difference need to be made here: first, the present study is not dealing with vernacular English but with an L2

---

though, Fischer makes it clear that "For the purposes of describing UE, I shall refer to it as an autonomous variety possessing its own distinctive features, rather than as a variant of Kenyan or Tanzanian English" (2000: 58).

variety of English, illustration for which will come from the speech of educated users of it; second, as the examples below indicate, the phenomenon is not about generalising the 3rd person to all persons, since all the subjects concerned are already in the third person.

(1) a. *The **inadequacies** of the traditional term "Pronoun" [...] **has** been discussed [...] by such **scholars** as Quirk & Greenbaum (1973: 22) **who replaces** it with [...] "Proform" [...]*
b. ***These corresponds** to English "this", "that" [...] respectively. Their plural **forms which corresponds** to "these" and "those" in English are...*
c. *The semantic difference between [the] **(a)-constructions** and their **(b)-counterparts** is that **the former is** ambiguous while **the latter is** not.*
d. *But according to Abney (1987) **determiners** are head functional projections and **selects** NP complements.*
e. *Further, their role within the DP [i.e. Determiner Phrase] is secondary as **they** only **modifies** the DP.*
(from an MA thesis by W.P., 1999)

(2) a. *These disorders indicate, therefore, that there are no external **factors that contributes** to the language deficit.*
b. *Some irregular verb inflections are surprisingly omitted as well, consequently going against Radford's notion that **irregular forms** stored **remains** intact [...]*
c. ***Function words** in (a) like article "the" **is** omitted and the verb "to be" [...] is likewise omitted.*
d. *[...] but **the words** "was incompetent" **does not** fit well with the initial parse.*
e. ***The noun "glass" and the verb "broken" does not** give a lexical ambiguity [...]*
f. *In garden-pathing, the verbs play a central role in parsing. **Verbs selects** different syntactic phrases types [...]*
(from a 5-page postgraduate paper by A.O., Jun 2011)

The lack of agreement in the two sets of examples clearly does not involve "invariant present tense forms due to generalization of third person –s to all persons", since the authors of those sentences also used correct plural forms for some of the subjects in the plural. Instead, it tends to be context-dependent, in two respects: first, it seems to be "sensitive" to the (lack of) proximity of the subject to the verb, which could be said to be a reflection of the eWAVE feature "F182: agreement [is] sensitive to position of subject (immediately adjacent to predicate) vs. not immediately adjacent to predicate". Second, relative pronouns, as well as the similarly anaphoric expressions *the former* and *the latter,* seem to attract a singular verb.

4.1.2 A plural verb used for a singular subject

This type of lack of number agreement is less common in KenE. Nonetheless, it occurs frequently enough to warrant illustration. For the purposes of highlighting variability in the language of the same KenE speaker, the two sets of examples below were also drawn from the same sources as the two in (1) and (2).

(3) a. *The basic argument against the case of this term is that* **the linguistic element** *it refers to* **are** *not always noun-substitutes.*
b. **Each** *of the above categories* **have** *a close relationship with the lexical category X° and is consequently called a projection of the X°.*
(from an MA thesis by W.P., 1999)

(4) a. *In conclusion, generally, the significant* **morphology remain** *in place [...]*
b. *Correspondingly, English* **agrammatism seem** *to omit majorly function words [...]*
c. **The verb "floated"** *with "with down the river"* **function** *as a verbal predicate of this sentence.*
d. **The brain potential,** *however,* **reflect** *word expectancy [...]*
(from a 5-page MA paper by A.O., Jun 2011)

As in the preceding case (of a singular verb used for a plural subject), the use of a plural verb for a singular subject seems to be sensitive to the (lack of) proximity to the subject as well. However, the very fact that the same speakers/writers can make both types of number-agreement errors confuses the issue of which rule(s) exactly they use and, hence, of the extent to which the variability in their application of the relevant number-agreement rules is systematic or free.

4.1.3 Lack of agreement between a noun and its determiners/pronouns

Although rarer than the lack of number agreement involving verbs, that between a noun and its determiner or pronoun is nonetheless revealing.

(5) a. ***This nouns*** *require singular verbs.*
   b. *I compared the **scores** to determine **its** quantitative strength.*
   c. *However, students of the Avant-Garde High School did not have **much problems** with item number one [...]*
   (from an MA paper by B.D., Mar 2011)

(6) *If there were any **problems** I encountered in the research I would also talk about **it**.*
   (from an MA paper by M.B., Feb 2011)

The singular demonstrative *this* in (a), the singular possessive determiner *its* in (b), the singular quantifier *much* in (c), and the singular personal pronoun *it* in (6) all refer to plural nouns, which makes the feature a mirror image of the use of a singular verb for a plural subject noun. (An utterance like *How **much marks** have been allocated to Question X?* is not uncommon during examination-moderation sessions at Kenyan universities.) It can thus be speculated that the abstract notion of "singular for the plural" is a strong construct in the minds of KenE speakers. Specifically with regard to the demonstrative *this*, it is a feature that has been reported in other varieties as well: see Kortmann and Lunkenheimer (2013), where it is feature F71; see also Bokamba (1982: 126–127), where it is discussed as a feature of West African English.

4.2 Addition of inflections to and omission of them from words

This section deals first with the well-known case of the plural *–s* added to non-count nouns, on the one hand, and, on the other hand, with cases where it is added to nouns, to pronouns and (rather strangely) to other categories of words within set phrases and idiomatic expressions. Second, it deals with various other inflections that tend to be "wrongly" added to all kinds of words in KenE.

4.2.1 The plural *-s* added to non-count nouns and to some idiomatic expressions

This feature corresponds to the eWAVE feature "(F 55): different count/mass noun distinctions resulting in use of plural for StE singular", as in *"these advices."*[2] Plurals such as *furnitures, equipments,* and *advices* have been reported to be "pervasive" in possibly the majority of L2 varieties of English. For example, out of the eight African L2 varieties that were included in the eWAVE survey (which also covers pidgins, creoles, and L1 varieties) the feature was rated as *A* (for "pervasive or obligatory") in five of them: Cameroon, Kenyan, Nigerian, Black South African, and Indian South African English. It was rated as *B* ("neither pervasive nor extremely rare") only in Ghanaian English, Tanzanian English, and Ugandan English.

But even though Schmied (2012: 462) judged the feature as not being pervasive in Tanzanian English, he had, in an earlier publication, remarked that "East African usage basically ignores the grammatical distinction of count vs. non-count nouns, which does not always correspond to the semantic one" (Schmied 2004: 932). While there is a lot of substance in this claim, at least concerning KenE, it needs to be qualified because the extent to which that distinction is ignored seems to depend on individual lexical items (as argued by Buregeya 2013: 5).[3] For example, while the plurals *furnitures, equipments, beddings,* and *damages* are common in KenE, *advices* (used by Ssempuuma 2012, to illustrate the feature in UgE) is less common, while *informations* (used by Schmied 2012 to illustrate TzE) is rare. Within KenE itself the rates of acceptability calculated by Buregeya (2013: 5) for both plurals suggest that *equipments* is more common than *furnitures*.

This argument of linguistic-context variation can be pushed further. It seems that for some words the lack of distinction between count and non-count nouns manifests itself more in the use of the article *a/an* than in the plural: for example, the singular form *an advice* is likely to be more often heard in KenE than the plural form *advices*. On the other hand, for some other words, the distinction will manifest itself more in the plural forms than in the singular ones: for example, hardly are the singular forms *an equipment, a furniture,* and *a bedding* used in KenE.

---

2 The related phenomenon, investigated in the eWAVE survey as "F48: Regularization of plural formation: extension of –s to StE irregular plurals", such as *criterias, phenomenas,* and *alumnis*, seems, contrary to what is suggested in Buregeya (2012: 469), actually extremely rare in KenE. What KenE seems to do, instead, is to use the irregular plural form for both the plural and the singular, e.g. *criteria* for both *criterion* and *criteria*. The irregular plural *alumni* is even "more special" in KenE: not only does it refer to 'many *alumni*' (and, incidentally, to 'many *alumnae*'), but also to 'one *alumnus*', and even 'one *alumna*'.

3 Hocking (1974/1984: 8–12) identifies a list of 49 uncountable words which he assumes are often used in the plural. But, in the present author's experience, the plurals of only the following 11 can be said to be common: *advice, equipment, behaviour, bedding, damage, furniture, hardware, land, luggage/baggage, money,* and *property*.

Further, it is worth pointing out that for a set of words that allow both a countable and an uncountable use, KenE tends to use the plural version, where Standard International English uses the singular version: *vocabularies, terminologies, ideologies, properties, questionnaires, consultancies, inconveniences, researches*, and *behaviours* all seem to be more often used than *vocabulary, ideology, property, questionnaire, consultancy, inconvenience, research*, and *behaviour*.[4]

Finally, there are miscellaneous set phrases and idiomatic expressions in which the plural –s has been added in KenE: *to bear **fruits**, to come out of the **blues**, My **names** are Andrew Joseph,* and ***sometimes** back*. And there is also the tendency, in informal spoken speech, for the educated youth to pluralize greetings when addressing many people: *Good **mornings**! **Hellos**!* and *How are **yous**?*

4.2.2 Addition of other inflections

The inflection *–ly*, affixed to adjectives to form adverbs of manner, has been affixed to the adverbs *often* and *anyhow*, to introduce *oftenly* and *anyhowly* into KenE. It has also been added to the adjective *jobless* to produce *joblessly*, and to the numeral adjective *several* to produce *severally*, which, in everyday KenE, means 'several times'.

There are also some cases where new words and expressions have been coined through the addition of some inflection: *(to be) worthy doing/to do sth* tends to be used for *(to be) worth doing sth*, and *a ru**nning** nose* for *a runny nose*.

4.2.3 Omission of the plural –s

This omission is manifested in the use of fixed expressions and idioms in the singular which are used in the plural in Standard International English: *master of ceremony* is used in KenE for *master of ceremon**ies***, and *to make noise about doing sth* for *to make nois**es** about doing sth*.

---

4 In addition to *behaviours*, Hancock and Angogo (1982: 316) also mention *bottoms, breads, bums, laps, minds, nighties, noses*, and *popcorns* as "some English words in Kenyan and Tanzanian colloquial speech [that] have a plural form but [which] are treated as singulars", but the present author has not yet come across these words used in this way.

4.3 Aspects of the noun phrase

This section describes the following aspects of the noun phrase: the pervasive omission (and the occasional addition) of articles, the use of the Noun + Noun structure for the genitive *'s* structure, the pluralisation of premodifying nouns, the use of some adjectives as nouns, and the use of the complementiser *that* after nouns that do not require it.

4.3.1 Omission and addition of the article

KenE is one of the L2 varieties data from which Sand (2004: 295) looked at in relation to article use. In one of her conclusions, she writes: "The most important feature is that all contact varieties irrespective of their substrate share a tendency to use definite articles in certain contexts where they are not required in British or American standard English". For a keen observer of KenE, it is hard to imagine what such contexts could be, because the overriding picture one gets from KenE data is that articles instead tend to be omitted, not overused. Sand (2004: 290–291) discusses five such "semantic contexts in which definite articles occur regularly in contact varieties but not in British or New Zealand English": a) "with collective nouns with a generic meaning, such as *society, people, men, women, boys* or *girls*"; b) "before nouns referring to institutions, such as *church, university, college, school* or *jail* [...]"; c) "when the proper name of a place or institution is used [...]"; d) in "temporal expressions, like days, months, seasons and holidays [...]"; e) in "deverbal nouns in *–ing* [...]". For each context, the author provides an example taken from the Kenyan component of the East African sub-corpus of the International Corpus of English (hereafter referred to as the ICE-K). But although corpus-based, some of the illustrative examples do not seem to be representative of KenE. That is the case of the sentence *"The most universalized celebrations is the Christmas that most people in the world are much concerned"* (ICE-EA(K) exam essay)", which Sand used to illustrate the use of the definite article in "temporal expressions".[5]

The widely held view that the tendency in African English is to omit articles from contexts where they are normally used in standard native English therefore remains more convincing. In relation to this, Mesthrie (2008b: 630) writes: "Articles are another area where New Englishes are united in their differences

---

[5] There is actually only one such instance in 8 hits of the word *Christmas* (as a festival) in the entire written component of the ICE-K, and none in the 10 hits of it in the spoken one.

from StE. Occasional absence of the article [...], whether definite or indefinite, is noted in all the L2 varieties represented [...]". For the specific case of KenE it can be asserted that while the absence of the indefinite article may be deemed "occasional", that of the definite article is definitely not just occasional; it is frequent.

4.3.1.1 Omission of the definite article

While reading news on the Kenyan Citizen TV (on the 1 p.m. news on 5 Jun 2012), the newsreader, J.M., started one sentence like this: *"The Treasury – Treasury, rather, has* [...]*"*. His "apology" for having used the article *the* where it would be deemed correct in Standard International English (hereafter StdIntE) is a telling illustration of what can be called the "definite-article-phobia" on the part of KenE speakers in general.[6]

As part of the eWAVE survey, the feature "F62: use of zero article where StE has definite article" was rated pervasive in KenE. However, as will be seen below, the pervasiveness of this omission of the definite article varies with linguistic contexts. Three of these where the definite article is most often frequently absent will be used for illustration: a) before abbreviations, b) before unique institutions, and c) in specific phrases (notably *the Nairobi area* and *the English language*).

Omission of the definite article before abbreviations

According to the relevant rule in StdIntE grammar, the article *the* should be used before abbreviations (such as *WTO*), as opposed to acronyms (such as *UNESCO*).[7] But consider the following example:

---

[6] The well-known Kenyan grammarian, Philip Ochieng, who runs a weekly column in the *Saturday Nation* about correct English usage, expressed his exasperation about the non-use of the definite article in the following terms:

[...] For example, the building in which *the* Finance minister works is not simply "Treasury" – as our reporters claim – but "*the* Treasury".

Yet, in all our newspapers – especially the rags which masquerade as "the alternative Press" – you are most likely to find such exasperating statements as: "*Treasury* yesterday said it had no money" [...]

(See Philip Ochieng, "Mark my Word", *Saturday Nation*, 18 Feb 2012, p. 14).

[7] However, this rule will apply only if the noun (for which the expected article should be used) is used in its countable sense, thus excluding the use of the article in e.g. ICT (Information and Communication Technology) and RP (Received Pronunciation).

(7) a. Ø **CIC** wishes to make the following statement [...]⁸
    b. There is no doubt that **the MCAs** have a legitimate and constitutional right to request a review of their terms. Indeed, Ø **CIC** has on several occasions requested **the SRC** to exercise their constitutional mandate [...] including Ø **MCAs** to ensure that ...
    c. These functions are not self-appointed [...] but attach to the offices of Ø **MCA** and Ø **CAs**.
    d. Ø **CIC** wishes to highlight the legal implications of the alleged indefinite adjournment or suspension of sittings by **the CA's**.
    e. The Commission urges Ø **MCA's** to fulfill their oath of office [...]
    f. To the people of Kenya, Ø **CIC** urges you to remain vigilant [...]
    (from an advertiser's announcement by the CIC Chairperson in the *Daily Nation*, 8 Nov 2013, p. 21)

Since the author of the text in (7) is known to pronounce *CIC* as /siːaɪ ˈsiː/, not as /sik/ – that is, as an abbreviation, not as an acronym – it is clear that in his grammar, and that of KenE speakers in general, even abbreviations can be pronounced as acronyms. However, variability is evident in his use and non-use of the definite article: this was used at least once before the other abbreviations, *SRC, CA,* and *MCA*.

Omission of the definite article before unique institutions
Consider the following data:

(8) *Message from the CEO*
    a. Ø Women Enterprise Fund was established with a clear mandate of providing sustainable and wholesome solutions [...]
    b. Ø Women Enterprise Fund promotes financial inclusion of women [...]
    c. Loans are provided at zero percent [...] thus making **the** Fund the financial service provider with the most equitable regional distribution channels in the country.
    d. Whereas **the** Fund is a flagship project in Ø.Vision 2030, and a clear demonstration of our government's commitment to the realization of the 3rd Millennium Development Goal on women empowerment [...]

---

8 In Kenya, *CIC* stands for *Commission for the Implementation of the Constitution*, *MCA* for *Member of the County Assembly*, *CA* for *County Assembly*, and *SRC* for *Salaries and Remuneration Commission*.

e. [...] **The** Fund will endeavour to do the best to serve you as trustworthy customers.
f. [...] Ø Women Enterprise Fund promotes economic empowerment and gender equality [...]
(from an advertiser's announcement in the *Daily Nation*, 9 Feb 2011, p. 38)

Two unique institutions (in Kenya) are concerned here: the *Women's Enterprise Fund* and the *Vision 2030*. For neither of them was the definite article used. Interestingly, it was consistently used before the shortened version, *the Fund*. It looks as if the use of the premodifying phrase *Women Enterprise* obviated the need to use the definite article. Yet, one would have expected a premodifier to automatically make the head noun even "more definite" and, thus, to make the use of the definite article even more likely.

Omission of the definite article before specific phrases
The phrases in question are: *majority of (people), Nairobi area* (or *region*), *English language,* and *reason.* (Here *Nairobi* and *English* stand for any place and language, respectively.)

– *Majority of* ...
It is only fitting to start with the following "warning" from Hocking (1974/1984: 217), about the use of the word *majority*: "NEVER use *majority* without any article: **Majority of people are not aware of this*. This is the common mistake, but it must always have one article or the other, and usually *the*". (The emphasis, through the use of capital letters in *NEVER,* is Hocking's own.) If there is a warning that has gone completely unheeded by the users of KenE, it is well and truly this one, because the omission of the article before the word *majority* is undeniably one of the features par excellence of KenE.[9]

Below are some examples (also illustrated with in Buregeya 2008: 35–36) taken from a variety of Kenyan newspapers:

---

[9] More or less the same feature has been reported in Ghanaian English (GhE) by Huber and Diko (2008: 375): "The omission of an article in *majority (of)/minority of* can be described as default usage in Ghana". The difference between KenE and GhE is that dropping the article before *minority of* is, strangely enough, not common in KenE.

(9) a. Ø **Majority of** secondary schools [...] have defied the [...] directive to reduce fees.
(*The East African Standard*, 12 Jan 2000, p. 2)
b. *He noted that surveys [...] have shown that Ø **majority of** schools [...]*
(*The East African Standard*, 25 Feb 1999)
c. *A spot-check by Kenya Times indicated that Ø **majority of** the touts [...]*
(*The Kenya Times*, 15 Jul 1999, p. 28)
d. *[...] but particularly because of their belonging to the party that has been given the mandate by Ø **majority** Kenyans to rule them.*
(*The Kenya Times*, 12 Jul 2000, p. 6)
e. *Ø **Majority of** those being retrenched are in the age brackets of 25–40.*
(*The Kenya Times*, 5 Dec 2000, p. 4)
f. *[...] the education of the girl child was a big success in primary schools but Ø **majority** [drop out] during the transition to secondary schools.*
(*The East African Standard*, 15 Jul 2000, p. 12)

– **Nairobi area** (and, to a lesser extent, **Nairobi region**)
Consider the examples in (10), all drawn from an article in *The Standard* (2 Apr 2013, p. 6):

(10) a. *A woman and her children at Ø **Kakola area** in Ahero yesterday following heavy rains. RIGHT: Flooded homes in **the area**.*
b. *TOP: A vehicle destroyed by floods at Ø **Juanco area** in Ngong town yesterday.*
c. *He added two other vehicles were swept at Lemelepo River in **the area** but the occupants were not injured.*
d. *They feared a temporary bridge **in the area** might be swept away by floods.*

As in the case of *Women Enterprise Fund* vs *the Fund*, what is interesting in the examples in (10) is the fact that while the article was omitted before the noun *area* when this was premodified by the name of a place, it was used when no such premodifier was used.

– **English language**
Consider the following examples (all from a PhD thesis proposal by N.B.W., Oct 2011):

(11) a. *Building on work on Ø **English language** in her book for teachers [...]*
  b. *In the East African region, Tanzania fares badly in Ø **English language** and moreover, English in comparison to other subjects in the curriculum.*
  c. *These differences in religious inclinations determine the attitude and beliefs learners have about **the English language** today.*
  d. *Despite these challenges, some students pass in **the English language** and pursue it at higher levels.*
  e. *This belief has for long affected the learning of Ø **English language**.*
  f. *[...] this study assesses the beliefs and motivation the learners of **the English language** have towards learning the language.*
  g. *Students taking Ø **English language**, specifically linguistic courses, in the Department of Languages and Linguistics [...] will form a case for study.*
  h. *The questionnaires distributed by the researcher will be in Ø **English language**, however, where need for clarification arises, Kiswahili might be used as well.*

Despite the variability in the use vs. non-use of the article *the* in the examples above, the indication is clearly that the omission of it before the structure "name of language + the word *language* itself" is the rule rather than the exception.

– **Reason:** ... (and, but to a lesser extent, **Question is:** ...)

The use of the nouns *reason* and *question* without the definite article occurs when speakers want to introduce the reason for what they have been saying.

(12) a. *Although many people were standing near bags its 2 [accused persons] who were arrested. [...] Ø **Question is** [:] are the 2 accused persons who had possession of bags?*
  (S1BCE06K)
  b. *[It is] Broca's aphasia [that] is at play [here]. Ø **Reason:** [...]*
  (from an MA paper by K.P., Jun 2007)
  c. *The type of aphasia at play is Broca's aphasia. Ø **Reasons:** [...]*
  (from an MA paper by O.I.O., Jun 2007)

4.3.1.2 Addition of the definite article

While the overriding tendency in KenE is to omit the definite article, there are two cases where this is actually used where it is not in StdIntE: before the phrases *Standard (...) English* and *Almighty God*. The latter phrase is almost always used orally, in prayers. When it comes to written uses of it, it will almost certainly be found in the acknowledgements section of postgraduate theses/dissertations, as in the following:

(13) *First, I give thanks to **the Almighty God** for providing me with abundant grace throughout this research period.*
(from a PhD thesis by S.M.N., Aug 2014)

Regarding *the Standard English*, here are some examples:

(14) a. *One of the important illustrations from history is based on **the Standard English**. **Standard English** is a variety that [is] usually used in print [..]*
b. ***The Standard English** has grown to be the statusful and prestigious variety of English over the ages and a consensus [..] was arrived at what is **Standard English** and what is not.*
c. *The vocabulary and grammar of **the Standard English** had a consensus but the pronunciation did not.*
d. *However, there is one accent associated with **the Standard English** and this is the RP. [ ]*
e. *It is the accent associated with **the Standard English**.*
(from an MA paper by N.T., Jan 2013)

The examples in (14) above reveal the reverse phenomenon of using the definite article when the noun *English* is premodified by *standard* from the previous one (of *English language*) where it tends to be omitted when *English* is postmodified by the noun *language*.

4.3.1.3 Omission of the indefinite article

Omission of the indefinite article in KenE from where it is expected in StdIntE seems to be a much less frequent phenomenon (and on the whole should not be regarded as a feature of KenE) than omitting its definite counterpart. However, the indefinite article is systematically omitted in at last three set phrases/idiomatic expressions (i.e. *on Ø par with, Ø song and dance,* and *make Ø noise*) and is frequently omitted after the predeterminer *such*.

Regarding *such*, here are many instances (out of many more in the same document, the "Kenya Citizenship and Immigration Regulations, 2012") where the indefinite article has been omitted after it:

(15) a. *15. Points of entry and departure*
   [...]
   (b) a place specified as appoint [sic] of entry in the Fourth Schedule at any time other than the time specified in relation to **such Ø place** *in that schedule [...]*
   b. *16. Report [sic] of entry*
   (2) [...] the person-in-charge of the ship or his or her agent shall –
   [...]
   (b) prevent the disembarkation of any person to whom paragraph (1) applies, until **such Ø time** *when an immigration officer shall authorize disembarkation.*
   c. *19. Permanent residence*
   [...]
   (3) A permanent residence certificate issued in respect of a person who is not present in Kenya, at the time of application, shall cease to be valid if **such Ø person** *fails to enter Kenya within one year from the date of issue.*

However, besides the instances where the indefinite article has been omitted, in the same document there are others (though much fewer) where it has also been used, as in (16) below:

(16) *[16] (3) [...] the person-in-charge of the aircraft or his or her agent shall –*
   [...]
   (b) prevent any person to whom paragraph (1) applies from leaving the precincts of the airport until **such a time** *when the immigration officer shall authorize the person to leave.*

4.3.2 The noun + noun structure used for the genitive's structure

This feature echoes the eWAVE feature "F77: omission of genitive suffix; possession expressed through bare juxtaposition of nouns", as in *"My daddy brother"*. In the eWAVE survey, the feature was rated as "neither pervasive nor extremely rare" in KenE. That was because, as Buregeya (2012: 470) suggested, the omission of the genitive 's "seems to be a feature of plural nouns and proper names", but not of common nouns in the singular. The suggestion was made on the basis that a structure like *my daddy brother* (for *my daddy's brother*) is indeed not common in KenE.

Example (17) is a good illustration of the tendency to use the N's + N and the N + N structures for exactly the same meaning: on the KTN news of 15 Aug 2014 the following two lines scrolled down on the television screen.

(17) a. *[The] guard:* **Governor's bodyguards** *accosted me.*
b. *[Mr] Moit: I was held by* **Nadith bodyguards**.

Both the nouns *governor* and *Nadith* refer to the same person (as do *the guard* and *Mr Moit*). But while in (a) the N's + N structure was used, in (b) it is the N + N that was, by the same person and to express exactly the same meaning.

Frequent phrases in KenE in which N+N tends to be more often used than N's + N are: *women groups* for *women's groups* (a case first discussed by Zuengler 1982: 116 and then by Buregeya 2008, 2012),[10] *women representatives* for *women's representatives* (who have been part of the Kenyan National Assembly since 2013), and *children affairs* for *children's affairs*. (It is worth recalling the multiple use of the phrase *Women Enterprise Fund*, instead of *Women's Enterprise Fund*, in example [8] above.[11]) Intriguingly, the phrase *men groups* is hardly used in KenE, although *men's groups* is not common either.

But there are already two types of structure about which there is practically no confusion at all in KenE, because, seemingly, the N's +N is simply absent from them. One such structure is the plural noun expressing duration, e.g. *three years' experience*; the other is the expression of measurement used before the noun *worth*, e.g. *a USD million's worth of goods*, as in the following example:

(18) *"[...] Uganda imports $700 million (Sh70 billion) worth of goods from Kenya [...], the President said."*
(*Daily Nation*, 13 Aug 2015, p. 4)

It should be added that using the genitive *'s* is a written rule that tends to be ignored not only in L2 varieties of English like KenE, but also in L1 varieties of it. It is one of those phenomena which Swan (2016, paragraph 318.4) calls "small, less important distinctions", and which are likely to disappear from English. He writes: "When confusions like these become widespread, they can lead to language change. This may well happen with the possessive *'s* form:

---

10 Even though in the written component of the ICE-K *women's groups* appears a record 44 times (against only 3 for *women groups*), almost all of them are from the same academic text entitled "Politics and Women's Groups" (see W2A018K).
11 Another telling detail is that the Republic of Kenya's government ministry in charge of child welfare during the 2008–2013 term was called "Ministry of Gender and Children Affairs".

more and more people are leaving out the apostrophe or putting it in the 'wrong' place, so that this spelling convention might one day lose its importance and even disappear".

4.3.3 Pluralisation of the premodifying noun

Closely related to the confusing use of the N + N and the N's + N structures is the pluralisation of the premodifying noun. The general StdIntE rule is that in an N + N sequence, the first N should be kept in its singular form, even if it has a plural meaning, as in *child labour*. For a non-native speaker of English, the application of this rule is bound to be a difficult task for two main reasons: first, there is a non-negligible number of phrases that are exceptions to the rule (Swan 2016: paragraph 125.4 lists some fifteen of them, including *a savings account, a customs officer,* and *arms control*). Second, there are differences in usage which have been reported in the two native varieties that influence KenE the most: Biber et al. (1999: 594) note that "plural premodifying nouns are more productive in BrE than AmE" and that "this difference is most evident in news". So, in KenE it is not unusual to encounter *a books fair* alongside *a book fair*, and *children welfare* alongside *child welfare*. Consider the following example from the written component of the ICE-K:

(19) *According to a survey done by the Children Welfare Society of Kenya in Mombasa, Malindi, Kilifi, Kiambu and Busia, Mombasa has the highest number of child prostitutes mainly in the tourism industry.*
(W2B012K)

In (19) we have both *children welfare*, which violates the rule above, and *child prostitutes*, which, on the face of it, does not violate it, but which in fact makes it even more confusing because, if the meaning of the phrase is that the children were prostitutes, then *children prostitutes* should have been used instead, as when we say *women lawyers*.

4.3.4 Some adjectives used as nouns

Consider the following examples (borrowed from Buregeya 2008: 67):

(20) a. *Allan is a **second born** in a family of five [...]*
    (*The East African Standard*, 4 Jan 2000, p. 1)

b. *Here she is assisted out of her house by her **second born**.*
(*The East African Standard*, 4 Jan 2000, p. 24)
c. *The [Minister] is garlanded by a pupil of Bondeni Girls **Primary**, Mombasa.*
(*Daily Nation*, 30 Nov 1999)
d. *Structurally, [it] proposes a 12-year basic education system, comprising one year of **pre-primary**, seven **primary** and four **secondary**.*
(*The East African Standard*, 4 Jul 2000, p. 2)
e. *The principal of Kabungut Boys **High** says Mr Kitur has done the school proud.*
(*The Standard*, 1 Sep 2006)

With the exception of *second-born*, all the other adjectives in bold type refer to education. (Another education-related adjective used in the same way is *secretarial*, which is frequently used on its own in advertisements like *We offer secretarial*.) Mesthrie (2008c: 497) noted a similar phenomenon in Black South African English, namely "[a] striking characteristic is the use of adjectives as nouns". He gives five examples, three of which relate to education: *primary* ('primary school'), *tertiary* ('tertiary education'), and *religious* ('religious studies').

But while it can be easily assumed that the non-use of a noun after *second-born* is modelled on that of *first-born* (which can be used also as a noun, and, hence, can stand on its own), it is not clear why only some adjectives related to education can "afford" to be used without their accompanying nouns. It might be because even without these nouns the meaning is more or less clear. Nevertheless, one would still wonder why KenE does not equally drop the noun *season* after *rainy* and *dry* in a construction like *The rainy is preferable to the dry*, where *season* would be easily recoverable if it were left out.

4.3.5 The complementiser *that* used after nouns that do not require it

In KenE *that*-complementation often appears after nouns that do not require it in StdIntE,[12] as the examples below show:

---

[12] Strangely, Hudson-Ettle (1998) gives no room at all, in her discussion (in section 5.3.1.1) of "*that* nominal clauses" in the "English used and spoken in Kenya", to this use of the "conjunction" *that* after nouns that do not require it.

(21) a. **Matters** *arising from the minutes*
 – **That** *the first issue of the Faculty newsletter had been published.* [...]
 b. **Communication** *from the chair*
 – **That** *there were several promotions and new appointments in the Faculty.* [...]
 c. **Approval** *of examinations results for 2012/2013*
 – **Tha**t *the results were not discussed* [...]
 d. *Any other* **business**
 – **That** *the agenda for meeting should be followed to save on time.*
 (from the minutes of a University-of-Nairobi Faculty-of-Arts Board's meeting, 25 Jul 2013)

The nouns *matters, communication, approval,* and *business* are not among those that would take a *that*-complement clause in StdIntE. However, using them the way they were in (21) is typical of the style of taking meeting minutes in KenE.

It should be added that even after nouns such as *recommendation*, which can take a *that*-complement clause, Biber et al. (1999: 648) report corpus findings showing that "There is a pronounced tendency for the noun phrases taking noun-complement clauses to be definite and singular" and that "This tendency is strongest with *that*-clauses [...]". In the light of this quotation, the *that*-clauses in (22) below would be rather unusual in StdIntE.

(22) **Recommendations**:
 [i] **That** *an examination processing schedule for each semester* [...] *be prepared* [...]
 [ii] **That** *examination processing* [...] *should be completed* [...]
 [iii] **That** *no internal examiner, from whom examination marks are still due, shall have his/her request for leave of absence approved* [...]
 [iv] **That** *processing of examinations by internal examiners should be an important factor* [...]
 (from a Faculty-of-Arts document, University of Nairobi, 16 Jun 1999)

4.4 Aspects of the verb phrase

This chapter identifies the following aspects of the verb phrase as those where KenE behaves in its particular way compared with StdIntE: marking the progressive aspect on stative verbs, overusing the modal *shall*, using *could* and *would* for *should*, using *would* for *will* and other forms, using *will/shall* in conditional and temporal clauses with *if*, lack of (tense) backshift in indirect speech, omitting obligatory complements after certain verbs, placing the *for*-introduced PP before the direct object NP, using certain verbs with PP complements instead of NP ones, using certain verbs with NP complements instead of PP ones, violating selection restrictions with some verbs, using the complementiser *that* after verbs that do not require it, complementation with *as follows*, using the copula *be + as a result*, using certain intransitive verbs transitively, omitting the infinitive marker *to* after the verb *enable* + direct object, not marking the accusative on the pronoun *who*, using the infinitive for the modal *should*, using *what you do* for *what you should do (is)*, using continuous tenses after *this is the first time*, using *can be able* for the modal *can*, mistaking past-tense forms for past-time meanings, using *never* for *did not*, and using the infinitive marker *to* for the preposition *to*.

4.4.1 The progressive -*ing* marked on stative verbs

This feature corresponds to eWAVE "F88: Wider range of uses in progressive *be + V-ing* than in StE: extension to stative verbs". In the eWAVE survey, its attestation rate was 63%, and its pervasiveness rate was 65%. This looks like a (relatively) high frequency. But, as one of their conclusions, Hilbert and Krug (2012), who studied the use of the progressive in Maltese English, report the following surprise finding:

> Our data show that the recurring "overuse" claim from the literature on progressives in non-ENL varieties is not easily or universally applicable. [...] What we do find are stative verbs used in the progressive aspect, though primarily with a limited number of verbs, notably *have* and *be*. These are high-frequency verbs and thus statistically to be expected to figure prominently. (2012: 133)

What is reported in the first sentence of this quotation is a "surprise" finding vis-à-vis the 65 % pervasiveness rate above. It should be noted, though, that elsewhere Hilbert and Krug (2012: 115) report that "Qualitatively, MaltE differs from BrE markedly in the use of the progressive with stative verbs. In the British data, hardly any stative verbs can be found in the progressive. In fact, what we are finding is that *be* and stative *find* do not occur in the progressive aspect at all". This latter quotation sounds more of what researchers on the topic would have expected. However, Hundt and Vogel (2011), who specifically sought to answer the question of whether the "overuse of the progressive in ESL and Learner Englishes [was] fact or fiction," did not find that overuse either. They report that "In [their] ESL corpora, unusual combinations of the progressive with stative verbs are also relatively rare. In fact, we found [...] only a few in the Singaporean and Kenyan corpora [...]" (2011: 156).

With specific reference to the KenE corpus, there must be more than just "a few" cases. For example, for the verb *see*, Aldrup (2014: 23) identified 26 occurrences of it used in its "simple tense forms with progressive aspect" (i.e. in its stative meanings) in the (spoken) component of the ICE-K. She compared these to the number of times (789) the verb *see* had been used in its "simple tense forms", and computed the verb *see*'s "share of progressive forms in %", which she found to be only 3.2%. She reported that "The frequency count shows that StE combinations of stative verbs with simple tense forms are much more pervasive in KenE than their use in combination with progressive aspect" (2014: 23). From this she concluded that the feature (F88) was "not extremely frequent compared to [the] StE [structure]" (23).

However, a different methodological approach needs to be followed: the conclusion of whether the feature in question is pervasive or not should not be based on the ratio of its occurrence to that of its expected StE equivalent, since the aim is not to investigate the extent to which StE forms have been replaced by the non-StE ones. The comparison should instead centre around how often the same non-StE forms occur in StE in similar discourse contexts. Such comparison would, for example, relate the twenty-six occurrences identified by Aldrup (2014) in the spoken component of the ICE-K to Hilbert and Krug's observation that "In the British data, hardly any stative verbs can be found in the progressive" (2012: 115).

But there is at least one non-contentious conclusion that can be drawn from Aldrup's (2014) "Table 5: Frequency count of F88: 'Wider range of uses of progressive *be + V-ing* than in StE: extension to stative verbs" (see pp. 23–24), namely that the rate at which the progressive is used with stative verbs is lexically-conditioned: it was highest (26.7%) for *imagine* and lowest (0.1%) for *want*. (The table compares rates for fifteen verbs.) This type of variability was explicitly referred to by Hundt and Vogel (2011) and Hilbert and Krug (2012). Hundt and Vogel (2011: 160) write: "[...] when comparing ENL, ESL and EFL, it is important to take variation *within* ENL, ESL and EFL into account before generalizing to the type of variety as such". For their part, Hilbert and Krug (2012: 130) report that "In each variety [i.e. MaltE, BrE, and AmE], *I'm really liking...* and *Are you understanding...?* are rated [by questionnaire respondents] to be very common". They also report that the use of a structure like *Are you understanding my point?* is "primarily a phenomenon of speech" (2012: 109), which makes the mode (spoken vs. written) of the text in which a given progressive stative was used another determinant of variability, in addition to the type of lexical item used.

Buregeya (2013: 18) adds a third potential type of variability: the *linguistic context* in which the stative verb was used. He reports the results of two MA students' (unpublished) studies which suggest that the progressive is most likely to be used on a verb like *know*[13] in two particular contexts: a) in an interrogative structure and b) when the verb appears after a modal auxiliary. For example, the sentence *Could you be knowing the way to Kitengela?* was chosen as the correct option by 22/30 (i.e. 70%) of respondents, who were asked to fill the gap in *Could you __ the way to Kitengela?* with a) *be knowing*, b) *know*, and c) *have knowledge of*. Another group of respondents were asked to indicate whether the following two sentences were correct or incorrect: a) *Could you be knowing the principal?* and b) *Are you knowing the principal?* Twenty (i.e. 67%) of the thirty respondents indicated that sentence (a) was correct, but not a single one of them did regarding sentence (b).

Below are examples (from the present author's large collection) of the use of the progressive on stative verbs in KenE.

(23) a. *As a result, they **would be having** the same percentage. If the interviewer meant the length of time one has been in politics, then [this candidate] **should be having** a lower percentage than [the other two]. [...] Unfortunately some of [interviewees], **could not be knowing** the candidates.*
(from an MA research paper, Feb 2009)
b. *"By the time the parties are coming to court for hearing, the judges **will be knowing** what kind of case the they have", said Chief Registrar of Judiciary...*
(*The Standard*, 25 Mar 2013, p. 4)
c. *Again it is not easy for the researcher to describe epenthesis phenomena of all loan words in Ekegusii because [...] he **may not be knowing** them.*
(from an MA research paper, Jan 2012)
d. *The patient **was having** anomia, that is, a problem of recalling or naming things [...]*
(from an MA paper by P.O.N., May 2011)
e. *Hi doc. I **am not seeing** my sociolings results, What hpnd?*
(an SMS from an MA student, 6 Oct 2011)
f. *By the way, **I'm not seeing** any evidence of demolition here.*
(from an SMS by a former MA student, 23 Aug 2014)

---

[13] This is particularly interesting for the verb *know*, which is mentioned by Biber et al. (1999: 472) and Hewings (2013: 222) as one of those that rarely occur with the progressive aspect in BrE and AmE. (Biber et al. also mention *see*.)

g. *[If someone]* **is not meeting** *those conditions, then [...]*
   (said on TV by the Principal Secretary, Ministry of Transport, 24 Dec 2013)
h. *I don't know why, but on this **I'm not believing** you.*
   (said by KTN news presenter K.E., 1 Aug 2014)
i. *The term "context"* **is not being** *specific. Exactly which context?*
   (from an MA student's paper, Dec 2014)
j. *The main problem is that the verbal prefix "re" and the adverb "again"* **are performing** *exactly the same semantic function.*
   (*Daily Nation*, 3 Jan 2015)

At a glance, it also seems that the stative is also more likely to occur when the verb is preceded by the negative *not* than when it is not.

All in all, it is only by taking the different types of variability into account that the apparent contradictory findings on the pervasiveness or otherwise of the use of the progressive on stative verbs will be put into its right perspective.

4.4.2 The modal *shall* overused with 2nd and 3rd pers. subjects

The modal verb *shall* is normally associated with 1st person subjects, both in the singular and the plural, even though even in this linguistic context "*Shall* is in present-day English (especially in AmE), a rather rare auxiliary and only two uses [...] are generally current [...]" (Quirk et al. 1985: 229). But the focus in this section is about *shall* used with 2nd and 3rd person subjects. About this use, Quirk et al. (1985: 230) say the following:

> *Shall* is in very restricted use with 2nd and 3rd person subjects as a way of expressing the *speaker*'s volition, either in granting a favour: [as in] You *shall* do as you wish [...] or in giving orders [as in] You *shall* do exactly as I say. [...] In these cases *shall* is archaic and "authoritarian" in tone.
>
> [...] A further restricted use of *shall* with a 3rd person subject occurs in legal or quasi-legal discourse, in stipulating regulations or legal requirements. Here *shall* is close in meaning to *must* [...]

The rare use of *shall* is also reflected in the corpus-based frequency figures reported by Biber et al. (1999: 486) for the "nine central modals" (*will, would, can, could, may, should, must, might, shall*): *shall* was found to be the least frequently used, occurring only about 250 times per million words, against 3,500 times for *will* (the most frequently used modal). It is further reflected in the fact that Hewings's (2013) grammar contains six units (15 to 20) dealing with "modals and semi-modals", all of which are mentioned in the headings of the units, with the exception of *shall*.

The claimed "overuse" of *shall* in KenE should be understood against this background. Its use with 2nd person subjects can be said to be frequent, while its use with 3rd person subjects can be said to be pervasive, particularly in written KenE. (A quick browse through the spoken component of the ICE-K will show that most of the uses of *shall* go with the 1st person pronoun, either *I* or *we*.) Example (24) illustrates the use of *shall* used with 3rd pers. subjects, and (25) the use of *shall* with 2nd pers. subjects.

(24) a. *The conference **shall** take place between 6th–8th August, 2014 [...]*
 b. *This international conference **will** be hosted by the Institute of African Studies [...]*
 c. *The conference **shall** take place on Main Campus of Kenyatta University [...]*
 d. *Authors of successful abstracts **will** be contacted by February 15, 2014.*
 e. *An ISSN publication **will** be produced with all the papers [...] that **will** be presented [...]*
 f. *[...] the conference papers [...] **shall** be submitted to a [...] peer review process [...]*
 g. *The selected articles are the ones that **shall** appear as part of published [...] proceedings.*
 h. *Oral and poster presentations [...] **will** be used [...]*
 (from a "Call for Papers" by the Institute of African Studies, Kenyatta University, Jan 2014)

(25) a. *You are now her daughter and **you shall** live in her house.*
 (W2F012K)
 b. *I think you are extremely as imaginative + hence **you shall** get far in life.*
 (W1B-SK24)

Clearly, in none of all the instances in (24) where *shall* was used would it have been required in BrE or AmE: none of them was meant to express an obligation, in the sense of *must*. They all just state events that will take place in the future. Wherever they were used, *will* would have been a more appropriate choice. It is interesting to note that the composer of the text used *will* as well, with the same meaning as *shall*, and in the same linguistic contexts (both were used with 3rd person subjects and in both active and passive structures). In (25), while *you shall* in (a) might be construed to mean a promise, that in (b) cannot be.

4.4.3 *Could* and *would* used for *should*

This section is about instances where the modal *should* ought to have been used to give advice. Below are some illustrative examples.

(26) a. *[...] variations which would result in exceeding the Contract Price by more than 10%* **would have** *the prior concurrence of the World Bank [...]*
(W1B-BK08)
b. *In the spirit of being mindful of the welfare of our brethren, we* **would have** *given this milk free of charge to these children's homes [...]*
(W2E017K)
c. *The title is not appropriate here. It* **could have** *been "suggestions", not "the suggestions".*
(from an MA paper by O.M.J., Jun 2009)

4.4.4 *Would* used for *will* and other modal verbs

Admittedly, the "misuse" represented in this feature is subtle to notice. That is why Hocking (1974/1984: 156–7), who first pointed it out, had to write a very long explanation (shortened in the quotation below) to help the reader notice it:

> Apart from the common special uses of *would* [...] the word can ONLY be used *in connection with an "if" clause IN THE PAST TENSE*.
> [...]
> ANY USE OF "WOULD" THAT IS NOT CONNECTED WITH AN "IF" CLAUSE, EXPRESSED OR CLEARLY IMPLIED, IS MEANINGLESS.
> [...]
> (Another way of explaining this that some people find easier to grasp is to say that *would* can only be used in a sentence that deals with an imaginary condition [...].)

With Hocking's highly prescriptive explanation in mind, consider the following examples taken from the written component of the ICE-K.

(27) a. *Most hospitals are situated in urban areas so that whether a woman resides in an urban or rural area, if she has a medical problem she* **would** *have to go to an urban area.*
(W2A028K)
b. *A teacher who doesn't get on well with the fellow teachers* **would** *always want to quarrel the learners.*
(W1A012K)

c. *It is wrong to assume that the speaker is the poet himself. [...] You **would** be safe to assume that the speaker is someone other than the poet himself*
(S2B078K)
d. *[...] the total fertility rate [...] is the average number of children a woman **would** have at the end of her reproduction period taken to be 50 years*
(W2A013K)
e. *I bet that by just being clever at guessing, you are unlikely to understand that weather report. [...] You **would** have to understand [...] the announcer's mother tongue to have even a faint idea as to what message was.*
(W2B003K)

The appropriate modal verbs should be *will* in examples (a) to (c), *can* in (d), and *need to* in (e).

It is important to point out that the use of *would* specifically for *will* has been reported for a number of L2 varieties of English (see Schneider 2015: 106). Focusing on the use of *will* in Ghanaian English (GhE), Schneider (2015: 106) writes:

> [Deuber et al. 2012] show that for a number of New English varieties the boundaries between the two modals *will* and *would* are blurred in contrast to the ENL varieties, such as BrE or AmE, where the two modals have distinct functions. A conflation of the two modals in written GhE has been reported by Owusu-Ansah (1994) and Ngula (2009 and 2012).

This conflation in GhE is manifested in particular in "the use of WOULD with non-past, non-hypothetical 'intention' and 'prediction' readings" (Schneider 2015: 89). It is this particular aspect that can be said to characterize KenE as well, as illustrated by the three examples in (27 a-c) above. The other (two) aspects reported by Schneider (2015) cannot be said to be characteristic of KenE at all. They read like this: a) "While past and hypothetical uses of WILL are nearly absent in ICE-GB, especially hypothetical uses are extremely frequent in the data from GhE" (Schneider 2015: 21); b) "[...] the hypothetical and related functions (i.e. tentativeness/politeness) of WOULD [have been] taken over by WILL in GhE" (108). In a nutshell, what is being claimed here for KenE is that while *would* has taken over some of the uses of *will*, the reverse is not the case.[14]

---

[14] Another statement made by Schneider (2015: 105) which, until it has been tested, will sound as a huge claim in relation to KenE is this: "The use of WILL to express 'habit' is drastically higher in spoken GhE than in spoken BrE".

4.4.5 *Shall* and *will* used after *if* and conjunctions of time

The use of the modal *will* "in dependent temporal and conditional clauses" is another aspect reported by Schneider (2015) to have been reported in previous studies. In the case of KenE, it is not just *will* that is used in this way, but also *shall*, since, as discussed in section 4.4.2, the latter is frequently used where *will* is expected in BrE and AmE. This section is about *will* and *shall* being used where the simple present, or the present perfect, is expected to be used for events/actions in the future. This is because "The use of the simple present for future time is much more common in subordinate clauses, particularly in conditional and temporal clauses" (Greenbaum and Quirk 1990: 50) and "The present perfect is used instead of the future perfect, to express the idea of completion [as in] *I'll phone you when I've finished.* (NOT ... when I will have finished.)" (Swan 2016: paragraph 231.3).

Below are some examples of *shall* and *will* used in KenE after *if* and temporal conjunctions:

(28) a. *Meanwhile, I'm having a mild problem and I wanted to request for some financial "soft loan"* ***if you will be*** *in a position to do so.* (W1B-SK21)
 b. ***If*** *you* ***will*** *have not complied,* ***if*** *you* ***will*** *ignore the law, you will do so at your own peril.*
 (said by the Justice and Constitutional Affairs Minister, on TV, 23 Apr 2012)
 c. *[...] or* ***if*** *in the sole opinion of the Publisher the quality of the Project as evidenced by the edited script* ***shall*** *not be of a sufficient standard, the Publisher shall be at liberty [...]*
 (from an editing contract by the Moran Publishers, 3 Mar 2011)
 d. *It is hereby expressly declared and agreed that* ***if*** *the rent* ***shall*** *be in arrears for more than fourteen days* ***after*** *the same* ***shall*** *have become due [...] or* ***if*** *the tenant* ***shall*** *fail to [...] observe any of the covenants [...]*
 (from a "Tenancy Agreement" text, Nov 1998)

The use of *shall* after the conditional *if* and after *after* (and other temporal conjunctions) in examples (c) and (d) is a frequent feature of the language of contracts in Kenya. In these examples *shall* clearly does not mean obligation or duty, and thus was not warranted at all.

4.4.6 Lack of (tense) backshift in indirect speech

Tense "backshift in indirect speech" is the phrase used by e.g. Greenbaum and Quirk (1990: 296) to refer to the change in the tense of the (subsequent) verb form in an indirect-speech construction. This change corresponds to the eWAVE "F113: Loosening of sequence of tenses rule", exemplified by "*I noticed the van I came in*" used instead of "*I noticed the van I had come in*". This feature is also another frequent one in KenE. Evidence for it can be obtained from virtually any piece of writing that contains indirect/reported speech. Here is one example:

(29) *Justice [X]* **said** *that the suit* **was** *premature since the process* **is** *ongoing and the public* **can** *participate during the vetting by parliament. He* **said** *that the law* **recognises** *legislators as the representative of the people.* (*The Standard on Saturday*, 8 Jun 2013, p. 3)

This single example is typical of what one will expect to find in KenE in relation to "tense harmony" (as the phenomenon is also sometimes called) in reported speech: the lack of it in most cases, and some application of it in a few cases, like the past tense form *was* in the same example.[15] The pervasiveness rate for the eWAVE feature F113 is reported to be 65%, but it is probably even higher in KenE.

4.4.7 Obligatory complements omitted after certain verbs

Hocking (1974/1984: 185) points out the following five verbs: *reach, enjoy, afford, discuss,* and *get*, and then goes on to say about them that "These verbs are peculiar: they can *never* be used without an object after them". But in KenE they are frequently used without one. Several other verbs might as well have been on Hocking's list. Among them are: *revenge*;[16] *sacrifice,* used in KenE to mean 'to sacrifice oneself' (*You've really sacrificed to give your children a good*

---

15 The rule of tense harmony in reported speech allows the verb of the reported speech to stay in the present when "the situation described in the *reported* clause is a *permanent/habitual situation,* or still exists or is relevant at the time we are reporting it [...]" (Hewings 2013: 70). This is not the case, though, with any of the verbs kept in the present tense in example (29).
16 Specifically about *revenge*, Hocking gives the example **People who get cheated may revenge*, and goes on to say that "*Revenge* is NOT a verb in ordinary modern English; it used to be, but now it is only a noun" (1974/1984: 235).

education); *spend*, used in KenE to mean 'to spend the night at a hotel' (*When he visits Nairobi, he spends at the Hilton hotel*); and *appreciate*. Regarding this latter, the sentence/utterance *I really appreciate* is one of the most frequent ones in spoken KenE and, nowadays, in mobile phone short messages, such as the following which the present author received from his postgraduate students:

(30) a. *Thank you very much mwalimu [teacher]. I really **appreciate** Ø.*
       (J.P.O., 9 Feb 2014)
   b. *I don't know how best I can **appreciate** Ø but let God grant you all ...*
       (R.K., 9 Feb 2014)
   c. *Once again thnx a lot for the concern u hve shown. I really **appreciate** Ø.*
       (H.A., 13 Mar 2014)

In fact, in sentence-/utterance-final position, no direct object should be expected after *appreciate* in KenE.

But there are many more verbs that are frequently used in KenE without the complements they require in StdIntE, as the examples below show.

(31) a. *Not all governors call themselves "Your Excellency". It's other people who **call** Ø.*
       (said by one Kenyan governor, 19 Feb 2015)
   b. *[...] as long as two things are not [put] on the table [for negotiation]. One, going back to Analog [TV transmission], because we are not **going** Ø.*
       (said by the Cabinet Secretary, Ministry of Information & ICT, 16 Feb 2015)
   c. *They see that the amount of money they used to get is going to be shared with others, and they don't **want** Ø.*
       (said by the DG of the Communications Authority of Kenya, 16 Feb 2015)
   d. *A creoloid has native speakers while a pidgin does not **have** Ø.*
       (from an MA paper, Dec 2013)
   e. *[They] remained seated inside to avoid contact with their counterparts outside as it would influence the results if they went out to **discuss** Ø.*
       (from an MA paper, Mar 2014)
   f. *Kindly collect your cheque book at NIC Bank [...] Please **ignore** Ø if you have already **taken** Ø.*
       (an SMS received from the NIC Bank, Dec 2012)
   g. *You'll call on another line, I'll not **touch** Ø.*
       (said by a presenter on QFM, 4 Oct 2012)

h. *The study will just [be a highlight] of the differences that* **manifest** *Ø in language usage of the men and women.*
(from a PhD proposal, Sep 2011)
i. *Ministers who have* **returned** *Ø yesterday are [...]; those who have not* **returned** *Ø are [...]. Mr K. vowed not to* **return** *his car [...]*
(*Saturday Nation*, 31 Oct 2009, p. 33, talking about govt. ministers who were expected to return their "gas-guzzlers" for more economical cars)

The wide range of verbs involved in the examples above is an indication that practically any verb that requires an obligatory complement (be it an NP, a PP, or some adverbial) is likely to be used without it in KenE. It should be pointed out here that the eWAVE survey contains a feature, "F42: Object pronoun drop", which has been rated pervasive in KenE. This feature can be considered to be just one aspect of the much wider phenomenon of omitting obligatory complements.

4.4.8 The *for*-introduced PP placed before the direct object NP

This is typically a feature of spoken KenE. Utterances such as *Make for them copies, Sign for me this form, Play for me this song,* and *Buy for her flowers* are very common in KenE. (Passive structures using the same pattern are also sometimes heard, such as *She was bought for flowers.*) The StdIntE rule "broken" here refers to what in transformational grammar is called "strict adjacency principle", which states that "when a Verb subcategorises both an NP and a PP Complement, the NP complement must come immediately after the Verb, and hence must precede the PP complement" (Radford 1988: 350–351).

Two interesting observations need to be made about this phenomenon. First, the prepositioning of the PP before the NP, in KenE, tends to happen when the object of the preposition is a pronoun: utterances such as *Make for the students copies*, where the object of the preposition *for* is an NP (*the students*), are quite rare. Second, the V + PP + NP structure under consideration typically involves the preposition *for*. Utterances such as *Send to me money* and *Send through me the money* hardly occur in KenE. Notice that even the following written examples which the present author came across (in the *Daily Nation*, 25 Aug 2006, p. 2) involve only the preposition *for*.

(32) a. *The best thing I will do is to* **prepare for him an egg**.
 b. *We would like him to [...]* **secure for us scholarships**.

4.4.9 PP complements used after certain verbs instead of NP ones

This feature involves the following verbs (there could be more of them) and the prepositions they take in KenE: *comprise **of**, contradict **with**, demand **for**, discuss **about**, divorce **with** [one's wife/husband], emphasise **on**, investigate **on**, leverage **on**, pass **in** (an exam), request **for**, research **on**, stress **on**, test **on**,* and *total **to**.* (The phrasal verb *advocate for*, which was mentioned by e.g. Schmied 1991a, 2004b, will be excluded from this list because it is recognized as AmE e.g. by the *Longman Dictionary of Contemporary English*, 5th edn, 2009). Adding prepositions to those verbs, thus giving them PP complements instead of NP ones, is, for some of them, notably *discuss*,[17] a phenomenon that has been widely documented in varieties of English beyond Kenya and even Africa. For example, Schmied (1991a: 67) discusses it under the heading "Phrasal/prepositional verbs are used differently" and refers to Platt/Weber/Ho (1984) who discussed verb phrases like *discuss about* and *stress on* "Not only for African English!" (1991a: 68).

While some of those verbs, particularly *discuss about,* occur frequently in everyday language, the frequency of occurrence of some others seems to depend on registers. The following examples, taken from papers written by MA students for a Research Methods course, show how e.g. *test on* can be prevalent in the research register.

(33) a. *Eight sentences **tested on** the words commonly misspelt as one word and eight **tested on** the words commonly misspelt as two words.*
 b. *Question Four **tested on** spelling of the words "after all".*
 c. *Question Number 5 **tested on** "in spite of".*
 (from an MA paper by N.P.G., Apr 2007)

(34) a. *That is why I wanted to **investigate** more **on** the topic of misspellings [...]*
 b. *The table represents the results of Section one of my questionnaire which **tested on** both the derivation and misspellings of the derived words.*
 c. *I recommend that future researchers review and **research on** the teaching approach on spellings [...]*
 (from an MA paper by P.K., Apr 2007)

---

17 One telling detail showing how *discuss about* is an entrenched sequence in East African English comes from the fact that in the *Swahili-English Dictionary*, published by the Tanzanian institution *TUKI* in 2001, the meaning of the Kiswahili verb *zungumzia* is 'discuss about, talk about'.

4.4.10 NP complements used after certain verbs instead of PP ones

Perhaps the most easily recognizable illustration of this feature lies in the use of the single verbs *pick* and *fill* for the phrasal verbs *pick up* and *fill in/out*, respectively. This is how the Kenyan grammarian Philip Ochieng' reacted to one instance where *pick* had been used instead of *pick up*: "When the phone persisted in the *Nation* newsroom, somebody shouted: *'Pick your phone!'* I applauded the sense of responsibility. But the language appalled me. For he had confused *'pick'* with *'pick up'*". (Philip Ochieng, "Mark my Word", *Saturday Nation*, 25 Sep 2007, p. 15)

The same "mistake" involves also a few other verbs, the prominent of which is *quarrel*, often used without the expected preposition *with*, a point made by Hocking (1974/1984: 243), saying: "**He quarrelled me* is wrong". And in (35) below is illustration of this KenE use from the written component of the ICE-K; all three examples come from W1A012K.

(35) a. *Projection is where one fails and would want to show that by <-/**quarraling**> other for example where a **wife is quarrelled by the husband** and she goes to beat the children or being rough to them.*
   b. *A teacher who doesn't get on well with the fellow teachers would always want **to quarrel the learners**.*
   c. *An example is where a learners [bullies] or is always **quarrelling others** of opposite sex.*

4.4.11 Selection restrictions violated with certain verbs

Some verbs are used in KenE in a way that violates the selection restrictions which would normally be expected to be observed in StdIntE. Four such verbs were used in the examples below: *to abet, to facilitate*, and *to interrogate*, which violate "object-selection" restrictions, and *to perform*, which violates "subject-selection" restrictions. In their (frequent) KenE structures *to abet sb* and *to facilitate sb*, *abet* and *facilitate* are given an animate object where they would be given an inanimate one (*to abet sth* and *to facilitate sth*) in StdIntE. For its part, the verb *interrogate* is given an inanimate object in the structure *to interrogate sth* (in its *added* KenE meaning of 'to raise questions/doubts about').

(36) a. *[He] accused the [government] of **abetting corruption** and intimidating wananchi and their leaders agitating for upright leadership.*
   (*Daily Nation*, 3 Feb 2015, p. 4)

b. *"Ordinary Kenyans to blame for **abetting corruption**"*
   (This is a headline in *The Standard*, 27 Mar 2015)
c. *The recent interception of a shipment of arrows [...] is strong indication that [it] aids and **abets violence** in Kenya.*
   (W2E014K)
d. *But see the point still stands if society [...] paid enough taxes to **facilitate such homes** I think then there would be no kid in the streets*
   (S1B022K)
e. *In the meantime the commission [...] has said a further delay of the final results had been effected to **facilitate the election team** [...] complete the probe on the alleged fraud*
   (S2B002AK)
f. *I agree that as we **facilitate these municipalities** we should do so knowing that they are not going to be small [...] majimbo [...]*
   (S1B057HK)
g. *There is need **to interrogate** the teachers' practical skills before they join the profession.*
   (from a draft journal article by K.A., Aug 2018)

As for the verb *perform*, it is sometimes given an inanimate subject in a context where logically an animate one would be expected, as in the following sentence:

(37) *In the recent years, when Kiswahili experts were asked to explain why **Kiswahili performs poorly**, they say that the grammar section is the one that has given them a challenge.*
(from an MA research paper by K.N., Feb 2015)

In StdIntE, the structure *why students perform poorly on Kiswahili* would be the appropriate one.

4.4.12 The complementiser *that* used after verbs that do not require it

Biber et al. (1999: 663–666) report corpus findings showing that the complementiser *that* can be used after a good number of verbs (159 of them) belonging to various semantic domains (mental verbs, speech act verbs, and other communication verbs). But in KenE many other verbs not mentioned in Biber et al.'s list are used with *that*-complementation as well. That is the case of *appeal, alert, cheat, clarify*, and *elaborate*, which are used in the examples below.

(38) a. *I am **appealing that** Kanu stops spreading the gospel about who from which area is being groomed for the Vice-Presidency [...]*
(S1BHN05K)
b. *I would like **to appeal to our people that** we use the funds that are allocated to the Ministry to make sure that we increase immunisations [...]*
(S1BHN15K)
c. *I immediately proceeded to HFCK I **alerted Mr. [..] that** I lost my identity card in the last week of December, 1992 [..]*
(S1BCE02K)
d. *Why do you go about **cheating people that** you can heal them?*
(S1A024K)
e. *His body is suspended from a piece of cloth in his cell **to cheat the world that** he committed suicide.*
(W2B009K)
f. *The Attorney General [...] today **clarified that** it was the intention of the government to register immediately the AGIP*
(S2B002AK)
g. *I would **elaborate that** they not only preserve Bukusu traditional culture, but also Kenya's culture as a whole.*
(from an MA paper by G.W., Feb 2011)

4.4.13 *As follows* used instead of an object or a complement clause

Closely related to the complementation with the complementiser *that*, and usually involving this latter, is the complementation with *as follows*. In StdIntE this phrase is normally used after a copula verb (*The names in the list are as follows*), or a passive structure (*It can be described as follows*), but not in a position where either an object (whether an NP or a PP) or a *that*-complement clause should have been used. But KenE uses *as follows* in these latter two positions quite often. For example, a rent contract in Kenya will have a statement like the following: *The tenant **agrees** with the landlord **as follows**: [...]*, while an affidavit will have a statement like *I [...] solemnly make and oath and **state as follows**: [...]*.

The following is an example from "ordinary" language in KenE:

(39) *The purpose of this memo is to **inform you as follows**:*
   – ***That** all members of staff should strive to update all their personal websites [...]*

– ***That*** *all coordinators [...] should hand in soft copy briefs about [the programmes they coordinate].*
(from a lecturer, Dept. of Linguistics, University of Nairobi, 4th Feb 2011)

4.4.14 *Be + as a result of* used for *be + a result of*

A good starting point to introduce this section is to mention these two examples given in the *Oxford Advanced Learner's Dictionary*, 9th edn., 2015:

(40) a. *She died **as a result of** her injuries.*
b. *The failure of the company was **a** direct **result of** bad management.*

These two examples show that in StdIntE the phrase ***as a result of*** is used after a verb (e.g. *die*) that denotes an event, while the phrase ***a result of*** is used after a copula verb like *be*.

In KenE usage, even the phrase *as a result of* is used, quite frequently, as a complement of the copula verb, as the following examples show:

(41) a. *[...] it emerges that the current tension within Narc Kenya **is as a result of** [his] reservations about using Narc Kenya as his re-election vehicle [...]*
(*Sunday Nation*, 1 Apr 2007, p. 17)
b. *As I mentioned earlier, varieties of English may **be as a result of** borrowing [...]*
(from an MA paper, Apr 2007)
c. *The mediation **is as a result of** international concerns over the violence that has rocked the country [...]*
(*People Daily*, 16 Jan 2008, p. 5)
d. *The publication of this directory **is as a result** of suggestions and enquiries from our customers*
(W1B-BK23)

4.4.15 The infinitive marker *to* omitted after *enable* + direct object

This feature is a specific aspect of eWAVE feature "F208: deletion of *to* before infinitives". Buregeya (2102: 471) rated this feature among the rare ones and suggested that "this feature seems to be the preserve of only one verb in Kenyan English, *to enable*". Limited to this particular verb the feature becomes pervasive. But rarely does it involve other verbs, including its synonym *to allow*. (The present author has so far come across, in written KenE, only the following example involving *to allow*: "State incentives can **allow** more Kenyans Ø **own** homes", from *The Standard on Saturday*, 8 Jun 2013.)

Below are some of the very many examples involving *to enable*.

(42) a. *Employers have been urged to pay retrenchees their dues in full* **to enable** *them Ø* **continue** *with their lives uninterrupted.*
(*The Kenya Times*, 5 Dec 2000, p. 4)
b. *This observation would* **enable** *the language teacher* **to come up with** *[a] methodology that would* **enable** *the students Ø* **improve** *their language.*
(from an MA research paper by S.N.J., Apr 2009).
c. *We are supposed to finish marking regular and special/supplementary exams this week to* **enable** *the University Ø* **make** *a list of graduands.*
(an sms from the chairman, Dept. of Linguistics, Univ. of Nairobi, 31 Oct 2013)
d. *[...] (b) To acquaint the student with modern methods of library organisation and administration* **to enable him** *effectively Ø* **organise***, develop and manage a library [and] (c) To provide the student with the knowledge and skills to* **enable him to assist** *teachers and pupils utilize effectively the resources available in the library.*
(W2D010K)

Example (42 d) is an indication that some KenE speakers (or maybe all of them?) have the two structures in their grammar (i.e. use of *to* and omission of it) after *to enable*, but the claim being made here is that omitting it will be the more frequent option.

4.4.16 Some intransitive verbs used transitively

While the use of certain transitive verbs intransitively in KenE (see 4.4.7 above) concerns potentially any transitive verb, very few intransitive verbs tend to be used transitively while keeping their usual intransitive meaning. The most common one is *to rain*, specifically in the passive phrase *to be rained on*.[18] Utterances like *I was rained on* are very common in KenE speech (even though not a single occurrence of *rained on* appears in the spoken component

---

18 The *Oxford Dictionary of English (ODE)* has the passive phrase *to be rained off* (i.e. for an event 'to be cancelled' because of rain), on which *to be rained on* might have been modelled.

of the ICE-K). And here is the only example that appears in the entire ICE-K sub-corpus.

(43) *I arrived home at 9.30 night **having been rained on** like nobody's business*
(W1B-SK46)

One other verb to point out is *to collapse*, which, unlike *to rain*, has actually both a transitive and an intransitive meaning in StdIntE. Consider the following example of its use in KenE:

(44) *I don't want my friend J.O. to go down in history as the one who **collapsed** [the] NASA [political coalition].*
(said by Wiper Party Leader, 20 Mar 2018)

In StdIntE, *to collapse* will be used transitively in its meaning of 'compressing' e.g. a document, while in the example above it clearly refers to its intransitive meaning of 'causing to disintegrate'.

4.4.17 The subjective-case *who* used for the objective-case *whom*

Quirk et al. (1985: 367) point out that "*Whom* is largely restricted to formal style, and can be avoided altogether in informal style, through the use of *who, that,* or zero". But they later add (1985: 368) that *whom* must be used *after* a preposition (and thus, "*This is the *person to who* you spoke" is ungrammatical). So, what is particular about KenE usage is simply the fact that *who* tends to replace *whom* even a) after a preposition, as examples (45a,b) show, and b) in a formal style, as examples (45c,d) show.

(45) a. *Mr. Speaker, Sir, [he] has only mentioned six people whereas he should have substantiated by say who was allocated which plot and sold it **to who**.*
(S1BHN02K)
b. *The aim lacks the school Z mentioned in the title and the written compositions we are not told will be tested **on who**.*
(from an MA paper by A.O.O., Jan 2011)
c. *Top officials contradict each other on new constituencies triggering the question of who is **fooling who** and if Kenya has two "governments".*
(*The Standard*, 19 Nov 2010, p. 1)
d. *Who is trying to **save who** from what?*
(*Saturday Nation*, 25 Dec 2010, p. 13)

4.4.18 The infinitive used for modal verbs *must* and *should*

In StdIntE, "Headlines often use infinitives to refer to the future [as in] *HOSPITALS TO TAKE FEWER PATIENTS*" (Swan 2016: paragraph 292, f). In this case, the infinitive replaces the modal *will*.[19] In KenE it is often used to make recommendations, as in (46), or to give instructions, as in (47) below.

(46) *In a nutshell, the study found out that students can improve on their spellings if the following is put in place:*
  - *Spelling **to major** as a topic in the syllabus.*
  - *Students **to be encouraged** to read alot of Eng materials inorder to get a wide exposure to the language.*
  - *All teachers **to be involved** in correcting spellings in students work.*
  - *Administrations **to mind** their spellings in the notices they hang on the school notice boards [..].*

(from an MA research paper by A.W., May 2003)

(47) *TO OUR ESTEEMED CUSTOMERS*
*In order to serve you better, all applications are advised to present themselves personally for our services. Those submitting applications on behalf of organizations **to produce** letters of accreditation and copies of their staff identity card.*
(A notice in the passport section of the Immigration Department, Nyayo House, Nairobi, seen by the present author on 22 Jul 2013)

In StdIntE the bold-faced infinitive in (46) should be replaced by *should* while that in (47) should be replaced by *must*.

4.4.19 *What you do* ... used for *What you should do is (to)*...

Somewhat similar to the structure in the previous section is *What you do*... (as in *What you do, write him a note*), a structure used instead of *What you should do is (to)*... Since, in this structure, the *what*-clause is grammatically

---

[19] In KenE this use will be found beyond headlines, as in this example: "[Parish] elections at Outstations will be conducted next Sunday [...]. Three (3) representatives from our Small Christian Communities [...] **to participate** in these elections" (from *The Sunday Bulletin*, 27 Jan. 2019, produced by the Our-Lady-of-Guadalupe Parish, Nairobi).

meant to serve as a subject, and semantically meant to be a piece of advice, the complete (and StdIntE) version of it should contain both *should* and the copula *is*. The KenE *What you do…* seems to be a frozen structure, practically involving only the second person. (Its possible counterparts involving other grammatical persons, such as *What I do, write him a note* and *What he/she does, write him a note,* hardly occur, if at all.) *What you do…* is pervasive in spoken KenE, which is why it is quite strange that not a single occurrence of it appears in the entire ICE-K sub-corpus. However, this contains at least one structure, in (48) below, modelled on *What you do…*.

(48) *So therefore* **what we do we negate** *the expansion, isn't it?*
(S2B057K)

4.4.20 Continuous tenses used after *this is the first time*

It would not be a wild claim to say that hardly any KenE speaker will say *This is the first time I've seen this*. They will say **This is the first time I'm seeing** this. The present continuous tense sounds logical because we are talking about something happening as we speak. But it turns out that this logical rule is not the one usually followed in StdIntE, if we take the rules stated below as the reference. First, Hewings (2013: 6) writes:

> After the pattern **It/This/That** *is/will be* **the first time** … we generally use the present perfect in the next clause:
> – *That's the first time* **I've seen** Jan look embarrassed. (reporting a past event)
> – *It won't be the first time* she **has voted** against the government. (talking about a future event)
> [...]

Swan (2016: paragraph 56.1) extends the rule to beyond the expression *the first time*:

> We use the present perfect in sentences constructed with **this/it/that is the first/second/third/only/best/worst** etc.
> – *This is the first time that* **I've heard** *her sing*. (NOT ~~This is the first time that I hear her sing.~~)
> [...]
> – *This is the fifth time you've asked me the same question* (NOT ~~This is the fifth time you ask…~~)

Below are KenE examples where a continuous tense was used instead of the present perfect.

(49) a. *[They] were equally surprised when they saw the document because it was **the first time they were hearing** of this document [...]*
(*Sunday Nation*, 13 Jan 2008, p. 7)
b. *Most probably, this is not **the first time you are hearing** of the term "zero-grazing" [...]*
(W2B039K)
c. *This is not **the first time such things are happening** but I wish it was the last time*
(S2B024KB)

One more reason (than the "logicalness" of the continuous tense) why non-native speakers of English are most likely to be confused by the rule stated above lies in the fact that, according to Swan (2016: paragraph 56.2), "Present (simple or progressive) and future tenses are both possible with *This is the **last*** ... and similar structures". The author gives this example: "*This is the last time **I pay** / **I'm paying** for you.* (OR *This is the last time I'll pay for you.*)". Since there is no obvious reason why the expression *this is the last time* and other "similar structures" should allow other tenses than those used after *this is the first time*, it is only natural that the two rules governing the choice of the tense to be used in this particular structure are simplified by choosing the more "logical" of them.

4.4.21 *Can/could be able* used for just *can/could*

Although the majority of educated KenE speakers, if asked, are likely not to accept *can be able* as grammatical (only 39 % accepted it in Buregeya 2006: 216), the structure is used on a daily basis by highly educated people speaking on television and radio. The pervasiveness of it in speech is such that one can safely predict that no amount of consciousness-raising about it will reduce it from the language. Nobody could have warned about the use of it in stronger words than Hocking's (1974/1984: 44):

> ***can/could be able**
> This is quite wrong. *Can* means *be able to:* **can be able* therefore means *be able to be able*. This is a serious mistake, because it plainly shows that the writer is not thinking what he is doing. Usually, when people make this mistake, they should have written *will be able* or just *can*.

[...]
Can be possible contains the same kind of absurdity. [...]

However strong Hocking's warning was, it has hardly achieved any success in spoken KenE.[20] If it has achieved some, this must be in written KenE. For example, there are 17 occurrences of *can be able* in the spoken component of the ICE-K (though, surprisingly, not a single one of *could be able*), 8 in the written-to-be-spoken one, and only 1 in the written. The following are some uses of *can be able* and *could be able*:

(50) a. *[...] the police ought to have held an identical parade after the arrest of [an] appellant to test whether the complainant **could be able** to identify him*
(W1C008K)
b. *I would like to hear what the hon. Member is saying so that **I can be able** to give guidance to the House*
(S1BHN14K)
c. *Ekegusii is an SVO language. Meshack **cannot**, in many instances, **be able** to incorporate the rule. [He] **cannot be able** to stick to this rule as seen above.*
(from an MA paper by P.O., May 2012)

4.4.22 Past-tense forms equated with past-time meanings

One manifestation of this equation relates to cases where a past tense form used to express the *present* conditional meaning is equated with a past conditional meaning, as in the following example:

(51) *If she only **spoke** up [...] Don't let a matatu driver lead you to an early death.*

The text in this example is a message which was posted in some public transport buses by the Kenya National Transport Safety Association and its partners as part of their campaign called "Speak up against reckless *matatu* [i.e. public-transport minibuses] drivers". The authors of the text meant to say: 'if only she

---

[20] However, Hocking's warning must have deterred the use of *Can be possible*, if ever it was prevalent at the time: it is hardly used, whether in speech or writing, in KenE.

had spoken up against the driver, she would not have died in the accident'. So, the message in (51) should have been expressed using the past conditional structure *if she had spoken up*.

Sometimes KenE also uses *would* instead of its past tense counterpart *would have*, and *could* instead of *could have*. Consider these examples:

(52) a. *This was done to avoid discussion amongst them, which **would** interfere with the results.*
(from an MA paper by W.M.W., Apr 2009)
b. *I received a call from C.I.C.I.O. Nairobi to go and identify some wires suspected to be stolen. [...] I went to C.I.C.I.O. Nairobi and found wires which were put in 2 bags. [...] On inspection I found they were copper wires which we use with our telecommunications. In [the] state in which they were in they **could** not be used, as they were coiled and burnt*
(S1B067K)

In (a), *would have interfered* is the appropriate structure, while in (b) *could not have been used* is the appropriate one.

4.4.23 *Never* used for *did not*

This feature corresponds to the eWAVE "F159: Never as a preverbal past tense negator", illustrated with "*He never came*" for "*He did not come*". It was rated as pervasive in KenE. In view of its attestation rate (83%) and its pervasiveness rate (71%) in the eWAVE survey, it is a feature that should be expected in (at least) some other varieties of English in Africa. Indeed, while describing morphosyntactic aspects of Ghanaian English, Huber and Dako (2008: 370) noted that "At times, *never* expresses negative completive aspect [as in] *I **never** knew you were in town* (for 'I didn't know you were in town')". And it must be because of the pervasiveness of the feature in varieties of English across the world that the *Collins English Dictionary*, 10th edn, 2009, has the following note on the usage of *never*: "In informal speech and writing, *never* can be used instead of *not* with the simple past tenses of certain verbs for emphasis *(I never said that; I never realized how clever he was)*, but this usage should be avoided in serious writing". The dictionary gives no indication of what those "certain verbs" are. Nonetheless, KenE seems to use *never* for *did not* in a wider range of verbs than those envisaged by the dictionary, and, more importantly, even in serious writing, as the examples below suggest:

(53) a. *I **never attended** the fundraiser nor did I see her off though I wrote her a small crumpled note asking forgiveness*
(W1B-SK28)
b. *The [respondents] said that the messages were not worth reading because they **never went** further on to tell them as to what they should do [...]*
(W2A017K)
c. *In cross-examination he said he **never saw** [anyone] remitting Kshs. 10/= but he could not remember the total remittance for the whole day*
(W1C007K)
d. *Three respondents **never added** the sound anywhere.*
(from an MA research paper by K.K.J., Mar 2011)
e. *[They] are the only ones I marked. I also **never bothered** to mark the sentences in (i) because they **never showed** the use of the morpheme ma-.*
(from an MA paper by K.E.M., Apr 2013)

4.4.24 The infinitive marker *to* used for the preposition *to*

Because of their formal similarity, the infinitive marker *to* is, inevitably for non-native speakers of English, sometimes confused with the preposition *to*. Since the latter will impose a gerund (*-ing*) ending on the following verb, using the infinitive *to* instead of it produces forms that would be ungrammatical in StdIntE, forms like those in bold face in the examples below (both taken from the *University of Nairobi Research Policy*, revised edition, 2013):

(54) a. *Thus, the University of Nairobi commits itself **to protect** and **preserve** [...]* (p. 18)
b. *Major avenues of consideration will include:*
– *Proactive approach **to seek** and **expand** fellowship/donor support [...]*
(p. 20)

In StdIntE, we would expect *commits itself to protecting and preserving* in (54a) and *approach to seeking and expanding* in (54b).

4.5 Aspects of the prepositional phrase

The preposition is used differently in KenE from StdIntE in the following aspects: a) a different preposition is used; b) an unnecessary preposition is added; c) a necessary preposition is left out; d) a preposition is repeated in a relative clause construction; e) one preposition is shared by two conjuncts requiring different prepositions; f) some prepositions or prepositional phrases seem to be non-existent in KenE. Aspects (b) (e.g. *to discuss about sth*) and (c) (*to quarrel sb*) will not be discussed in this section, as they have already been in the previous one (aspects of the verb phrase). There is only one case of (c) which was not discussed earlier: the addition of *from* to *off*, in *to jump off from a bus*, discussed by Mwangi (2003: 234). Some structures illustrative of (b), e.g. *to cope up with sth*, will be discussed, as part of idioms, in the next chapter (on lexis and semantics), instead.

4.5.1 Use of a different preposition

The best illustration of this aspect comes from Mwangi (2004: 29). She suggests that the prepositions *at* and *on* "are losing out in various contexts to *in*", as in the following cases: *in the meeting* (vs. *at the meeting*), *in the party* (vs. *at the party*), *in the conference* (vs. *at the conference*), *in the island* (vs. *on the island*), and *in the coast* (vs. *on the coast*). The following can be added as well: *in a bus/train* (vs. *on a bus/train*), *in the continent* (vs. *on the continent*), and *in the market* (vs. *on the market*). And, apparently, it is not just *at* and *on* that are losing out to *in*; other prepositions seem to be, too, as the four instances in (55) suggest:

(55) a. *My research is aimed at finding out if students use ungrammatical English question tags in their [...] texts and narrows its investigation* **in** *five key areas.*
 b. *As to why the respondents responded well* **in** *the statement containing "it is" may partly be explained by the fact that [...]*
 c. *Comparing the performance of the respondents* **in** *the positive polarity tag [...] "it is"* **in** *which 63.3% of the [sample] provided a grammatical tag [...]*
 (from an MA research paper by S.Z., Apr 2014)

The preposition *in* was used for *to* in (a), for *to* in (b), for *on* in the first instance in (c), and for *for* in the second instance in (c).

KenE tends to use a different preposition in miscellaneous other cases: a) those involving verbs: *to admit sb* **at** *a hospital* for *to admit sb* **to** *a hospital, to admit a student* **into** *a university* for *to admit a student* **to** *a university, to be aligned* **to** for *to be aligned* **with**, *to be anchored* **on** for *to be anchored* **in**, *to* comply *to* for *to comply with, to converge at* for *to converge on, to dovetail into* for *to dovetail with, to go a long way in doing sth* for *to go a long way towards doing sth, to pride oneself in* for *to pride oneself on, to result to* for *to result in, to sensitize on* for *to sensitize to, to translate to* (also AmE) for *to translate into,* and *it depends with* used for *it depends on/upon*; b) those involving nouns: *attendance of* (a meeting) for *attendance at,* and *on the queue* for *in the queue*; c) those concerning other prepositions (which have been replaced): *during weekends* for *at weekends* (BrE) or *on weekends* (AmE), *in/within the premises* for *on the premises, on his/her/its part* for *for his/her/its/their part,* and *on the cutting edge* for *at the cutting edge.* It should be added that the frequency with which the so-called KenE prepositions tend to replace the BrE/AmE ones varies with individual prepositions: some (like *for his part, to admit sb at a hospital* and *to result to*) seem to be more entrenched in KenE usage than others (like *to depend with*). Moreover, Mwangi (2003: 230) found that the differences between KenE and BrE (or AmE) usage were more noticeable in speech than in writing.

4.5.2 Repetition of the preposition at the end of a relative clause

The repetition of prepositions in KenE usage is a phenomenon that was studied by Hoffmann (2011b), who compared preposition pied-piping and preposition stranding in both KenE and BrE. He illustrated with the following examples from the ICE-K.

(56) a. *Top managers **with whom** they will be doing business **with** (ICE-EA: W1BBK 25)*
   (Example 4.1a in Hoffmann 2011b: 126)
   b. *The thing is **to whom** this drug is going **to** and the use of it is to be put into (ICE-EA: S1B025K)*
   (Example 4.63 in Hoffmann 2011b: 172)
   c. *… in [the] state **in which** they were **in** they could not be used as they were coiled and burnt (ICE-EA: S1B067K)*
   (Example 4.72b in Hoffmann 2011b: 175)
   d. ***For what** purpose is it **for** (ICE-EA: S1B041K)*
   (Example 4.72c in Hoffmann 2011b: 175)

What is not StdIntE grammar in the constructions in (55) is the fact that the preposition has at the same time been pied-piped (i.e. moved along with the *wh*-element from the end position) and stranded (i.e. left behind at the end of the clause). Incidentally, in his discussion (see pp. 123–124) of the way prepositions were presented in two textbooks widely used to teach English in secondary school in Kenya, Hoffmann (2011b) noted that KenE had no preference for either preposition pied-piping or preposition stranding. He writes: "In both textbooks preposition stranding and pied piping are thus presented as possible options, without any further stylistic restrictions" (2011b: 124). It would thus seem that this lack of preference is the main source of the confusion as a consequence of which many KenE speakers use the same preposition both where it has moved it and where it is supposed to have moved from.

4.5.3 One preposition is shared by two conjuncts requiring different ones

This phenomenon can be illustrated by the examples in (57):

(57) a. *[...] despite [pronunciation] being taught Ø and exposed **to** similar conditions and environment [...]*
(from an MA research paper by M.V.A., Apr 2015)
b. *The quality policy shall be communicated Ø and understood **by** all staff within the Ministry for efficient and effective implementation and maintenance of the QMS* [sic].
(from a "Quality Policy Statement" from the Ministry of State for Immigration and Registration of Persons, 2008)

A different preposition, specifically *in*, would be expected in StdIntE after the verb *taught* in (a), since the author must clearly have meant to say *taught in similar conditions* rather than *taught to similar conditions*, which would be ungrammatical. Similarly, the preposition *to* would be expected after *communicated* in (b).

4.5.4 Omission of prepositions and PPs

This phenomenon is partially represented by the eWAVE feature "F216: Omission of StE prepositions", the typical example of which is *"He came out Ø hospital; She went Ø town; We're going there Ø Tuesday"*. This eWAVE feature is only a partial representation of the phenomenon under discussion because it is limited to omitting "locative prepositions and prepositions before temporal expressions". In this limited scope, KenE rarely omits prepositions.

However, it very frequently does so, notably in speech, in the following linguistic contexts: a) clause-/utterance-finally and b) in phrases that are meant to involve a relative pronoun (*about which/whom, of which/whom, for which,* etc.), as (58) illustrates.

(58) a. *[Let us build] a country that we are proud Ø*
   (said by a govt. minister and reported on the KTN news, 31 Jul 2010)
   b. *Whether or not we should do away with [it] completely is a matter we need to consult Ø*
   (said on TV by the Education Cabinet Secretary, 9 Apr 2015)
   c. *(i) A life you don't prepare for you will be a misfit. (ii) Any area of life that you want to go up Ø [...] (iii) The area of life that you need discipline Ø [...]*
   (said by a preacher at a university graduation reception, 5 Dec 2014)
   d. *Why resign over something you are not the cause Ø?*
   (said by a govt. minister and reported on the KTN news, 7 Oct 2006)
   e. *[After we have done that], then that corruption, the numbers Ø will go down.*
   (said by the Deputy Inspector General of Police [heard on radio], 25 Feb 2015]
   f. *Those ones, we don't worry Ø*
   (said by a former Vice-Chancellor of the University of Nairobi, 13 Jul 2011)

The preposition *of* was expected in (a), *about* was expected in (b), *in* was expected in both instances in (c), and the prepositional phrase *for which* was expected in (e), *of it* was expected in (d), while *about them* was expected in (f).

Similarly, KenE frequently drops the preposition in a third linguistic context, namely sentence-/clause-initially. This will be most evident in written language, as in the following example:

(59) *Ø The second section they were to fill in the correct pronominal concords [...] and then write the sentences in plural. Ø The fourth section the students were supposed to use the nouns [...] to form sentences, and Ø the last section the students were to write the plural form of the sentences given.*
   (from an MA research paper by P.K., Mar 2011)

Clearly, the preposition *in* would be expected, in StdIntE, in the empty slots marked *Ø*.

It is worth pointing out that part of what is illustrated above has been discussed in Cameroon English by Mbangwana (2008: 419) under the label "preposition 'chopping' in relative clauses", illustrated by these examples: [i] *He is being followed by an old man **which the name is not given** Ø* and [ii] *We have produced an album **which we want you to buy a copy** Ø*. A structure like *which the name is given*, for *whose name is given*, is pervasive in KenE, as will be seen in section 4.9 below.

4.5.5 Are there non-existent and "dead" or "vanishing" prepositions in KenE?

The title of Mwangi's (2004) paper, "Prepositions vanishing in Kenya", could not have been any more thought-provoking. Perhaps her biggest claim, made in Mwangi (2003: 229), was that *underneath* "no longer exists as a preposition in KenE". She should have said that "it is extremely rare",[21] because the present author came across, in 2007, an instance of *underneath* used in the following extract from an MA student's research paper: "*[...] it always passes out as a tip of a bigger problem of comparison underneath*". And (60) below, which contains *underneath*, actually appears in the written component of the ICE-K.

(60) *The vehicle swayed a little this way, then that way, and as if lifted by an incredibly powerful hand from **underneath**, jerked itself out of the ditch and back on to the road.*
(W2F008K)

Further, Mwangi (2003: 229) predicted that "the other prepositions that could also go out of use in KenE are *off*, *past* and *beneath*". There is no solid reason to believe that they will. Regarding the preposition *past*, in particular, it is most likely to stay in use at least in the lexical bundles expressing time, such as *past midnight*. (In this connection, the bundles *past 3.00 pm* and *past 11 pm* both appear in the written-to-be-spoken component of the ICE-K, while *half past eleven* and *twelve past four* appear in the spoken component.) Concerning the preposition *beneath*, it appears at least three times in the spoken ICE-K, in the phrases "*beneath that skirt*", "*beneath the gender differences*", and "*beneath them*". (And it can be expected to survive at least in a collocation like *beneath the surface*.) As for the preposition *off*, Mwangi (2003: 234) pointed out that it was used in KenE (though redundantly in relation to StdIntE) in combination

---

[21] In Mwangi (2004) she was less categorical about *underneath*, as she simply included it in the prepositions that "are rare in KenE and could eventually go out of use" (2004: 29).

with *from*, to show 'source', as in *to get off from a bus*. Note that it was used non-redundantly at least once in the spoken ICE-K, in the phrase *"at Kabati Market in Kandara off that highway"* (S2B019AK).

Mwangi was essentially talking about one-word prepositions. However, in addition to these, there are those about which Biber et al. (1999: 75) say that "Some multi-word sequences function semantically and syntactically as single prepositions". The authors point out two-word prepositions (e.g. *as for*), three-word prepositions (e.g. *as well as*), and four-word prepositions (e.g. *as a result of*). To relate their long list of such multiple-word prepositions to Mwangi's (2003) observations and claims, some of them are indeed very rare in KenE; they are likely to be occasionally found in very formal texts, like legal ones. Those are expressions such as *by reference to, by way of, in back of, in consequence of, on the part of, upwards of, owing to,* and *preparatory to*. (One wonders if *preparatory to* exists at all in KenE.) Some of those multi-word prepositions have a (slightly) different equivalent in KenE: thus, just *except* tends to be used for *except for, as at* for *as of, upto* for *up to, with regards to* for *with regard to, in regards to* for *with regard to,* and *in respect to* for *in respect of*.

4.6 *(as) compared to* used for *than* as the second element of the comparative

As noted in Buregeya (2012: 472), the use of *"(as) compared to"* instead of *than* as the second element of the comparative, even though not one of the eWAVE features, is one of the really pervasive features of KenE.[22] It could even be labelled "the feature par excellence" of KenE. Examples to illustrate it will be easily found both in speech and in writing. One good illustration is the series of constructions in (61) below; they were all drawn from the same text (a 5,800–word long draft journal article, Dec 2011) written by a university lecturer.

---

[22] It is quite surprising that the structure *more . . . compared to* has not been reported in other varieties of African English. The closest the present author has come across by way of literature on the comparative structure is this: "As in other varieties of English in Africa, comparative structures are occasionally simplified", in that *"than* is preferred to *rather than* while in [. . .] the superlative form *most* is left unstated" (Mesthrie 2008c: 495). This statement echoes that by Schmied (1991a: 75–76): "Other possible cases of grammatical 'Africanisms' might [include]: [. . .] a tendency to 'simplify' comparative constructions, either by omitting the comparative particle *than* or, more often, the inflection *–er/-est*".

(61) a. *This complex sentence is arguably more cohesive than the other sentence types [...].*
b. *[...] comparative reference tends to be **less** in casual talk **as compared to** demonstrative and personal reference cohesion.*
c. *[...] reference cohesion in the [complex sentence] in informal discourse is **more** back-referring **as compared to** the one that would be forward-looking.*
d. *Sentence (1) seems **more** effective in communication [...] **as compared to** sentence (2).*
e. *This teacher is better than that other.*
f. *[The three sentences] are **less** cohesive **compared t**o the complex sentences [discussed above].*
g. *The cohesion patterns of sentence (18) [...] are **higher compared to** [those of] sentence [19].*
h. *The high presence of reference elements makes [sentence (a)] a **more** closely knit [...] text entity in cohesion terms **compared to** [sentence (b)].*
i. *The first person pronouns [are] used **more** [...] for situational **rather than** textual reference [...]*

These examples illustrate the typical usage of the comparative structure in KenE: the same individual is likely to use both the StdIntE structure *more/less ... than* and the KenE, *more/less ... (as) compared to*, with the latter probably being more frequent than the former.

The following example illustrates two arguably less frequent structures also used in KenE to express the comparative: a) *more/less ... as opposed to* and b) just *than*, i.e. without the first element of the comparative structure being mentioned.

(62) a. *We tend to remember sentences that have **simpler** structures **as opposed to** those that with complex structures [...]*
b. *For example, "Tom will beat the dog" will be remembered Ø easily **than** [its] negative counterpart [...]*
c. *A sentence that undergoes several transformations will pose a Ø challenge [...] in terms of comprehension **than** one which exists in its simple form.*
(from an MA paper by A.A.O., Jun 2007)

Another interesting aspect of the comparative structure is the addition of the indefinite relative pronoun *what* after *than*, a feature investigated in the eWAVE survey as complementation with *"as what/than what* in comparative clauses" (see F204). It was rated by Buregeya (2012: 468) as pervasive in KenE, but only the second option, i.e. *than what*, since *as what* is definitely not a feature of KenE. For example, there is not a single use of *as what* as the second element of the comparative in the entire ICE-K . Below are just two examples from the ICE-K of *than what* as the second element of the comparative (There are 10 occurrences of it in the spoken component of the ICE-K and 3 in the written one.)

(63) a. *They have been saying* **less than what** *they mean or* **more than what** *they mean [...] or something else other* **than what** *they actually mean* (S2B080K)
b. *Stretched further, this observation points at meeting (elite) cultural expectations* **more than what** *the situation demands* (W2A032K)

4.7 Non-use of subject-auxiliary inversion in questions

This generic feature encompasses two specific ones covered in the eWAVE survey: "F228: No inversion/no auxiliaries in wh-questions", as in *"What you doing? What he wants?"*, and "F229: No inversion/no auxiliaries in main clause yes/no questions", as in *"You get the point? You liked the idea?"*. Both features have been rated as highly pervasive, with a 79% rate for the former and 81% one for the latter. They can be argued to be pervasive in KenE as well. However, with specific reference to F228, a typical *wh*-question in spoken KenE is that which places the *wh*-word not at the beginning of the utterance (as in the eWAVE example), but at the end, as in *He wants what?* It is this latter that is indeed pervasive in (spoken) KenE. And so is the lack of inversion in *yes/no* questions.

Thus, KenE speakers will probably say *You are coming with us?* and *You are going where?* more often than they will *Are you coming with us?* and *Where are you going?* (This implies that *You are going where?* is not typically an echo-question in KenE, as it is in StdIntE.) The only questions that have kept the *wh*-element at the beginning in spoken KenE seem to be those which, in the process of L2 acquisition, are usually learnt very early on as formulaic expressions, such as *What's this?*, *How are you?*, and the usual KenE greeting *How have you been?* Note, though, that a formulaic expression like *What's your name?*, which one expects to be very frequent in the language, is frequently replaced by *Your name is who?* (and not, quite interestingly, *Your name is what?*) and *You are who?* (As noted in Buregeya 2001: 1, *You are who?* is a question which receptionists like asking visitors when they want them to identify themselves by name.)

Written KenE is likely to contain more instances of the *wh*-question word being placed at the beginning of the question, but they are probably not enough to make the structure a typical feature of it. Nonetheless, as Buregeya (2001: 18) comments, "Although [the non-use of subject-auxiliary inversion in questions] does not seem to be so common [...] in written Kenyan English, its use cannot certainly go unnoticed in one particular book called *Driving Test Guide for Kenya* (produced by the East African Road Safety Training Centre, revised & reprinted, 1997 [...]". All the examples below were taken from the book in question.[23]

(64) a. *Q. 13.* **Where** *normally* **you may** *find continuous solid yellow lines in the middle of the road?* (p. 21)
b. *Q. 15.* **Where one should** *not overtake another vehicle?* (p. 22)
c. *Q. 17. Within* **what period one should** *forward the insurance documents at a police station when asked to do so by a police officer?* (p. 23)
d. *Q. 20. Within* **what period an accident should be** *reported at a police station?* (p. 24)
e. *Q. 31.* **What will be the thinking, braking and overall stopping distances** *when a car is driven at 80 kph?* (p. 26)
f. *Q. 38. Within* **what period a driver is required** *to produce driving licence at a police station when asked by a police officer?* (p. 27)

It is worth adding, however, that the same series of questions also contains many in which the inversion rule was observed, as in *"Q. 42. What do you do when you are involved in an accident?"* (p. 30).

The no-subject-auxiliary inversion feature has been reported in some other African varieties as well: while discussing what he refers to as *"Wh*-word and constituent questions" in Cameroon English, Mbangwana (2008: 421–424) writes: "Sala (2003: 196) shows how *wh*-movement does not occur in CamE. Questions are generated at the base, that is in situ" (2008: 421). Mbangwana distinguishes between *"*Wh- in root clauses" (*"You are going where?"*) and *"*Wh- word in subordinate clauses" (*"He told you that he was going where?"*) (422). He adds that *"Yes/no* questions show the same word order as ordinary statements [...]", as in *"You are breaking your fast?"* (423).

---

[23] Those same questions are still stated in exactly the same way in the revised edition of 2014.

4.8 Use of resumptive pronouns

This is eWAVE feature "F194: Resumptive/shadow pronouns", the typical example of which is *"This is the house which I painted it yesterday"*. Its pervasiveness rate is 55%, which more or less reflects its current B-rating in KenE; that is that of a feature that is "neither pervasive nor extremely rare". Buregeya (2012: 474) rated it as rare in KenE. However, at the time he did not seem to have realised that rare though the feature might be in written KenE, it was not in speech. Here are some examples of its use:

(65) a. [...] *civil society groups,* **who** *we know* **them** [...]
(said by the Majority Leader in the Kenyan National Assembly, 9 Feb 2014)
b. *When people think* **some of us we** *[cannot run for president]* ...
(said by a presidential aspirant interviewed on Citizen TV, 9 Sep 2011)
c. **Some of them, they** *are running [looking for their parents]*
(said by a Citizen TV reporter on the 9 p.m. news, 13 Sep 2011)
d. [...] *and* **these people** *are we can say* **most of them they** *are aged*
(S1B043K)
e. *And they are very much uh I mean* **most of them they** *are very arrogant*
(S1B010K)

What looks interesting is that in KenE resumptive pronouns tend to occur after a partitive structure (*some of them/of us, most of them*). Future research could look at whether indeed there is a specific linguistic context (or more than one) which tends to attract them.

In Cameroon English and Nigerian English, such a linguistic context has already been observed: resumptive pronouns are associated mainly with relative clauses, as expressed in Alo and Mesthrie's (2008: 328) observation that "NigE allows resumptive pronouns in non-subject relativisation [as in] *The guests whom I invited them have arrived*" and Mbangwana's (2008: 425) observation that "[Resumptive pronouns] are most common in CamE relative clauses [as in] *The other teacher that we were teaching English with* **her** *went away*".

4.9 Non-use of the relative determiner *whose*

This feature is closely related to the omitting of a prepositional phrase discussed above in 4.5.4, since *whose* is semantically the equivalent *of whom* and *of which.* But it is dealt with separately here because, as the illustrative examples below will show, there are instances where *whose* will be required but where it is not clear which prepositional phrase it has replaced.

The non-use of *whose* discussed in this section is instead of the type presented in the eWAVE feature "F192: Use of analytic or cliticized *that his/ that's, what his/what's, at's, who his*", the typical example of which is *"the man what's wife has died"*. While these cliticized forms would look quite strange in KenE, two of the analytic ones, *that his* and *who his*, would not, as they would produce a structure like *the man who his wife has died*. While this structure does not actually occur in KenE, it reflects the Swahili structure[24] on which the KenE structure seems to be modelled, but to which it does not correspond word for word. There is no word-for-word correspondence because KenE will either simply drop *who his* (so that the equivalent of the typical eWAVE example becomes *the man [the] wife has died*) or insert some text between the relative pronoun and the possessive determiner as the examples in (66) show.

(66) a. *[...] I don't call **the people the phone numbers** I don't know*
(said by MA student H.A., 1 Mar 2015)
b. *These are **the characteristics that** the researcher wants to ascertain **their effects** on a given phenomena.*
(from an MA research paper by A.T.O., Feb 2011)
c. *My study is going to explore the possible linguistic [...] origins of misspelling [...] i.e. morphological, syntactic, phonological and **others which** I am not clear of **their origin**.*
(from an MA paper, Mar 2003)

Example (a) illustrates the *dropping* possibility while (b) and (c) illustrate the *inserting* one.

In the end, it can be easily hypothesised that if the eWAVE feature F192 were presented as "the non-use of *whose*", both its attestation rate and its pervasiveness would be higher than they are currently, namely 24% and 59%, respectively. After all, the learning, in L2 English, of a relative clause introduced

---

[24] A structure like *the man who his wife has died* will be translated into Swahili as: *Mwanaume* ('the man') *ambaye* ('who') *mke* ('wife') *wake* ('his') *amekufa* ('has died'), i.e. *the man who wife his has died*.

by *whose* has been predicted (see Lightbown and Spada 2013: 54)[25] to be very difficult and for some individuals to be impossible to achieve.

4.10 The pronoun (subj.) + pronoun (obj.) sequence used in subject position

This feature (illustrated by *Me I like music*) is a more generic variant of the eWAVE feature "F28: Use of *us* + NP in subject position", illustrated with "*Us kids used to pinch the sweets like hell*". The *Me I* ... structure was rated as a B-feature (i.e. neither pervasive nor extremely rare) in Buregeya (2012: 469). The author claimed that the pronoun + pronoun sequence "was extremely common in everyday speech" and thus should be treated differently from the eWAVE feature F28.

In principle, the pronoun (subj.) + pronoun (obj.) sequence covers all the personal pronouns: *me I, you you, her she/him he/it it/, us we,* and *them they*. In reality, though, the sequences involving *you* (e.g. *you you like pizza*) and *it* (e.g. *it it likes meat*) are either extremely rare (plausibly for the former) or simply non-existent (plausibly for the latter) in KenE. And while the sequence is very common in spoken KenE, it seems to be extremely rare in written, if we go by the fact that no examples of it seem to be available in the written component of the ICE-K. There are quite a number of them in the spoken component, although depending on which pair of pronouns is involved: some 20 instances of *me I*, 6 of *us we*, 4 of *them they*, 3 of *her she*, 0 of *him he*, and 0 of *you you*.[26] Below are some of those instances.

(67) a. **Me I** *feel if we are responsible citizens, yeah, the best thing is to do [...]* (S1B021K)
b. *No it doesn't end but* **me I** *don't know what she is doing at home* (S1A005K)

---

[25] Lightbown and Spada (2013: 54) refer to the "accessibility hierarchy for relative clauses in English", a 6-level hierarchy on which the difficulty in learning relative clauses in English increases depending on the function of the relative pronoun involved. The "possessive" relative clause, illustrated by the sentence "*I know the woman whose father is visiting*", is in 5th position on the hierarchy, meaning that it is the second most complicated relative clause structure to learn.

[26] The following two *it it* sequences appear, but they simply seem to be the result of the hesitation and repetition expected in speech: [a] *And the people have thought that philosophy must be uh* **it it** *creates trouble* (from S1B023K) and [b] *So* **it it** *may uh really depend on the student* (from S1BINT4K).

c. **With me I** could not be disturbed by what they said
(S1BCE09K)
d. But you see **with us we** are so rigid rigidly adhered to the Queen's language
(S1BINT7K)
e. I think uh we were able **even us we** were able to hear Nyerere on the radio addressing the nation in Kiswahili language
(S1B002K)
f. Those ones have been used to seeing each other but here **for us we** need to change
(S1A024K)
g. I don't like the idea of people generalizing ati [that] uh **them they** do it
(S1A006K)
h. Now those guys **them they** are given uh lunch those sides
(S1A012K)
i. **Even her she** was wearing a mini
(S1A003K)
j. She wanted to send me and **me I** refused and **her she** didn't want to know
(S1A004K)

An observation which would be interesting to further investigate is that the examples above seem to suggest that some KenE speakers need to introduce the pronoun sequence with the adverb *even* or with a preposition (like *with* or *for*), even though the two pronouns are still clearly positioned in a subject position, not in an adjunct or object-of-a-preposition one.

The claim made above that the feature under discussion is extremely rare in writing can be substantiated by the finding (made by Buregeya 2006: 216) that educated KenE speakers seem to be aware that despite the relative pervasiveness of the structure in speech, it is not acceptable in writing. Buregeya (2006) reports that in a sample of 103 respondents to a written questionnaire, only 2% accepted the sentence *Us we will contribute [up to] ten thousand shillings each* as correct. A further study by Buregeya (2013) reports (p. 5) that only 21 out of 218 respondents (i.e. 10%) accepted the same sentence, 40 out of 218 (i.e. 18%) accepted *Them, they were lucky: they had started [writing] their theses when the strike occurred*, while 7 out of 123 (i.e. 6%) accepted *Me, I don't know what the [phenomenon] is*. What is intriguing is that the *Me I* structure, which seems to be more frequent in speech (if we refer to the ICE-K data) than the *us we* and the *them they* structures, was the least accepted of the three.

4.11 The plural pronoun *we* used instead of the singular *I*

Okombo (1987: 48) refers to this structure as "the use of a plural pronominal subject form in cases where there are only two participants constituting the subject of a sentence and one of them is mentioned in the sentence after the 'with' as in 'we were with Kamau' [for *I was with Kamau*]". This is a structure encountered more often in speech than in writing, and, as suggested in this quotation, it is usually composed of the pronoun *we*, the copula verb *be* and the preposition *with*. But, as can be seen in (68a), other lexical elements can be involved as well (the verb *schooled* and the preposition *together*).

(68) a. *My very close friend **we were once schooled together** here in Nairobi.* (S1B028K)
   b. *[...] that discussion took two hours and when **we were standing with** Mr [X] outside there in that corner then we discussed for another two hours* (S1A009K)

4.12 *Isn't it* used as an invariant question tag

This is one manifestation of the eWAVE feature "F165: Invariant non-concord tags". While F165 covers the variants of *isn't it?*, namely *innit?* and *in't it?*, these latter two do not occur in KenE at all. (The form *isn't it* is also the only one reported in other, non-pidgin L2 African varieties of English: see Mbangwana 2008: 423, for Cameroon English; Alo and Mesthrie 2008: 327, for Nigerian English; Huber and Dako 2008: 371 for Ghanaian English.) *Isn't it* is a very pervasive, universal question tag in KenE: in fact, it is virtually the only tag used in KenE[27]; the other tags are extremely rare. To put things into some perspective, while the spoken component of the ICE-K contains 50 instances of *isn't it* as a tag, it contains only 2 of *don't you* and 1 of *hasn't he*. It does not contain a single one of *hasn't she, hasn't it, haven't you, couldn't you, can't he/she/it, aren't they,* and *won't you*.[28]

---

[27] It is actually surprising that *isn't it* is not one of the very many structures described by Hocking (1974/1984).
[28] Frequency counts were done only for just those negative question tags because "The tags are most often added to a positive statement, as positive clauses are in general more common than negative clauses" (Biber et al. 1999: 211).

Here are some examples of *isn't it* used where a different one would be used in StdIntE.

(69) a. *Last time we did our test,* **isn't it?**
 (S2B057K)
 b. *She sort of you know uh ruled the island behind the scenes,* **isn't it?**
 (S1A025K)
 c. *After your last lesson you must go home,* **isn't it?**
 (S1B028K)
 d. *Then you know people get influenced by what they see first,* **isn't it?**
 (S1B010K)
 e. *He is a foreigner,* **isn't it?**
 (S1A016K)

Interestingly, as in the case of the *Me I...* structure discussed in section 4.10, a majority of educated KenE speakers (62/103, i.e. 61%) judged *isn't it* as a mistake in the sentence **The equipments have cost alot of money, isn't it?* They corrected it to *haven't they?,* or *hasn't it?,* depending on whether they had corrected **equipments* to *equipment* as well (see Buregeya 2006: 216).

4.13 *No/not/none ... nor* used instead of *no/not/none ... or*

The present author's attention was drawn to this feature by the following notice: **"No** *hawking, preaching* **nor** *begging in this bus"*, posted inside the buses of the Double "M" Bus Services operating in the City of Nairobi. This structure is visibly a kind of double negation, but one in which the second element is specifically *nor*, which means that the structure in question must be an overgeneralization of the StdIntE structure *neither ... nor*. It involves, as the first element, not just *no*, but also *not* and *none*. It is a double negation structure different from the better-known ones, like that in the sentence *"He won't do no harm"*, used to illustrate the feature "F154: multiple negation/negative concord" in the eWAVE survey, one which was rated "rare" in the case of KenE. The *no/not/none ... nor* can be said to be pervasive in KenE.

Unlike many of the features described so far which have been claimed to be more typical of spoken KenE than written, this one seems to be (perhaps) more typical of written than spoken. The following are a few of the very many examples that appear in the written component of the ICE-K.

(70) a. *We personally do **not** protest **nor** harm anybody in your organisation*
(W1B-BK51)
b. *Do **not** put different tablets, **nor** pills, in the same container.*
(W2D002K)
c. *We would **not** have known about the existence of the present two collections, **nor** about the fact that one of his plays has taken pride of place [...]*
(W2B010K)
d. ***None** of the employees nominated, **nor** the employees, were identified.*
(W2E020K)
e. *There is **no** place for industry [...] and consequently **no** culture of the earth; **no** navigation, **nor** use of the commodities that may be imported by sea*
(W2A011K)
f. *Here, the target is **not** often the individual occupier or owner of land **nor** even any particular parcel of land or area.*
(W2A040K)
g. *Therefore he was **not** there **neither** for the ritual **nor** the celebrations and nobody ever said anything about them to him*
(W2F012K)

The last example, where *not, neither* and *not* are all used at the same time, offers the clearest clue that the *no/not/none ... nor* structure is most likely an overgeneralization of *neither ... nor*.

4.14 Non-use of *It is I who am* and *It is you who are*

According to Quirk et al. (1985: 766), StdIntE usage concerning the structure *It is I who am/It is you who are* is the following:

> In relative clauses and cleft sentences, a relative pronoun subject is usually followed by a verb in agreement with its antecedent: *It is I who am to blame* [...] But 3rd person concord prevails in informal English, where the objective case pronoun *me* is used: *It's me who's to blame.* Similarly, 3rd person singular may be used in informal English in these constructions when the pronoun *you* has singular reference: *It's you who's to blame.*

A structure like *It is I who am to blame* is almost unthinkable in KenE. In relation to this particular structure, KenE does not distinguish between the formal and the informal style: it has only one rule for both, that for the informal style in StdIntE.[29]

(71) a. **It is you who is** the president [who must show leadership]; it is **you who is** the minister [who must show leadership]
(said by Prof. P.L.O.L., one of the most eloquent English speakers in Kenya, addressing a leadership conference in Mombasa, 3 Aug 2011)
b. *Many others are disabled and you should be extra careful and* **you who is** *in the showground walking uh you should be extra careful [...]*
(S2B023K)
c. *Then there is one who is an African like* **you who is** *a young kid trying to learn English*
(S1B006K)

4.15 *Those ones* used instead of *those, these, they,* etc

This is what Hocking (1974/1984: 244) says about the use of *these ones* and *those ones*:

> A very odd little fact about English that is usually not realized is that you can say *this one* and *that one* but not **these ones* or **those ones*. For some reason these phrases can only be made plural if there is an adjective in front of *ones*: *I think I'll take those red ones*. **I think I'll take those ones* is quite definitely wrong. If you do not want to use an adjective you have to say *these* or *those*, without *ones*: *I think I'll take these*.

Quirk et al. (1985: 387) do not discuss *those ones* as such; they simply state that "Substitute *one* can be easily combined with determiners and modifiers", as in "*those ones* I like" and "*the old one* in the kitchen". Biber et al. (1999: 354) pass no judgement about whether *these ones* and *those ones* are correct, either: they simply compare the distribution of occurrences (in the Longman Corpus of Spoken and Written English, hereafter the LSWE corpus) of the two structures with those of others involving the pronoun *one*. They report that while, in the conversational register, *this one* occurs about 300 times per million words, *these ones* occurs only less than 25 times per million words, and that while *that one* occurs about 600 times per million words, *those ones* appears only less

---
[29] Swan (2016: paragraph 174.3) proposes only "two possibilities": the "object form + *that*", as in *It's me that needs your help*, which he terms "very informal", and the "subject form + *who*", as in *It is I who need your help*, which he terms "very formal". Neither of them tends to be used in KenE.

than 25 times. These relative frequencies suggest that the plural versions are hardly used in speech.[30]

Let us put things into some perspective by comparing figures from the ICE-K with those from the LSWE: in the spoken component of the ICE-K (though not all of it is of the conversational register), which has 289,625 words – excluding the "written to be spoken" part (see Hudson-Ettle and Schmied 1999: 57), *those ones* appears 20 times. This corresponds to 1 occurrence in about every 14,500 words in the ICE-K, compared to 1 in about 40,000 in the LSWE corpus; that is, about three times more in KenE than in StdIntE. For its part, *these ones* occurs only twice (in the 289,625 words-long spoken component, i.e. 1 occurrence in about 145,000 words), which is even less frequent than in the LSWE corpus. So, in the end, it is only *those ones* that is typical of KenE.

Here are some examples of its use:

(72) a. *Yeah [. . .] I didn't know exactly what they meant by clearing*
[. . .] The utensils
*[. . .] Yeah **those ones** were not there*
(S1A001K)
b. *Take a case where it's the maid who bathes the boy*
[. . .] What if it's the maid who washes the boy
[. . .] The boy has faked an age whereby just wash yourself that time the maid gets in [. . .] In that case is true
*[. . .] Uh Let me tell you **those ones** happen to kids who are spoiled [. . .]*
(S1A003K)
c. *[..] What about if the books that have titles written in uh big print you put them right at the back of the display. And you have **those ones** written in small print brought just near [..] the glass of the window so that **those ones** which are in the back cannot be read from afar [. . .]*
(S1B005K)
d. *So [..] he seeks for refuge in drug taking. So maybe among **those ones** who come from that calibre of those who are pressed to drugs by poverty and frustrations that are money-related [..]*
(S1B004K)

---

[30] The frequencies reported by Biber et al. (1999) for the fiction register inform us that *this one* and *that one* occur about only 50 times each per million words, that *these ones* and *those ones* occur less than 25 times each, and that both in the news register and the academic register each one of the four structures occurs less than 25 times per million words.

e. *You've seen a lady in a mini-skirt okay [...] And you know of course we are mature personally you know already [...] that one now you are harassing me because now I know what* **those ones** *are meant for you know [...]*
(S1A003K)

A close look at these examples shows that Hocking had a point: it transpires from them that in KenE the expression *those ones* is used beyond the context illustrated by Hocking's words quoted above, that is, a context where a choice is required to be made between alternatives: seemingly, the expression is a "universal" proform used in lieu not only of other proforms (*those, these, they, those who*) but also of nouns, and even with some unspecified reference. And this is what makes it peculiar usage in StdIntE and precisely gives it its KenE character.

4.16 Miscellaneous structures

This section deals with KenE features that could not be easily classified under the NP, VP, or PP aspects, or the other various sections of this chapter.

4.16.1 *The much (I can do)*

Hocking (1974/184: 109) discusses the structure **the much I can do*. In his characteristic prescriptive tone, he writes the following about it:

> This is a common mistake, but there is absolutely no such expression in English. The mistake no doubt arises from remembering the common expression *the most I can do*, meaning *all that I can do*, but remembering it wrong. **The much* never occurs in English.

The much DOES occur at least in KenE, where it is far from being uncommon in speech, and even sometimes in writing, as the following example shows.

(73) *It is a tradition of sorts for presidents to just fire their appointees without any explanation and to let Kenyans speculate* **the much** *they want [...]*
(*The Sunday Standard*, 22 Jun 2003, p. 13)

4.16.2 *Other* repeated in the *other* ... *than* structure

This is a common feature of KenE, both spoken and written. Below are some examples.

(74) a. *[...] if you have a visually handicapped child who has **no other** complications **other than** the vision then [...]*
(S1B043K)
b. *In fact watching performances from **other** cultures **other than** our own also brings us face to face with the new art forms [...]*
(S2B030BK)
c. *So can we maybe look at uh can we maybe cite **other** factors **other than** politics that have uh popularised English [...]*
(S1B011K)
d. *Some students indeed used **other** words **other than** articles before some nouns.*
(from an MA paper by K.M., Mar 2012)
e. *[At the purification stage], borrowed words from **other** languages **other than** the dominant language are removed [...]*
(from an MA paper by J.O., Jan 2013)

4.16.3 *Basing on* used for *based on*

In KenE, the present participle inflection *–ing* is often used on the verb *base* instead of the past participle inflection *–ed*.

(75) a. *And now **basing on** that one this is what now the this is where they get the argument [...]*
(S1B012K)
b. ***Basing on** these percentages, it is only in the word "cassette" that over 50% of subjects stressed the correct syllable.*
(from an MA paper by K.N.M, Mar 2011)
c. *A large number will be selected **basing on** the fact that only volunteers will respond [...]*
(from an MA paper by E.K.O., Feb. 2011)

4.16.4 *As such* used for *therefore*

This is what Hocking (1974/1984: 141) says about this use of *as such*:

> *As such* is a popular phrase that is almost always used wrong. It does NOT mean *therefore*. [...] You can only use *as such* when you have just said that *something* IS A NOUN – that is, after statements like *He IS an OLD MAN, She IS a good COOK* [...] and so on. As such CANNOT be used after other verbs (such as *have*), or after the verb *be* and an adjective. It is used only after *be* and a noun [as in] *He is a criminal and as such he is a menace to society* [...].

In short, Hocking is saying that *as such* has to refer to a preceding noun, and thus has the meaning 'in the exact sense of this word' (as defined by the *Oxford Dictionary of English*, 3rd edn, 2010).[31] That is quite an elaborate rule, indeed, one that KenE speakers seem to have been incapable of learning, if ever it was brought to their attention. Examples of the use of *as such* for *therefore* abound both in spoken and written KenE. Here are some of them:

(76) a. *In evolutionary terms, the achievement of civilization represents a definitive stage in the development of society and culture;* **as such,** *it contrasts with savagery and barbarism* [...]
(W1A007K)
b. *Discourse therefore is generally defined as language in use or language in communication.* **As such** *certain assumption are made in Discourse analysis.*
(W1A019K)
c. *Mr. Speaker, Sir, that is not part of the original Question neither is it related to it and* **as such** *I cannot react to it.*
(S1BHN01K)
d. *Sometimes when a riddler gives a riddle the respondent is not able to give an answer.* **As such** *the riddle does not end there.*
(S2B075K)

---

31 The *Collins English Dictionary*, 10th edn, 2009, deals with *as such* on its own and defines it thus: "[...] [a] in the capacity previously specified or understood: *a judge as such hasn't so much power* [b] in itself or themselves: *intelligence as such can't guarantee success*". These examples are consistent with Hocking's rule, even though they do not contain a form of the verb *be*.

4.16.5 *All what* used for *all that*

The best way to start talking about *all what* is to remind ourselves that Hocking's (1974/1984) book, which has been extensively referred to in this chapter, was first published as *All What Was Taught and Other Mistakes*. This title seems to suggest that the structure *all what*, used for *all that*, struck the author more than any other structure. In an absolutely angry tone, Hocking wrote this:

> It is one of the worst of all mistakes to write things like **I think I still remember all what I was taught about this*. After the words *all* and *everything*, the word *that* MUST be used – definitely not *what*. This mistake is considered absolutely illiterate, so be careful never to make it. (1974/1984: 177)

The examples below, from both spoken and written KenE, are an indication that *all what* is *not* "absolutely illiterate", after all. Clearly, some of the examples were produced in careful writing; e.g. example (d) was originally from *The Sunday Standard*.

(77) a. *So,* **all what** *we need is the chance!*
   (S1B037K)
   b. *[...] You see you're not getting the point properly here. I remember [X] stressing that you give* **all what** *you have* **all what** *you can do to ensure that these children come up from the streets.*
   (S1B039K)
   c. *All you have to do is to time Good Friday when he is crucified and do* **all what you want**.
   (W1B-SK32)
   d. *When it is asserted that strict, predictable rules of private property and free contract are necessary to protect the functioning of the market [...] it can be shown that the actual rules are not* **all what** *they are claimed to be [...]*
   (W2B016K)

The use of *all what* has been reported in at least one other African English variety: Alo and Mesthrie (2008: 329) comment that "Jowitt (1991: 120) notes that in popular NigE [...] *what* is used as a relative pronoun after *all* [as in] *All* **what** *he said was false*".

4.16.6 Post-verbal adverbial *there* used for dummy *there*

This is a feature reported in Indian English by Bhatt (2008: 560) and illustrated with *"Bread is there"*, used for *"There is bread"*. Plausibly, the same feature was borrowed by KenE, in which it is frequent in speech, and can also be found in written KenE, as the examples below indicate.

(78) a. *The law **is there**. But you see these children they cannot [...] There is nothing else they can do because it's not their fault.*
(S1B022K)
b. *[...] Certainly there are more in the developing countries [than] in the developed countries but the problem **is there** and therefore [...]*
(S1B030K)
c. *Local public barazas, for most people said they attend them. The audience **is there** so that what is left is to get the knowledgeable people in each area to address the gathering*
(W2A017K)
d. *The course for computer **is there** but [it's] one thousand shillings per month. Unless I start on January [whereby] I will be reading for hours*
(W1B-SK39)

4.16.7 *How it is called* used for *What is it called*?

This is a feature of spoken KenE, even though the spoken component of the ICE-K contains only one example of its use. (Note in passing that two occurrences of *What is it called?* appear in the same component.)

(79) *[A] Oh I know [...] the one which is not supposed to boil*
*[B] Yeah [...] **How is it called?***
(S1A002K)

4.17 Features which KenE shares with AmE rather than with BrE

4.17.1 Past participial *gotten* vs. *got*

The AmE past participle *gotten* (from the verb *to get*) is very frequently in KenE as well, especially in speech. (Ten uses of it appear in the spoken component of the ICE-K, against only one in the written-to-be-spoken sub-component, but not a single one in the main written component.)

(80) a. *All was not well and he tried to throw the chips back but [X] had **gotten** hold of him*
(S1BCE10K)
b. *If I may reply to that I mean I've listened to rock-and-roll before I've never [...] **gotten** mad I've never [...] **gotten** possessed by demons*
(S1B026K)
c. *The study will employ the survey method in data collection. It will rely on information **gotten** from teachers of English and pupils [...]. Charts, tables and figures will be used in the analysis of the data **gotten** from the informants, teachers' documents and course books.*
(from a PhD proposal by K.M.S., Jul 2015)

4.17.2 AmE *as much as* used for BrE *much as*

Some dictionaries (e.g. the *Oxford Advanced Learner's Dictionary*, 10th edn, 2015)[32] specify that where BrE uses *much as* (to mean 'although'), AmE uses *as much as*. KenE uses the AmE variant a great deal, especially in speech. As an indication of this, *as much as* ('although') appears 10 times (against only 3 times for *much as*) in the spoken component of the ICE-K, while it appears only once in the entire written component, where *much as* appears 9 times. Below are some examples.

(81) a. *[...] and we want to say that **as much as** we value our customs [...] if we are to recognise changes that have taken place where we are here and now [...]*
(S1B024K)
b. *So, **as much as** we are advocating uh that we want everybody to become educated we want everybody to become literate [..]*
(S1B011K)
c. ***As much as** I do not want to interrupt the Hon. [X], this is a very important Motion with a purpose [...]*
(S1BHN05K)

---

[32] Quirk et al. (1985) do not discuss *much as*. But they discuss *as much as* in its meaning of "quasi-coordinator", as in "John, *as much as* his brothers, was responsible for the loss" (1985: 982) and in its use as "comparison of equivalence", as in "I agree with you *as much as* (I agree) with Robert" (1137).

4.18 Parallels between KenE and other African L2 varieties of English

Earlier in the discussion of some KenE features mention was made of some African varieties in which the same phenomena have already been reported in the literature: the use of mainly education-related adjectives as nouns (*Her daughter is in primary*) has been also reported in BlSAfE, while the following three features have been reported also in GhE: the use of the modal *would* for *will* (*A student who plagiarises would be expelled*), the use of *shall* and *will* after *if* and conjunctions of time (*You will get the book when you will have paid for it*), and the use of *never* for *did not* (*He never attended that meeting*). The omission of prepositions and PPs has been reported in CamE (*That's the book you need a copy Ø*), the use of resumptive pronouns (*Those are the same people some of whom they don't pay taxes*) in NigE and CamE, and the use of *isn't it* as an invariant tag (*They have always claimed they are innocent, isn't it?*) in CamE, GhE, and NigE.

But there is literature on African English varieties which reports the use of more such features than just the ones mentioned in the previous paragraph. Indeed, the eWAVE survey, in eighteen of its 235 features that are among (or are at least related to) the sixty-odd features discussed in this chapter, reports a pervasive use (corresponding to an A-rating in the survey) of some of them in a number of African varieties. For example, the use of the plural *–s* on non-count nouns (a feature corresponding to eWAVE "F55: different count/mass noun distinctions resulting in use of plural for StE singular") has been reported to be pervasive in five other varieties (in addition to KenE) out of the eight "indigenized L2 varieties" of English in Africa that are part of the eWAVE survey. The five are: BlSAfE, Indian South African English (IndSAfE), CamE, NigE, and GhE. The following features were also reported to be pervasive in more than one African variety: the omission of the definite article in CamE and NigE (cf. eWAVE "F62: Use of zero article where StE has definite article"); the lack of (tense) backshift in indirect speech in IndSAfE and CamE (cf. "F113: Loosening of sequence of tenses rule"); the use of *than what* as the second element of the comparative in IndSAfE and NigE (cf. "F204: *As what/than what* in comparative clauses"); the lack of subject-auxiliary inversion in *wh*-questions in IndSAfE (cf. "F228: No inversion/no auxiliaries in *wh*-questions"); and the lack of subject-auxiliary inversion in *yes/no* questions in IndSAfE and CamE (cf. "F229: No inversion/no auxiliaries in yes/no questions").

A curious observation that can be made from the previous two paragraphs is that there is no mention of Ugandan English (UgE) and Tanzanian English (TzE) as varieties linked with anyone one of those features reported to be pervasive in KenE. This *could* be interpreted to mean that the two varieties are indeed quite distinct from their geographical neighbour, KenE. But, at the same time, the fact that KenE would seem to be closer to CamE and IndSAfE than to its two geographical neighbours is counterintuitive (and calls for further research). No explanation seems handy for the *apparent* greater closeness of KenE to CamE than to UgE and TzE. However, some plausible speculation could be easily put forward as to why it could be closer to IndSAfE than to the latter two: both KenE and IndSAfE must carry the influence of Indian English (IndE), from the Asian subcontinent. The influence of IndE on IndSAfE sounds a natural thing to claim. But the same influence on KenE is not a wild claim either, as there has been a non-negligible Indian-English speaking community in Kenya for a century (especially in the city of Nairobi).[33]

4.19 Summary and conclusion

This chapter can best be summarised through a table recapitulating all the morphological and syntactic features of KenE discussed in it and indicating whether they are mainly spoken, mainly written, or characteristic of both written and spoken KenE, and also indicating which features in the eWAVE survey are related to the KenE ones, even if only partially.

In conclusion, if the structures summarised in Table 4.1 are claimed to be features of KenE, theoretically this should mean that they are not rare at all. That is, if we borrow the eWAVE feature-rating terminology, they should get a least a B-rating. And that is precisely the present author's standpoint, one based on the following two considerations: first, a feature that has an idiosyncratic behaviour in a given variety needs to be dealt with individually, rather than as part of a larger pattern that will inevitably eclipse its idiosyncratic behaviour and thus cause the rater to dismiss the feature as non-existent, or as

---

[33] In fact, if we take the eighteen eWAVE features close equivalents of which were discussed in this chapter (see Table 4.1) as the reference, a search on the eWAVE map of varieties and features will reveal that both KenE and IndE share the same A-rating for seven of them (against eight shared with IndSAfE and nine shared with CamE). To put things into perspective, KenE does not share a single A-rating with both UgE and TzE, simply because neither of these scored a single A-rating on them. (In fact, UgE did not score a single A-rating on any of the 235 varieties investigated in the eWAVE survey, while TzE scored only one A, for feature "F45: Insertion of *it* where StE has zero", as in "*As it is the case elsewhere [...]*".)

Table 4.1: Summary of the morphological and syntactic features of KenE.

Section in the chap.	Name of feature: example is typical of speech (S), of writing (W), or of both (S &W)	Related eWAVE feature (its rate of attestation in varieties around the world)[a]
4.1.1	Sing. verb for plur. subject: *The topics has been discussed* (S & W)	F182: Agreement sensitive to position of subject (12%)
4.1.2	Plur. verb for sing. subject: *The topic have been discussed* (S & W)	–
4.1.3	No agreement between noun and its determiners/pronouns: *The topics and the discussion of it* (S & W)	–
4.2.1	Plur. –s added to non-count nouns and some idiomatic expressions: *"Victoria furnitures"*; *to bear fruits* (S & W)	F55: Different count/mass noun distinctions resulting in use of plur. for StE sing. (54%)
4.2.2.	Other inflections added: *anyhowly, severally; to be worthy doing* (S & W)	–
4.2.3	Omission of inflections: *master of ceremony* (S & W)	–
4.3.1.1	Omission of the definite article: *It is Ø IEBC which organises elections in Kenya*; *"Ø University of Nairobi is a corruption-free area"*; *Ø majority of people in Ø Nairobi area* (S & W)	F62: Use of zero article where StE has definite article (58%)
4.3.1.2	Addition of the definite article: ***the** Almighty God* (S & W)	–
4.3.1.3	Omission of the indefinite article: *to be on Ø par with; if such Ø person at such Ø place* (S & W)	–
4.3.2	Noun + noun structure used for N's + N structure: *women groups; three years imprisonment; a million worth of goods* (S & W)	F77: omission of genitive suffix; possessive expressed though bare juxtaposition of nouns (57%)
4.3.3	Pluralising the premodifying noun: *a book**s** fair; the Child**ren** Welfare Society* (S & W)	–
4.3.4	Using some adjectives as nouns: *She's his **second born**; She's in **primary*** (S & W)	–

Table 4.1 (continued)

Section in the chap.	Name of feature: example is typical of speech (S), of writing (W), or of both (S &W)	Related eWAVE feature (its rate of attestation in varieties around the world)[a]
4.3.5	Using the complementiser *that* where not required after nouns: "***Matters** arising from the minutes **that** the first issue...*" (W)	–
4.4.1	Marking the progressive aspect on stative verbs: *I'm not **seeing** any evidence of it here* (S)	F88: Wider range of uses of progressive *be + V*-ing than in StE: extension to stative verbs (63%)
4.4.2	Overuse of *shall*: "*There **shall** be a Faculty Board meeting next week*" (S & W)	–
4.4.3	*Could* and *would* used for *should*: "*The title is not appropriate here: it **could** have been 'suggestions'*" (S & W)	–
4.4.4	*Would* used for *will* and other modals: "*A teacher who doesn't get on well with the fellow teachers **would** always want to quarrel [...]*" (S & W)	–
4.4.5	*Shall* and *will* used after *if* and conjunctions of time: *If by tomorrow **you will have** not submitted your term paper, it will not be accepted.* (S & W)	–
4.5.6	Lack of (tense) backshift in indirect speech: *He **said** he **will** come the following day* (S & W)	F113: Loosening of sequence of tenses rule (66%)
4.4.7	Obligatory complements omitted after certain verbs: *I really appreciate Ø.* (S & W)	F42: Object pronoun drop (37%)
4.4.8	The *for*-PP placed before the direct object NP: *Buy **for me** lunch* (S)	–
4.4.9	PP complements used after certain verbs instead of NP ones: *Let's **discuss about** that issue later* (S & W)	–
4.4.10	NP complements used after certain verbs instead of PP ones: *He'll **quarrel you** if you arrive late* (S & W)	–

Table 4.1 (continued)

Section in the chap.	Name of feature: example is typical of speech (S), of writing (W), or of both (S &W)	Related eWAVE feature (its rate of attestation in varieties around the world)[a]
4.4.11	Selection restrictions violated: *They will **facilitate you** to do it* (S & W)	–
4.4.12	Using complementiser *that* after verbs that do not require it: *Let him not **cheat** you **that** he'll help you get it* (S & W)	–
4.4.13	Complementation with *as follows*: *This is to inform you **as follows*** (W)	–
4.4.14	Using the copula *be* + *as a result of*: *His death may **be as a result of** a heart attack* (S & W)	–
4.4.15	The infinitive marker *to* omitted after *to enable* + direct object: *That will **enable** us Ø do it* (S & W)	F208: Deletion of *to* infinitives (34%)
4.4.16	Some intransitive verbs used transitively: ***We were rained on*** *while playing* (S & W)	–
4.4.17	*Who* used for *whom*: *Who said what **to who**?* (S & W)	–
4.4.18	The infinitive used for modals *should* and *must*: *All the staff **to wear** name tags* (W)	–
4.4.19	*What you do* used for *what you should do* is: *What you **do, write** him a note* (S)	–
4.4.20	Continuous tenses used after *This is the first time*: ***This is the first time I'm seeing*** *this* (S)	–
4.4.21	*Can/could be able* used for *can/could*: *So that we **can be able** to move ahead* (S)	–
4.4.22	Past-tense forms equated with past-time meanings: ***If they reacted*** *early,* ***they would have*** *rescued him* (S & W)	–
4.4.23	*Never* used for *did not*: *He **never** attended that meeting* (S & W)	F159: *Never* as preverbal past tense negator
4.4.25	The infinitive *to* used for the preposition *to*: *They need **an** appropriate **approach to** increase their revenues* (S & W)	–

Table 4.1 (continued)

Section in the chap.	Name of feature: example is typical of speech (S), of writing (W), or of both (S &W)	Related eWAVE feature (its rate of attestation in varieties around the world)[a]
4.5.1	Use of a different preposition: *He was **admitted at** the Nairobi Hospital* (S & W)	–
4.5.2	Repetition of the preposition at the end of a relative clause: *the house **in** which he lives **in*** (S & W)	–
4.5.3	One preposition is shared by two conjuncts requiring different ones: *He **comments** and **quotes from** the Bible a lot* (S & W)	–
4.5.4	Omission of prepositions and PPs: *"Those ones, don't worry Ø"* (S & W)	F216: Omission of StE prepositions (70%)
4.6	*(as) compared to* used for *than* in the comparative: *It's a nicer day **compared to** yesterday* (S & W)	F204: *As what/than what* in comparative clauses (66%)
4.7	No subject-aux. inversion in questions: ***You're going where?*** (S) ***You get the point?*** (S)	F228: No inversion / no auxiliaries in *wh*-questions (72%); F229: " / " in main clause yes/no questions (92%)
4.8	Use of resumptive pronouns: ***Some of them, they** are naughty children* (S)	F194: Resumptive/shadow pronouns (47%)
4.9	Non-use of relative det. *whose*: *"I don't call **the people the phone numbers** I don't know"* (S & W)	F192: Use of analytic [...] *that his* [...], *what his* [...], *who his* instead of *whose* (24%)
4.10	Pronoun (subj.) + pronoun (obj.) sequence in subject position: ***Me I** like music* (S)	F28: Use of *us* + NP in subject function (50%)
4.11	Plural *we* used for singular *I*: ***We** went to the same school with Andrew* (S)	–
4.12	*Isn't it?* used as an invariant tag: *We all want peace, **isn't it?*** (S)	F165: Invariant non-concord tags (67%)
4.13	*No/not/none ... nor* used for *no/not/none ... or*: *"**No** hawking, preaching **nor** begging in this bus"* (S & W)	F154: Multiple negation/negative concord (80%)
4.14	Non-use of *It is I who am/It is you who are*: *It is **you** who **is** to blame* (S)	–

Table 4.1 (continued)

Section in the chap.	Name of feature: example is typical of speech (S), of writing (W), or of both (S &W)	Related eWAVE feature (its rate of attestation in varieties around the world)[a]
4.15	*Those ones* used for *those, these, they,* etc.: "***Those ones***, we shall deal with them perpendicularly [i.e. 'ruthlessly']" (S)	–
4.16.1	Use of *the much (I can do)*: That was ***the much*** they could do (S & W)	–
4.16.2	Repetition of *other* in the *other . . . than* structure: *You cannot use **other** books **other than** those recommended* (S & W)	–
4.16.3	*Basing on* used for *based on*: ***Basing on*** what has been achieved so far . . . (S & W)	–
4.16.4	*As such* used for *therefore*: *He has not applied for it; **as such** he cannot be shortlisted* (S & W)	–
4.16.5	*All what* used for *all that*: *That's **all what** we need* (S & W)	–
4.16.6	Post-verbal adverbial *there* used for dummy *there*: "*Night runners in Kenya? They are **there**!*" (S)	–
4.16.7	*How is it called* used for *what is it called*? (S)	–
4.17.1	AmE *gotten* used for BrE *got*: *He couldn't buy it then because he **hadn't gotten** money yet* (S & W)	–
4.17.2	AmE *as much as* used for BrE *much as*: *Much **as** you'd like to employ him, he is a lazy man* (S & W)	–

[a] A dash (-) means 'no related feature in the eWAVE survey'.

extremely rare. A case in point is the omission of the infinitive marker *to* after the verb *to enable*: this feature is pervasive in KenE, but it will automatically become "extremely rare" if we talk about dropping the *to* after verbs in general. This chapter contains more cases of such lexically-conditioned pervasiveness (e.g. regarding the use, or non-use, of articles in *the Almighty God, majority of,* and *such person*). Second, the pervasiveness of a given feature should be related to its possible absence from the English variety being described rather than to its coexistence with its StE variant(s). Otherwise, one may find that not a single feature is pervasive in the L2 variety in question, in which case the whole concept of it being an indigenized variety will be called into question. (This might apply to UgE and TzE, if we go by their current eWAVE ratings for the host of features investigated.)

5 Lexis and semantics

Skandera's (2003) book is the most scholarly discussion of meanings of KenE vocabulary to date. Although it deals only with the meanings of idioms, it is relevant to this chapter in two respects: first, it identified special meanings of "Kenyan English idioms" (see chapters 8–10), idioms such as *wife inheritance, to draw a map of Africa/Kenya, slowly by slowly,* and *jua kali*. Second, it categorized the meanings of such idioms on the basis of the processes that explain how the meanings in question came about, which the present study will do as well.

Thus, this chapter will present the KenE vocabulary along three parameters: a) loan expressions from indigenous languages of Kenya, b) words and phrases that have been coined by Kenyan English users but which are not (yet) lexical entries in standard international English dictionaries, and c) those that are lexical entries in StdIntE dictionaries but have acquired additional meanings which do not appear in these same dictionaries. The chapter will then attempt to answer the questions of the extent to which KenE lexical items coexist with their StdIntE variants, of how much they can be used in formal and informal situations, and of the extent to which KenE vocabulary has been influenced by other varieties of English.

5.1 Loan expressions from indigenous languages of Kenya

A number of publications, including dictionaries, contain a varying number of words which have been borrowed by English from Kiswahili and some other indigenous languages of Kenya. From the scattered picture of how many such words there may be, this chapter first proposes a "common core" list of them and then attempts to explain the wide variation there is in the loan expressions into English.

5.1.1 Towards a common-core list of loan expressions in KenE

Table 5.1 below presents a common-core list of loan expressions compiled on the basis of an arbitrary criterion: only the expressions that have been proposed

---

Note: The content of this chapter is an updated and restructured version of Buregeya (2007).

in at least two of the eight sources which this chapter drew specific lexical items from were included in the list. The eight sources are: Zuengler (1982), Okombo (1987), Schmied (1991a), Bulili (2002), Atichi (2004), the *Oxford Primary Dictionary for Eastern Africa* (2008) – hereafter abbreviated as the *OPDEA*, 2008,[1] the *Collins English Dictionary*, 10th edn, 2009 – hereafter the *CED*, 2009, and the Kenyan component of the ICE, hereafter the ICE-K. (The two dictionaries, as well as Schmied 1991a, refer to the expressions under discussion as "East African", rather than as "Kenyan".)

The common-core list in the table above contains some sixty expressions. Not included are the Swahili words that are part of code-mixed set phrases which have become proper nouns referring to national holidays (*Madaraka* Day: 'self-governance' day, *Mashujaa* Day: 'heroes' day, and *Jamhuri* Day: 'independence' day); to buildings (e.g. *Sheria* House: the State 'Law' Office, *Afya* House: the Ministry of 'Health' building, and the *Magereza* Headquarters: the 'Prisons' Headquarters); to streets (e.g. *Biashara* street: the street of 'business'), etc.

5.1.2 Discussion

This section describes the nature of the wide variation there is across the eight sources and attempts to explain it. One striking observation is the extent to which they vary in terms of how many expressions they recognize as having been borrowed from indigenous Kenyan languages: at one extreme are Okombo's (1987) and Atichi's (2004) lists of just 14 expressions each, while at the other extreme is Schmied's (1991a) list of 67. Between the two are Zuengler's (1982) list of 25, Bulili's (2002) list of 27 and the *OPDEA*'s (2008) list of 43. It was not possible to go through the *CED* (2009) to establish how many words exactly are labelled "East African" in it. As for the ICE-K, we can get a rough idea of how many such expressions there are by referring to Budohoska (2014), who used the Concordance search tool in the "Ant.Conc.3.2.m search software" (2014: 35) to establish "a list of African loanwords in the ICE-K" (2014: 93). By selecting "only lexical items appearing more than two times and in at least two different texts" (93), she produced a list of 31 words, only 18 of which appear in Table 5.1.

---

[1] Although the smallest of them, this *OPDEA* will, for the purposes of this study, represent the entire family of Oxford English dictionaries, all of which recognize East African English vocabulary.

5.1 Loan expressions from indigenous languages of Kenya — 141

Table 5.1: List of KenE expressions borrowed from indigenous languages of Kenya[a].

Word	Donor language	Gloss	Zuengler (1982)	Okombo (1987)	Schmied (1991a)	Bulili (2002)	Atichi (2004)	OPDEA (2008)	CED (2009)	ICE-K
askari	Swahili	'soldier', 'guard'	–	X[b]	X	X	X	X	X	X
baba	"	'father'	X	–	X	–	–	–	–	X
baraza	"	'a citizens' meeting (usually) called by a government official'	X	X	–	X	X	X	X	X
boma	"	'an area with a fence around it to keep people or animals safe at night'	–	–	X	–	–	X	–	–
buibui	" / Arabic	'Islamic veil'	–	–	X	–	–	X	X	–
busaa	Luhya / Ekegusii	'a kind of home-brewed beer from sorghum or millet'	X	–	–	–	–	–	–	X
bwana	Swahili	'mister', 'master', 'lord'	–	–	X	–	–	–	X	X
chai	"	'tea'	–	–	X	–	–	–	X	X
chang'aa	Luhya (?) / Ekegusii (?)	'a very strong (illicit) liquor distilled from cereals'	–	–	–	X	X	–	–	X
daktari	Swahili	'doctor'	–	–	X	–	–	–	–	X
debe	"	'a tin container of 20 litres' (KKK, 2001)[c]	–	X	X	–	–	–	X	–

(continued)

142 — 5 Lexis and semantics

Table 5.1 (continued)

Word	Donor language	Gloss	Zuengler (1982)	Okombo (1987)	Schmied (1991a)	Bulili (2002)	Atichi (2004)	OPDEA (2008)	CED (2009)	ICE-K
duka	"	'shop'	–	X	X	–	X	–	X	–
githeri	Kikuyu	'a cooked meal from a mixture of maize and beans'	–	–	X	–	X	–	–	X
harambee	"	lit. 'let's pull together', used as rallying slogan in political rallies; 'fundraising'	X	X	X	X	X	X	X	X
irio	Kikuyu	'food'	X	–	–	–	–	X	–	X
jembe	Swahili	'hoe'	X	–	X	X	–	X	X	X
jiko	"	'a stove that runs on charcoal'	–	–	–	X	–	X	–	X
jua kali	"	'the informal sector' – lit. 'hot sun'	–	–	–	X	–	X	–	X
kachumbari	"	'a mixture of raw onions, tomatoes and strong pepper'	–	–	–	X	–	X	–	–
k(h)anga	"	'a piece of colourful soft-material clothing which women tie from the waist or the bust'	–	–	X	–	–	X	–	–
k(h)anzu	"	'a flowing robe worn (usually) for religious purposes'	–	–	X	–	X	–	X	–

5.1 Loan expressions from indigenous languages of Kenya

		meaning									
kiondo	Kikuyu	'a bag with long handles made from sisal leaves'	–	–	x	–	–	–	x	–	x
les(s)o	Swahili	'another name for *kanga*'	–	–	x	–	–	–	x	–	x
majimbo	"	'federal states'	–	–	–	x	–	–	x	–	x
ma(a)ndazi	"	'doughnut'	–	–	x	x	–	–	x	–	x
manamba	"/Sheng	'a tout on a public service vehicle'	–	–	x	–	x	x	x	–	x
manyat(t)a	Maasai	'a group of huts built almost in a circle with, usually with a fence around them'	–	–	–	–	–	–	x	–	x
matatu	Swahili	'a public service minibus'	x	–	x	x	–	–	–	–	x
mato(o)ke	Ekegusii / Luhya	'a meal made of boiled bananas'	–	–	–	–	–	x	x	–	x
miraa	Swahili (?) / Kimeru (?)	'another name for *khat*'	–	–	–	–	–	–	x	–	x
moran	Maasai	'a young warrior waiting to be an elder'	–	–	–	–	x	–	–	–	x
mtumba	Swahili	'second-hand sale article'	–	–	–	x	–	–	–	–	x
mwalimu	"	'a teacher'	–	–	x	–	–	–	x	x	–
mwananchi	"	'an ordinary citizen'	–	–	–	–	x	–	x	–	x

(continued)

Table 5.1 (continued)

Word	Donor language	Gloss	Zuengler (1982)	Okombo (1987)	Schmied (1991a)	Bulili (2002)	Atichi (2004)	OPDEA (2008)	CED (2009)	ICE-K
mzee	"	'an old man', 'a respectable man', 'a husband'	–	–	x	–	–	x	x	x
mzungu	"	'a white man'	–	–	x	–	–	–	x	x
ndugu	"	'a brother', 'a comrade'	–	–	x	–	–	x	–	–
ngoma	"	'dance', 'a drum'	–	–	x	–	–	x	–	–
nyama choma	"	'gilled/roasted meat'	–	–	–	–	–	x	–	x
nyatiti	Dholuo	'a stringed musical instrument popular in the Luo community'	–	–	–	x	–	x	–	x
panga	Swahili	'machete'	x	x	x	x	x	x	x	x
rungu	"	'a (wooden) club'	x	x	–	x	–	–	–	–
shamba	"	'cultivated plot of land', 'a farm'	x	x	x	x	x	x	x	x
shuka	"	'a piece of garment [...] that women cover their waist with' (OPDEA, 2008)	–	–	–	x	x	x	–	–

5.1 Loan expressions from indigenous languages of Kenya

Word	Source	Definition[c]	1	2	3	4	5	6	7	8
sufuria	"	'a wide-bottomed open aluminium pan for cooking, boiling water, etc.'	x	–	x	–	x	–	x	x
sukumawiki	"	(lit.) 'push the week'; ref. to 'spinach-like greens'	x	–	x	–	x	–	x	x
taarab	Swahili / Arabic	'a type of music that people in East Africa play, especially along the coast'	–	–	–	–	x	–	x	x
ugali	Swahili	'boiled maize meal'	x	x	x	x	x	–	x	x
uhuru	"	'freedom', 'independence'	x	–	x	–	–	x	–	–
uji	"	'porridge typically made from sorghum'	–	–	x	x	x	–	x	x
wananchi	"	'people', 'citizens'	x	–	x	x	x	–	x	x
wazee (plur. of *mzee*)	"	'old/elderly people'	–	x	–	–	–	–	–	x
wazungu (plur. of *mzungu*)	"	'white people'	–	–	x	–	–	–	–	x

[a] The definitions provided in this table are not specific to any one of the eight sources; they would most likely be accepted by all of them. Where they might not be, the source is indicated in brackets.
[b] X: cited in the source mentioned at the top of the column
[c] For *Kamusi ya Kiswahili-Kiingereza / Swahili-English Dictionary* (2001)

Although Budohoska's (2014) criterion is a solid one, it has left out the following words (included in Table 5.1) which are not uncommon in KenE: *githeri, mandazi, manyatta, manamba, makanga, moran,*[2] *mzungu, wazungu, taarab,* and *uji.* But Budohoska's (2014) list is bound to be slightly shorter than that in Table 5.1 for another reason: she has classified, e.g. in Appendix 4 (see pp. 182–183), the singular and the plural of a given word as one single word. This is indeed the convention in dictionaries. However, the practice in the eight sources has been to list singular words such as *shamba, mzungu, mzee,* and *mwananchi* as separate from their plural equivalents *mashamba, wazungu, wazee,* and *wananchi.* This practice seems to have developed from the tendency, on the part of some KenE users, to apply English morphology to the Swahili loanwords and mark the plural with the English suffix *-s,* and say *shambas* (which appears 3 times in the ICE-K written-to-bespoken component), instead of using the Swahili prefix *ma-* in *mashamba* or *wa-* in *wazungu.* For some other words, the English *-s* even gets affixed to what is already a plural in Swahili; thus, some people say *wazees* (which appears 3 times in the ICE-K spoken component) instead of its plural counterpart in Swahili, *wazee.*

Further, there is a sizable number of words and phrases which were not included in Table 5.1 because either they appear only in one of the eight sources or in none at all, but which, in the present author's view, are frequent enough and are used by people from all the various ethnic groups of Kenya to qualify as KenE loan expressions. Those are: *bodaboda* ('a bicycle/motorbike taxi'), which appears only in the *OPDEA* (2008); *chama* ('a revolving fund for women's groups'), sometimes pronounced as /tʃa'ma:/ and is different from the *chama* ('a political party', always pronounced as /tʃa:ma/) that appears in Schmied's (1991a) list; *fundi* ('a craftsman', 'an artisan'); *kikoi* ('a piece of coloured cotton cloth with lines on it that people [esp. women] wear'), which appears only in the *OPDEA* (2008); *Nyayo system* ('a political system associated with former Kenyan President Daniel arap Moi'); *insha* ('a school composition in Swahili'), which appears once in the ICE-K spoken; *(the Speaker's) Kamukunji* ('an informal meeting of members of parliament in Kenya convened by the Speaker of

---

[2] In fact, the word *moran* appears more than twice in the spoken and the written-to-bespoken components of the ICE-K. (In the latter component, it appears in two different texts, S1BHN11K and S1BHN09K.) At the same time, the criterion in question allowed words which, arguably, cannot be called KenE to make it to Budohoska's (2014) list. One of them is the Kalenjin, *not* Swahili, noun *orkoiyot* ('king, supreme chief, witch-doctor'), together with its plural form *orkoiik.* Other examples are the discourse fillers *ati* ('hey/say'), *sijui* ('I don't know'), and *nini?* (what?).

the National Assembly to discuss a given issue'; university students also commonly use *Kamukunji* for 'their unofficial meeting'); *kienyeji* ('indigenous'), as in *kienyeji chicken* ('an indigenous breed of chicken'); *kinyozi* ('barber', 'barber shop'); *makanga*, another name for *manamba* ('a tout on a public service vehicle'); *mama/mama X* ('mother', 'mother of child X'), which appears 17 times in the ICE-K[3]; *mama mboga* ('an ordinary woman, who toils to earn a living, esp. one who sells vegetables'; *mboga* means 'vegetables'), which appears once in the ICE-K spoken; *panya (route)* ('an illegal route through which illicit trade is done'), mentioned once in the ICE-K written component; and *Wanjiku* ('an ordinary citizen, in general', even though *Wanjiku* is in fact a female name). All these expressions are from Swahili, except for *Kamukunji* (borrowed from the name of a stadium where rallies took place to agitate for multiparty democracy in the early 1990s) whose origin is not clearly known, and *Wanjiku*, which is a typical Kikuyu name.

Another striking observation about the list in Table 5.1 is that only three (*harambee, panga, shamba*) expressions can be found in all the eight sources. Indeed, each of these has surprising "absences": Okombo's list lacks expressions such as *chang'aa, jembe, jiko, jua kali, moran, manyatta, sufuria,* and *sukumawiki*; Atichi's lacks *jua kali, majimbo, matatu, rungu, sufuria,* and, notably, *ugali*; Zuengler's lacks *askari, matatu, githeri, moran, uji, and manyatta*; Bulili's lacks *githeri* and *moran*, while Schmied's lacks *manyatta, mtumba/mitumba, moran, omena,* and *sukumawiki*. For its part, the *OPDEA* (2008), which states (on its back cover) that it is a dictionary "especially for primary schools in Eastern and Central Africa", does not contain *chang'aa, githeri, moran, rungu,* and *uji*. The *CED* (2009) does not contain *chang'aa, githeri, jiko, jua kali, manyatta, moran, mwananchi,* and *rungu*. As for the ICE-K, while it contains most of the words in Table 5.1, some in much lower frequencies than one might have expected (e.g. it contains only 3 hits of *mwananchi*, without a single one in its spoken component), and some others in much higher frequencies (e.g. *wananchi*, with 92 hits), it does not contain a single occurrence of such a frequently-heard word as *rungu*.

One explanation for the variation in the eight sources must have to do with the methodology used to collect the words included in their various lists. While Okombo (1987) and Atichi (2004) seem to have relied on their personal "beliefs" of whether a given word belonged to KenE or not, Zuengler (1982) and Bulili

---

3 Notice that while another two (Zuengler 1982 and Schmied 1991a) of the 8 sources have *baba* ('father') in their lists, neither of them has *mama*. Surprisingly, both words are referred to as Indian English, not Kenyan, or East African, by the *Oxford Dictionary of English*, 3rd edn, 2010.

(2002) seem to have decided that any word found in a single written source automatically qualified as a KenE one. Schmied (1991) consulted several written sources: from Dalgish's *Dictionary of Africanisms* (1982), which "is only a beginning",[4] to "large dictionaries of World English", in particular the *Concise Oxford English Dictionary* and the *Oxford English Dictionary* with its supplements. Concerning the *OPDEA* (2008), it can be assumed (because it is not indicated in the dictionary itself) that, like the other Oxford dictionaries, it relied on information from the British National Corpus and the Oxford English Corpus (as indicated e.g. on the back cover of the *Oxford Advanced Learner's Dictionary*, 9th edn, 2015). For its part, the ICE-K was compiled through an elaborate methodology (described in Hudson-Ettle and Schmied 1999) appropriate for compiling language corpora. It is worth pointing out, though, that regarding its representativeness for lexical studies, Schmied (2004b: 944) cautions us that "[this corpus] is, however, not really sufficient for lexical and collocational research, where a much larger corpus is necessary".

Another explanation for the variation across the eight sources can be sought from the inclusion, in their respective lists, of regionalisms, that is those lexical items that reflect what the present study considers to be "regional dialects" of KenE.[5] For example, only the *OPDEA* (2008) has the words *makuti* ('palm-tree leaves used to thatch houses') and *zeze* ('a one-stringed musical instrument of the violin type'), both of which are well known in the coastal region of Kenya, but not elsewhere in the country. The inclusion of regionalisms in certain dictionaries must in turn have stemmed from what can be termed "informant bias", which happens when a language informant from a given region of Kenya recommends, for inclusion, a word that is practically known in that geographical area.[6]

---

[4] The full reference for this dictionary is: Dalgish, Gerard M. 1982. *A Dictionary of Africanisms. Contributions of Sub-Saharan Africa to the English Language*. Westport, Connecticut/London: Greenwood Press.

[5] From Schmied's (1991$_b$) discussion of "subnational" features in the pronunciation of KenE, it can be argued that such dialects identifiable on the basis of pronunciation already exist.

[6] Such informant bias must be the main reason for inclusion, in the *Oxford Advanced Learner's Dictionary of English*, 8th edn, 2010, of *mwethya*, labelled an East African word (in fact from the Kikamba language of Eastern Kenya) and defined as 'a group of people who are involved with projects in a community, for example for building roads'. (It should be noted, though, that the word in question is not an entry in the dictionary's 9th edition, 2015). The same could be said about the word *nyanza*, which appears in the *CED*, 2009, as an East African word meaning 'a lake', and which is likely to be used in the English spoken in the south-western part of Kenya, along Lake Victoria.

A more robust criterion for inclusion should be the "frequency and distribution" (mentioned by the *CED* 2009: 1901) of a given word in a corpus. But not even this criterion has always prevailed: in the *CED* itself, in the appendix to its 7th edn, 2005, the word *matatu*, there referred to as "African" and defined as 'a loosely regulated and very popular form of public transport in Kenya, usually a minibus or converted truck', is listed among those being "tracked for frequency and distribution" as "candidates for inclusion in future editions". However, the word did not make it to future editions: it is neither an entry in the dictionary's 8th edition (2006) nor in its current 10th edition (2009). The editors of the *CED* must have concluded that *matatu* was one of those "expressions [that are] ephemeral coinages". But the reality about it is that not only has the word been mentioned in the literature for about three decades now (e.g. by Okombo 1987 and Schmied 1991a – the latter even informs us that the word was already "contained in [the] *Oxford English Dictionary* [...]" [1991a: 81]), it is still frequently used in KenE, in collocations such as *matatu drivers, matatu touts, matatu conductors, matatu operators,* and the *matatu industry*.[7]

5.2 Coinages of Kenya English

5.2.1 A list of specific coinages

Single words and phrases in this category do not appear as lexical entries either in general standard international English dictionaries such as the *Oxford Advanced Learner's Dictionary,* the *Oxford Dictionary of English,* the *Collins English Dictionary, Merriam-Webster Online: Dictionary and Thesaurus,* and *Webster's English Dictionary,* or in the specialised *Cambridge International Dictionary of Idioms* (1998).[8] Nonetheless, all of them were formed from existing Standard English words, except for *shrubbing*.

---

[7] Of all the words in Table 5.1, *matatu* in fact appears most frequently in the ICE-K, even though the frequency counts vary with authors: 96 (44 spoken + 44 written + 8 written-to-be spoken) for the present author, 91 hits (51 spoken + 40 written) for Budohoska (2014: 182), and 44 (25 spoken and 19 written) for Schmied (2007: 6).
[8] Where there was doubt, the frequency of occurrence of the relevant expression both in the British National Corpus (BNC) and the Corpus of Contemporary American English (COCA) was also taken into account. The online dictionaries such as *Wiktionary,* the *Free Dictionary,* and *Urban Dictionary,* in which seemingly any word (and any slang term for this latter) which has been used by some source, irrespective of how widespread it is in its usage internationally, is likely to appear, will be ignored in the present study.

In the list below, the coinages are arranged first by the word class of the key word: nouns and noun phrases, verbs and verb phrases, etc.; those that are not easily classifiable (like entire sentences) have been classified as "miscellaneous". The sources of the various coinages are indicated between brackets: *A* stands for Atichi (2004), *B* for Bulili (2002), *S* for Skandera (2003), and *AB* for the present author. The definitions given were provided by the indicated sources. In case the definition requires some illustration, an example provided by the indicated source is added.

Nouns and NPs
(1) *academics* [sing.] (AB) 'academic matters' (see e.g. the University of Nairobi's website where *Academics* is one heading); 'intellectual learning subjects at school' – *He's very good at sports but very weak at academics.*
(2) *a bed net* (S) 'a mosquito net'
(3) *a beachboy* (S) 'a boy or a man who is trying to entice tourists along the coast, often rather persistently, into staying at a particular hotel, going on a safari, or buying handicrafts'
(4) *a best maid* (AB) 'bridesmaid' (mentioned in Mwangi 2003: 16)
(5) *a bicycle kick* (in football) (AB) 'an overhead kick'
(6) *a bicycle taxi* (A) 'a means of transport', 'a bicycle that is hired for a charge that is based on the length and time of the journey'
(7) *the big five* (S) 'the five most sought-after, though not necessarily the biggest, animal species in Kenya's national parks and reserves: elephant, rhinoceros, buffalo, lion, and leopard'[9]
(8) *a bride price* (B) 'money or animals given to a bride's parents by the bridegroom'
(9) *a bride wealth* (B) [Note: same definition as for *bride price*]
(10) *a briefcase (political) party* (AB) 'too small a party to survive on its own'
(11) *a by-the-way* (AB) i.e. used as a noun to mean 'an afterthought'
(12) *a chase car* (AB) 'a car that is part of a motorcade'
(13) *chest-thumping* (AB) 'gloating over one's achievement' (usually said of politicians)
(14) *the City in the Sun* (S) 'a name for Nairobi'
(15) *cold water* (B) 'cold sweat'

---

[9] The expression *the big + number* is in fact productive in KenE and is used beyond animals: for example, after his re-election in 2017, President Uhuru Kenyatta said his second term was going to revolve around "the Big Four" pillars of his Kenya economic transformation agenda.

(16) *[a] come-we-stay [union]* (B) '[a relationship in which a couple live together as husband and wife but without being officially married yet]'
(17) *a co-wife* (S and B) 'a woman who is married to the same man as another woman in a polygamous society'
(18) *an end result* (B) 'results', 'end'
(19) *an extension worker/officer* (S) 'extension agent' (StdAmE)
(20) *a face towel* (S) 'face cloth, face flannel' (StdBrE)
(21) *failure to which* (AB) 'failure to do that'
(22) *a flag-bearer* (A) 'one who represents a group, party, country in a competition or election'
(23) *life chances* (S) 'opportunities one has to make the most of one's life'
(24) *the members' day* (S) 'refers to [Friday evening when especially men gather in bars to drink to end the working week]'
(25) *a minute* (AB) 'one item of a meeting's minutes'
(26) *mob justice* (A) 'an attack or harm meted out to a criminal or suspect by a crowd of people'
(27) *most (of the) times* (AB) 'most of the time'
(28) *a night runner* (AB) 'a man or a woman who practises witchcraft and runs at night as part of his/her witchcraft ritual'
(29) *an out-grower* (A) 'a small-scale farmer commissioned by a factory to grow a cash crop, outside its nucleus or premises with the support of that factory' [e.g. *a sugar cane out-grower*]
(30) *a parking boy* (S) 'a street child [or man] who presses drivers for money in return for guarding their parked cars'
(31) *a polite notice* (AB) This is a public notice usually meant to be a 'warning'.
(32) *a premise* (AB) 'a building', i.e. the singular of *premises* – "*The JKUAT Kitale CBD Campus will be moving to occupy a new premise known as Mega Centre this year [...]*" (from *Agritech News*, 46/57, p. 22)
(33) *at the present moment* (B) 'at the moment'
(34) *a proforma* [sic] (AB) 'a form used to raise funds (from the local community) for a project, e.g. to build a classroom'
(35) *queue-voting* (S) 'an electoral system whereby voters publicly line up behind a symbol or picture of [or the person himself/herself] they choose to vote'
(36) *a sessional paper* (AB) 'a government paper, esp. on economic policy, extensively discussed by the cabinet and the parliament before it is published for the general public'

(37) *(go for) a short* or *long call* (S) [this is] a euphemism for 'to go to urinate' and 'to go to defecate', respectively
(38) *a show-cause letter* (AB) 'a letter which an employee is asked to write to explain himself/herself'
(39) *shrubbing* (AB) 'pronunciation of English that is influenced by one's mother tongue, specifically a Kenyan indigenous language'
(40) *a sit-in CAT* (continuous assessment test) (AB) 'an in-class CAT'
(41) *a sitting allowance* (AB) 'an allowance that people, especially Members of Parliament, get for attending a meeting/a parliamentary session'
(42) *a slay queen* (AB) 'a young woman who seeks attention through affected speech and gestures' (Note: The opposite is *slay king*, but this is much less used.)
(43) *something small* (S and B) 'a bribe'
(44) *song and dance* (AB) used in its literal meaning – "His supporters [...] broke into song and dance when the judges ruled [in his favour]" (*The Standard*, 20 Feb 2014, p. 7). Note also that the KenE expression lacks the indefinite article which appears in *a song and dance* in both BrE and AmE.
(45) *strong tea* (B) 'tea without milk'
(46) *those sides* (AB) 'that place where you are/you live' (cf. StdIntE *in/round these parts*)
(47) *a turn-boy* (S) 'a person who collects fares on a bus or other public vehicle [or who assists a truck driver on long journeys]'
(48) *twilight girls* (AB) 'prostitutes'
(49) *twitching of an eyelid* (B) 'twinkling of an eye'
(50) *a vice versa* (AB) 'an alternative; the opposite' – *The vice versa is also true*.
(51) *a windbreaker* (S) 'windcheater' (BrE)
(52) *wife inheritance* (S) 'a tradition whereby a man automatically becomes the husband of his brother's wife if his brother dies'
(53) *a youth-winger* (S) 'a young party member'

Verbs and VPs
(54) *to add salt to injury* (S) 'to add insult to injury'
(55) *to add salt/pain to injury* (B) 'to add insult to injury'
(56) *to anchor sth in/into law* (AB) 'to give sth a legal foundation'
(57) *to ashame sb* (AB) 'to shame sb'
(58) *to be another one* (B) 'to be something else', '[to be] difficult to understand' (and S) '(to be) a one'

(59) *to be asking* (typically in *I'm asking/was asking*, said with a rising intonation) (AB) 'May I ask?/If I may ask/I'd like to know'
(60) *to be at least* (AB) 'to be better' – *His life is now at least.*
(61) *to be behind (the) news* (AB) 'not to be aware of the latest news'
(62) *to be cast in stone* (AB) 'to be carved/set in stone'
(63) *to be in for a rude shock* (AB) 'to be in for a rude awakening'
(64) *to be in hot soup* (S) 'to be in hot water, to be in the soup'
(65) *to be kidded* (AB) 'to have children' – *"If kidded* [indicate the] *No. of children* [and] *the age of the youngest child"* (from an application form from the St. Camillus School of Nursing)
(66) *to be [so] lost* (B) '[to] not [have been] seen for [quite] some time'
(67) *to be married somewhere* (AB) said of or by a woman 'to refer to where her husband comes from' – *I was born in Nairobi but was married in Mombasa.*
(68) *to be on sb's neck* (AB) 'to be a pain in the neck of sb'
(69) *to be on talking terms* (S and B) 'to be on speaking terms'
(70) *to be past tense* (S) 'to be no longer relevant, effective, important or existent'
(71) *to be saved* (A) 'to be born again, to accept Jesus as a saviour'
(72) *to be time-barred* (AB) (said of an application to a court of justice) 'to be filed too late'
(73) *to be welcomed* (B) 'to be welcome'
(74) *to be with* (S) 'to come together with, to meet, to see' – *I was with David recently, he is fine*
(75) *to beat one's drum* (AB) 'to blow one's own trumpet'
(76) *to borrow a leaf from sb* (S) 'to take a leaf out of/from sb's book'
(77) *to bring sb into the fold* (A) 'to make sb support ideas [...] of a group [...] to which one belongs'
(78) *to brush shoulders [with sb]* (B) 'to rub shoulders with sb'
(79) *to carry the brunt of sth* (AB) 'to bear the brunt of sth'
(80) *to clap for sb* (AB) 'to clap sb'
(81) *to develop cold feet* (S) 'to get/have cold feet'
(82) *to draw a map of Africa* (S) [Skandera (2003: 163) says that this idiom] 'refers to a girl's embarrassed motion of the foot, as if she were drawing something on the ground, when talked to by a boy she like'
(83) *to eat life with a long spoon* (AB) 'to live luxuriously'
(84) *to eat money* (B) 'to eat money up'
(85) *to enjoy someone* (B) 'to make fun of someone', 'to ridicule someone'

(86) *to extract blood from a stone* (AB) 'to try to do the impossible'[10]
(87) *to flag off* (S) 'to give the starting signal for'
(88) *to get a child/a baby* (S) 'to have a child, a baby'
(89) *to give one a hand* (B) 'to lend one a hand'
(90) *to give sb a push* (S) 'to accompany sb part of the way'
(91) *to grease sb's hand/hands* (S) 'to grease sb's palm'
(92) *to grow horns* (B) 'to be proud [or] stubborn'
(93) *to have beef with sb* (AB) 'to have a beef with sb' (: 'to have an issue with sb')
(94) *to have a clean heart* (S) 'to have a good heart'
(95) *to have a godfather* (S) 'to know an influential person'
(96) *to have a tall relative* (S) 'to know an influential person'
(97) *to have long hands* (S) 'to have a tendency to steal (small things)'
(98) *to lie low like an envelope* (S) 'to behave in an inconspicuous way, to keep a low profile'
(99) *to look at somebody with bad eyes* (S) 'to give sb the evil eye'
(100) *to make a mountain out of an anthill* (S) 'to make a mountain out of a molehill'
(101) *to midwife* (AB) 'to nurture, to bring sth to realization'
(102) (for sb, not sth) *to make sb else's day* (AB) 'to make sb very happy' – *You've just made my day.*
(103) *to milk sb dry* (AB) 'to bleed sb dry'
(104) *to move with speed* (AB) 'to act quickly'
(105) *to oversight* (AB) 'to play an oversight role'
(106) *to not be refusing that . . .* (AB) 'to not deny that . . .' – *I'm not refusing that he made a mistake, but he should be forgiven.*
(107) *to paint sb/sb's name black* (S) 'to blacken sb's name'
(108) *to paint someone black* (B) 'to taint somebody's name'
(109) *to part ways with sb* (AB) 'to part company with sb'
(110) *to pen off* (S) 'to stop writing, especially at the end of letters'
(111) *to perform a test item/an exam question/a sentence* (AB) 'to do it'
(112) *to pick (telephone calls)* (AB) 'to answer phone calls' – *I've been trying to call her for an hour but she's not picking.*
(113) *to play with sb's mind* (AB) 'to make a fool of sb by pretending to be cleverer than him/her'
(114) *to pull resources together* (AB) 'to pool resources'

---

10 Notice that for the same meaning the *Longman Dictionary of Contemporary English*, 5th edn, 2009, has the phrase *like getting blood out of a stone*.

(115) *to preach water and drink wine* (AB) 'to preach one thing but do something else'
(116) *to promise heaven on earth* (AB) 'to promise the earth / the moon'
(117) *to pull up one's socks* (AB) 'to pull one's socks up'
(118) *to push with sb* (S) [usually for young people] 'to have an amorous relationship with, to go out with sb'
(119) *to put one's act together* (AB) 'to get one's act together'
(120) *to put out of sb* (A) 'to be no longer on [speaking] terms [with sb]', 'to disagree [with] or hate somebody'
(121) *to put sth into consideration* (S) 'to take sth into consideration'
(122) *to raise the red flag* (AB) 'to raise the alarm'
(123) *to read from* (S) 'to spend time learning in or at' – *I am going to read from my room.*
(124) *to read from the same script (AB)* 'to be on the same page'
(125) *to result to* (AB) 'to resort to'
(126) *to sail in the same boat* (S) 'to be in the same boat'
(127) *to score everything* (AB) 'to have every answer on a test/exam correct'
(128) *to see fire/dust* (S) 'to deal with the unpleasant consequences of one's actions'
(129) *to see with one's mouth* (B) 'to gape', 'to be surprised'
(130) *to shift the goalposts* (AB) 'to move the goalposts'
(131) *to sing one's tune* (B) 'to dance to one's tune'
(132) *to sing somebody's tune/song* (S) 'to praise or support sb/sth enthusiastically (and sometimes uncritically)'
(133) *to smile all the way to the bank* (AB) usually said for 'to have been awarded the money one has been fighting for' (cf. StdIntE idiom *to be laughing all the way to the bank*)
(134) *to spread like bushfire* (S and B) 'to spread like wildfire'
(135) *to stay clear of/to stay away from (e.g. politics)* (AB) 'to steer clear of (e.g. politics)'
(136) *to stay with* (S) 'to keep' – "*You stayed with my notes for more than eight hours, and each and every minute means a lot to me*".
(137) *to talk nicely* (S and B) 'to give a bribe'
(138) *to take a cue from sb* (AB) 'to take one's cue from sb'
(139) *to test a question* (AB) 'to make a question an item on a test'
(140) *to turn the heat on sb* (AB) 'to turn up the heat on sb'
(141) *to up one's game* (AB) 'to redouble one's efforts' – "*NACADA must up its game to control the situation*" (Kenya's Deputy President, 12 Jul 2014).
(142) *to wreck havoc* (AB) 'to wreak havoc'

Adjectives and APs

(143) *as fast as lightening* (S) 'as quick as lightening'
(144) *ill-bent* (AB) 'hell-bent' – *Politicians ill-bent on propagating hate speech should be arrested.*
(145) *indisciplined* (AB) – 'undisciplined' (Note: The use of *indisciplined*, modelled on the noun *indiscipline*, is not a mere issue of misspelling in KenE.)
(146) *quite fine* (S) 'quite well'
(147) *second last* (AB) 'second from last' – *Look at the second last line at the bottom.*
(148) *smooth sailing* (S) 'plain sailing'
(149) *unbwogable* (AB) 'who cannot be intimidated'[11]

Adverbs and adverbials

(150) *a.m. in the morning* (B) 'in the morning'
(151) *latest* (AB) 'at the latest', apparently on the analogy of *soonest*, which can be used on its own, as in this example from the *CED* (2009): "*send money soonest*"
(152) *off-head* (S and B) 'offhand, by heart [or] without referring to prepared material'
(153) *p.m. in the evening* (B) 'in the afternoon, in the evening'
(154) *slowly by slowly* (S) 'little by little'

Prepositional phrase

(155) *of which* (AB) 'therefore', as when an immigration officer said: "*Of which, we don't know what to do about his application*" (3 Jul 2015)

Miscellaneous

(156) *All protocols observed!* (AB) 'I hope I have given each one of you concerned the respect he/she deserves' – *Your Excellency the President, Cabinet Secretaries, Honourable MPs . . ., Ladies and Gentlemen, all protocols observed.*

---

[11] The term was borrowed from a famous song by a Kenyan band called "Gidi Gidi Maji Maji", a song that was released not long before the 2002 general election in Kenya. The term was coined from a combination of English and Dholuo. The Dholuo verb *bwogo* means 'to intimidate'; the rest of the morphemes in *unbwogable* are visibly English. The word was extremely popular in 2002/3. But, all of a sudden, the term went out of use. It is hardly used by any politician nowadays.

(157) ... *(but) do I say!* (AB) 'needless to say'[12]
(158) *but one* (AB) 'the one before last' (e.g. *last week but one*: 'the week before last'), or 'the one after next' (e.g. *next week but one*: 'the week after next')[13]
(159) *can be able to* (S) 'can'
(160) *Don't count your chicks before they hatch* (AB) 'Don't count your chickens before they're hatched'.
(161) *Every marketplace has its own madman* (B) 'There is always a bad person among good people'.
(162) *Have a nice time* (S) 'have a nice day'
(163) *I'm coming* (AB) 'I'll be back in a moment/in a minute', as in the following conversation observed at the Yaya Centre shopping complex in Nairobi, 21 Dec 2013:
A: Girl aged A (8–10), dragging her father to a nearby shop: *I'm coming, just now*.
B: Another girl, playmate of A: *Where are you going?*
A: *I'm coming just now. Okay?*
(164) *It's there/they are there* (AB) 'It is/they are, it exists / they exist, it's a reality' –
A: *I've never believed in the people you call "night runners"*.
B: *Imagine they are there*.
(165) *A journey of a thousand miles begins with one step.* (AB) 'Small steps matter in achieving something big'.
(166) *A new broom sweeps better* (AB) 'Any change is beneficial' (Note: The KenE saying refers to more than just people, unlike the StdIntE proverb *A new broom sweeps clean*.)
(167) *out there* (AB) 'ordinary, common' – *For the people out there, those changes mean very little*.
(168) *Silence means consent* (AB) 'Silence gives consent' (mentioned in Schmied 2004: 941)
(169) *Strike the iron while it is hot* (AB) 'Strike while the iron is hot'
(170) *The subject above refers* (AB) 'With reference to the subject above...' – "*Our previous communication on the above subject dated March 15, 2018 refers*"

---

12 The expression ... *(but) do I say!* is mostly used by KenE speakers belonging to the Luo tribe while boasting about some achievement or quality. Although the expression looks like a question, it is not one: it is used after the speaker has actually said what he/she wanted to boast about.

13 Some people even say *yesterday/tomorrow but one* ('the day before yesterday/the day after tomorrow'). *But two* (e.g. *last week but two*) can also be heard; however, *but three* will be rare and *but four*, etc., even rarer.

(from an email from the University of Nairobi's Director of Security, 28 Mar 2018).
(171) *We shall meet/talk (again)* (S) [this is said as] 'a farewell formula'
(172) *When/where did the rain start beating us?* (AB) 'When/where did things start going wrong for us?'
(173) *You can take it to the bank!* (AB) 'You can take it as a fact'
(174) *You eat where you work, but you don't let your mouth shine* (AB) 'You make the most of the privileges offered by your job but you avoid letting that show'

5.2.2 Discussion

The coinages in the list above can be grouped into three categories. The first category is that of those that were formed through combining two or more elements, with the resultant structure producing either a compositional meaning or a figurative one. Thus, the structure of *co-wife* is the result of a prefix + a noun, that of *wife inheritance* the result of a noun + noun, that of *to have long hands* the result of a verb + a noun phrase, etc. But while the meaning of e.g. *wife inheritance* is compositional (literally referring to 'inheriting a wife'), that of *to have long hands* is figurative (referring to 'having a tendency to steal').

The second category is composed of expressions which were coined by partially altering an existing expression by replacing a given word (which would have been the "right" one in StdIntE) with the "wrong" lexical alternative (e.g. *sing* vs. *dance* in *to sing sb's tune*, meaning 'to dance to sb's tune'). Typically, this KenE alternative is semantically close to the StdIntE one, but in some cases, such as *to add salt to injury* vs. *to add insult to injury*, the two are close primarily phonetically (and secondarily semantically).

The third category of coinages concerns those like *to flag off* ('to give the starting signal for'), *to pen off* ('to stop writing, esp. a letter'), and *academics* (sing.) ('academic matters'), which were formed on the analogy of other structures of the same type, whether these latter contained some of the words in the coinages or not. Thus, while it can be easily argued that *flag off* was built on the component *flag* in the StdIntE phrase *flag down*, there is no existing phrase comprising the verb *pen*, on which *to pen off* would have been modelled. However, it would not be unreasonable to suggest that the KenE *to pen off* was modelled on the StdIntE *to write off*. As for the singular noun *academics*, the analogy must have involved borrowing the suffix *–s* used on nouns such as *economics* and *mathematics*.

A final comment about the coinages of KenE is that several of them will have had an ephemeral life, because they were related to realities which do no longer obtain in Kenya. This applies to *queue-voting* and *youth winger*, both of which refer to political realities in the reign of former President Daniel arap Moi, a reign which came to an end in December 2002. It also applies to non-political realities like that embodied in the phrasal verb *to pen off*, which hardly means anything in the age when writing letters with a pen is quite rare, and to the noun phrase *bicycle taxi*, which is bound to make room for *motorbike taxi* (i.e. the *bodaboda taxi* mentioned in section 5.1), as the latter mode of taxi will have totally eclipsed the former.

5.3 Additional meanings in Kenyan English

5.3.1 A list of specific expressions with additional meanings in KenE

Hancock and Angogo (1982: 318) noted that "Examples [...] in which international English words are used in special senses account for the bulk of lexical differences between East African English and other varieties; a complete list would fill many pages". However, the authors themselves did not discuss any such list. Skandera (2003) and Atichi (2004) did. The list below comprises the words whose additional meanings in KenE they discussed and those that were later gathered by the present author. The words in question are arranged by the word classes of their key words. For each expression in the list, the source is indicated after it in brackets: *A* for Atichi, *S* for Skandera, and *AB* for the present author. In case the definition requires some illustration, an example provided by the indicated source is added.

Nouns and NPs
(1) *a (police) abstract* (AB) 'a document issued by the police to attest to loss or theft of documents'
(2) *an academy* (AB) 'a private, prestigious (especially) primary school'
(3) *a (university) degree* (AB) specifically 'a Bachelor's degree'; it is never used to refer to a postgraduate degree – *"The study found that trained Diploma holders performed better than both degree and Masters holders"* (from an MA student's paper, 2010).
(4) *a casualty* (AB) 'a kind of form signed by the school from which a teacher is being transferred and that to which he/she being transferred'
(5) *a crusade* (A) 'a Christian public worship session that is not limited to members of their sect only'
(6) *a cut-off* (as part of an alarm system in a car) (AB) 'a cut-out'

(7) *a dame* (A) 'a young unmarried female' – *The young man came home with a dame.*
(8) *a docket* (A) 'the portfolio or jurisdiction of an official, especially of government' – *Prisons fall under the docket of the Minister for Home Affairs.*
(9) *a double-decker* (A) 'a bed with two levels' [i.e. 'a bunk bed']
(10) *a dummy copy* vs. *a live copy* (AB) with reference to the Kenya Certificate of Secondary Education examinations, a *dummy* copy is 'a photocopy of a student's copy which an examiner marks by way of practice before marking the "real thing"'; by contrast, this 'original copy' is referred to as the *live copy*
(11) *dues* (A) 'money that should be paid by somebody as a result of a court order'. The word *dues* is used in KenE even more frequently to refer to 'severance pay' (AB) – *He was summarily dismissed and paid his dues soon afterwards.*
(12) *an escort* (AB) 'some snack to have tea with' – *"I don't take tea without escort"* (Dr. C.A., p.c., 13 Jun 2014).[14]
(13) *an exhibition* (AB) 'one of a group of stalls sheltered in a bigger shop partitioned into such smaller shops'
(14) *a flower girl* (AB) 'someone whom others do not deem necessary to consult in a decision-making process'. (The phrase is usually used in the negative when people are complaining about not being consulted, saying *We are not flower girls.*)
(15) *my follower* (B) 'the sibling that follows me'
(16) *a flyover* (AB) 'a footbridge'
(17) *a foolscap* (AB) 'an A4-size, ruled paper, as opposed to plain, photocopying paper'
(18) *a gadget* (AB) this term is used to cover not just 'a small mechanical device or appliance' (the *CED* 2009) but 'a mechanical device or appliance of any size' – *Thieves broke into the house and stole a variety of gadgets, including a TV set.*
(19) *a hardware* (AB) 'a shop selling hardware'
(20) *a home guard* (S) – By way of definition of it, this what Skandera (2003: 135–136) writes:

In KenE, *home guard* (written with small initial letters, often as one word) refers to the approximately 20,000 Kikuyu tribesmen who were

---

[14] Hancock and Angogo (1982: 318) mention *escorter*, which they define as "something edible to accompany a beverage".

recruited to assist the British army in putting down the Mau Mau rebellion of the 1950s, and in policing the so-called protected villages [...].

(21) *hot drinks* (S) 'distilled alcoholic drinks'
(22) *a hotel* (AB) 'a restaurant; any place where meals can be bought' (Also mentioned in Schmied 2004: 942)
(23) *incidences* (AB) 'incidents' – *"Security has been maintained here in Mombasa, with no security incidences being reported"* (a K24 TV reporter, 6 Mar 2013).
(24) *an instructor* (at a university) (AB) 'any lecturer', and not, as the word is defined in AmE, just 'a teacher below the rank of assistant professor'
(25) *a joyrider* (AB) 'someone who joins a team or a party with no (significant) role to play in it'
(26) *a lady* (A) 'any woman' – *I gave the book to that silly lady.*
(27) *a locker* (AB) 'a student's desk which has provision for keeping books and stationery'
(28) *a logbook* (AB) 'a registration document attesting to one's ownership of a car'
(29) *Madam* (A) 'a title reserved for professional women'[15]
(30) *a matchbox* (S) '[this word] seems to refer not just to the box itself, but also to the matches contained in it' (p. 132).
(31) *a merry-go-round* (AB) 'a self-help system whereby women give each other money in rotation'
(32) *(no) otherwise* [used as a noun, but specifically with the negative determiner *no*] (A) 'an alternative, another option' – *We'll rely on our school bus because we have no otherwise.*
(33) *a rural home* (AB) 'where the grandparents live, in an area outside a big town' – *Our family live in Nairobi but our rural home is in Nyandarua.*
(34) *a sacred cow* (AB) 'a person who, because of his/her powerful position in society, is perceived to be above criminal investigations'
(35) *a safari* (A) 'any trip or journey made from one point to another [...] by road, air, rail, etc.'
(36) *a saloon* (A) 'a hairdressing shop', [i.e. 'a salon']
(37) *a saloon car* (AB) 'any motor car, whether of the saloon or hatchback or estate type'
(38) *a semester* (AB) 'any academic term of study' – *The University of Nairobi runs three semesters a year.*

---

[15] See more details about the use of *madam* in section 6.2.2.

(39) *a service charge* (S) 'a tax that [used to be] paid to the local governments for the provision of public services [...]'
(40) *slang* (AB) 'a mixture of languages, especially of English and some other language in informal speech, seen as corrupted language' – *That's not English; it's slang.*
(41) *slippers* (AB) 'flip-flops / thongs'
(42) *a (bus) stage* (AB) '*any* bus stop designated as such, *not* necessarily one with a fixed fare' (cf. the definition of *stage* in the *CED* 2009: 'a division of a bus route for which there is a fixed fare')
(43) *a stream* (AB) 'if a class is too big to be taught in one classroom and is divided into two or more groups, each one of these is a stream'
(44) *a supplementary (exam)* (AB) 'a university exam given as a resit' (Note that according to the *Oxford Advanced Learner's Dictionary*, 9th edn, 2015, the noun *make-up*, used alone, can also be used for this type of exam, while in KenE *make-up* is used not to refer to an exam, but to a continuous assessment test or a class session.)
(45) *a take-away (term paper, assignment)* (AB) 'a paper, an assignment which students are given to take home instead of doing it in class'[16]
(46) *torch-bearer* (A) 'one who represents a group, party, country in a competition or election'
(47) *transport* (A) 'an amount of money that enables somebody to travel by public means', 'fare'
(48) *a vote* (AB) 'money allocated to a department of a bigger organization'
(49) *working-class* (AB) 'the people who have a job, especially a well-paid one'

Verbs and VPs
(50) *to adapt (a figure/table/diagram from a publication)* (AB) 'to adopt it', i.e. 'to take it as it is without modifying anything in the original'
(51) *to ambush* (AB) 'to catch sb unprepared, especially for an interview'
(52) *to assume* (A) 'to ignore', '[to pretend to not] have seen or recognized a person' – *I tried to greet her but she assumed me.*
(53) *to attempt (an exam question)* (AB) 'to answer (an exam question)'
(54) *to avail* (A and B) 'to make something available; present something or oneself [...]'
(55) *to be compromised* (AB) (esp. for politicians and journalists) 'to be bribed'
(56) *to have been missing in action* (AB) 'said esp. of a politician who has not been seen in public for a long time'

---
16 *A take-away* is also used as slang to refer to 'a prostitute'.

(57) *to be pressed* (A) '[to be] in an urgent need to relieve oneself' – *I am [...] pressed; I have to go out.*
(58) *to be within* (AB) 'to be around, to be on the premises' – *You can wait for the chairman, he's just within.*
(59) *to befriend* (A) 'to get into an intimate relationship with a member of the opposite sex with the purpose of getting married to them'
(60) *to bounce* (A and B) 'to fail to [find] somebody or something at an [expected] place [...]' – *I bounced my brother yesterday,* [or] 'to fail to take place' – *We were there on time for our 10 o'clock class, but it bounced.*
(61) *to clear* (A) "to complete, to be through with an exercise, task or process'
(62) *to communicate* (AB) 'to get in touch' – *Bye for now. I'll communicate later.*
(63) *to demarcate* (A) 'to divide land into portions or sections'
(64) *to depict* (AB) 'to display' – *"They had been exposed to English language use longer and would therefore depict high levels of proficiency [...]"* (from an MA research paper, Mar 2013).
(65) *to enjoin* (AB) 'to be made a party to a legal case' – *The Law Society of Kenya has asked to be enjoined in the case filed to the court by X.*
(66) *to escort* (A) 'to accompany a friend, visitor [as] a courteous gesture of [seeing them] off'
(67) *to go to bed (with the government)* – (said especially for an opposition politician) 'to work/cooperate with'
(68) *to hibernate* (A) 'to be away from the public in order to rest, to be inactive'
(69) *to hustle* (AB) 'to look for a job'
(70) *to include* (AB) 'to be comprised of', i.e., 'with *all* the elements, and not just some, being counted in the list' – *The three arms of government include: the Executive, the Legislature and the Judiciary.*[17]
(71) *to interdict* (A) 'to [suspend] somebody for a while from [their official] duties [...] in order to investigate suspected or alleged misconduct [on their part]'
(72) *to interrogate sth* (not *sb*) (AB) 'to raise questions/doubts about sth')
(73) *to land* (A) 'to arrive, reach a place [without the idea of having travelled by plane or boat at all]' – *When we landed home, the guests were just leaving.*
(74) *to learn* (AB) 'to study, to attend a class, to follow a class session, to teach' – *She is learning at the University of Nairobi.* (Note: The noun

---

17 In the *Constitution of Kenya, 2010*, article 259, (4), (b), it was deemed necessary to define the term *includes* in the following way: "the word 'includes' means 'includes, but is not limited to'". This definition suggests that *to include* does not refer to 'all the elements of a group.'

learning is similarly used to refer to the activities of teaching and attending classes. A frequent headline in the Kenyan dailies is: *Learning paralysed as lecturers' strike bites.*)

(75) *to mainstream* (S) 'to place at the centre' – *They are keen to mainstream gender equality in all their activities.*

(76) *to miss* (AB) 'not to have' – *"Surely, as a photocopier operator you can't miss a paper clip"* (said by a customer to a photocopier operator, Feb 2014)

(77) *to offload* (AB) 'to lay off (workers)'

(78) *to offset* (A) 'to clear bills, debts'

(79) *to overlap* (AB) 'to drive past other vehicles on the wrong side of the road'

(80) *to portray* (AB) 'to display' – *"It is said that SLI children portray a language which is very similar to that of agrammatism in Broca's aphasia"* (from an MA paper, 2011).

(81) *to pothole* (B) 'to look for a job'

(82) *to prefer [e.g. a sample]* (AB) 'to select'

(83) *to record a statement (with the police)* (AB) 'to make a statement to the police'

(84) *to resort to* (AB) 'to result in'

(85) *to retaliate* (AB) 'to reiterate' ~ *"There's no cause for alarm. I can retaliate that"* (said by the minister in charge of internal security on the K24 TV news, 11 Jun 2013).

(86) *to retrench* (A) 'to lay off workers against their wish and before they are due for retirement'

(87) *to revert* (AB) 'to reply to the person who has written to you' – *"Let me check and revert"* (an sms from administrative secretary N.M., 27 Jul 2015).

(88) *to rewind* (A) 'to repeat a [year of study] at school or college/university'

(89) *to rhyme* (A) '[said] of things that look alike' – *Their shirts rhyme in colour.* [It also means 'to get along with somebody [...]' – *I don't rhyme with my maths teacher.*

(90) *to school* (as an intransitive verb) (AB) 'to study, to go to school' – *He schooled with Andrew at the Alliance High School.*

(91) *to see red* (S) 'to become the target of anger' – *"I'm warning you! If I catch you again around here [...] you'll see red!"* instead of *"[...] I'll see red!"*.

(92) *to shift* (AB) 'to move house'

(93) *to surcharge* (A) 'to deduct or withhold part of the money or benefits that [one] is entitled to [because of some misconduct or failure to discharge one's duties]'

(94) *to tarmac* (A and B) 'to look for employment [...]'

(95) *to transit (to sth)* (AB) 'to transition (into sth)'

Adjectives and APs

(96) *upcoming* (A) 'with a promising future [...]'
(97) *tried and tested* (Note: used for *people*) (AB) 'with a lot of experience in the field' – *We need a candidate who is tried and tested.*

Adverbs and adverbials

(98) *at least* (S) ['at most'] Skandera observes that "In StdIntE, *at least* is used to indicate that something is the minimum that can be done or expected [...]. Conversely, in KenE, *at least* can be used to indicate that something is the maximum that can be done or expected [...]" (2003: 150).[18]
(99) *majorly* (A) 'mainly, chiefly, principally'
(100) *never* (AB) 'did not' – *Yesterday, I never attended class.*
(101) *offside* (B) 'off-guard; not prepared'
(102) *severally* (A) 'more than a few but not very many' [i.e. 'several times']
(103) *up-country* (S) '[an expression used to refer to one's] ethnic home area' – *I had decided to spend [my holidays] upcountry [...].*
(104) *upstairs* (A) '[used to refer to the location of] human intelligence' – *John is very smart upstairs.*
(105) *whereby* (A) 'where'

Prepositions and PPs

(106) *according to [me]* (S) 'in my opinion'. About the use of *according to me*, Skandera adds the following comment: "While all of the Kenyan informants described this usage as acceptable and very common, StdIntE-speakers are not only certain to consider it an error, but they may also perceive it as pompous or presumptuous [...]" (2003: 155).[19]
(107) *by all means* (S) 'by any or every possible means'
(108) *by the way* (S) Skandera says the following: "[...] [this] idiom can, additionally, fulfil quite a different discourse function in KenE, namely to

---

[18] This meaning can be illustrated by the following utterance from a prominent woman politician in Kenya, N.C., when asked (in Aug. 2007) if some political parties were courting her own: "Nobody is courting me. And I don't know the word *courting*. **At least** I was courted once, and I got married once". It is obvious that she meant that the maximum number of times she was courted was just 1.

[19] This is a view supported by Swan (2016: paragraph 356), who also labels *according to me* as an error and explains this by saying that "we do not usually give our own opinions with *according to*". Note, though, that a native speaker of American English (James Rumford) who read a draft of this chapter commented (in June 2014) that *according to me* was "AmE". Also, a search in the COCA corpus produced 27 uses of this phrase from 1991 to 2012.

repeat, confirm, or summarize a point that has been made, or simply to add emphasis" (2003: 138), as in the following example:

[SPEAKER A:]: *Have a nice day.*

[SPEAKER B:]: *You too, by the way.* (2003: 139)

(109) *in the name of* (S) 'in order to', 'for the purpose of' – *A third mistake people make is that of taking black tea or coffee with sugar in the name of watching their waistline.*

Miscellaneous

(110) *cap.* (AB) an abbreviation for *chapter* in legal texts

(111) *either* (AB) 'whether' – *"Members of Parliament, either from CORD or from Jubilee, are supposed to check the government"* (a presenter on a morning chat programme on the Kenyan Citizen TV, 12 Feb 2014)

(112) *leave alone* (in the sense of 'not to speak of') (B) 'let alone'

(113) *Sample this!* (AB) 'Take this as an example!'

(114) *up* (AB) (while reporting sports scores) 'to each side, all' – *The two (basketball) teams are now 40 points up.*

(115) *where/when the rubber meets the road* (AB) 'where/when the real/serious work begins'

(116) *wow* (AB) Note: This interjection is used even in sad contexts in KenE, as in this example:

A: *Five people have died in that accident.*

B: *Wow!*

5.3.2 Discussion

The additional meanings of practically all the expressions listed above have resulted from the process of semantic expansion; that is, the expressions concerned have broadened their range of meanings.[20] The different meanings seem to have been formed through the following various sub-processes:

- analogy, whether metaphorical (e.g. *merry-go-round*) or logical (e.g. *slippers,* from the idea of slipping on a shoe);
- literal, compositional formation (e.g. *to be kidded* used for 'to have children' and *my follower* for 'the sibling who follows me');

---

[20] An evident example of the few that can be said to have narrowed their meanings is the noun *hotel*, which, in KenE, has restricted its meaning to only the part of it that sells meals.

- logical derivation (e.g. *to avail* used for 'to make available' and *severally* for 'several times');
- mistaking a word for a semantically similar one (*a stream* for 'one part of a large class', *a bus stage* for 'any bus stop', and *sample this* for 'take this as an example'); and
- mistaking a word for a phonetically close one (e.g. *incidences* for 'incidents', to *retaliate* for 'to reiterate', *saloon* for 'salon', and *either* for 'whether').

However, in some cases it is not obvious what sub-process was used for the additional meaning acquired: for example, it is not clear what the link is between *a casualty* and 'a kind of form signed by the school which a teacher is being transferred from and that to which he/she being transferred', or why *slang* means some corrupted 'mixture of languages'.

In some cases the new meaning is only remotely, if at all, related to the original meaning(s), as in the case of *docket*, whose dictionary meanings are: a) 'a document or label [...]', b) 'a list of cases [...]', and c) 'a list of items [...]'. The link between these three and the KenE meaning of 'area of responsibility' or 'ministerial portfolio', perhaps through the idea of portfolio, is really tenuous. In other cases, the meaning simply consists in a slightly different shade of meaning, as in the case of *a bus stage* for 'any bus stop' or that of *a hardware* for 'a shop that sells hardware'.

To end this section with Hancock & Angogo's (1982: 318) suggestion that "a complete list [of international English words with additional meanings in KenE] would fill many pages", it could be argued that a great source of difficulty in knowing such words and, especially, their added meanings, lies in the fact some of the latter belong to the in-group jargon of specific occupational groups and are thus not known to the larger speech community. A case in point is the verb *to rewind*, which appears in the list above with the widely-known added meaning of 'repeating a year of study at school/college/university', but which has another added meaning of 'wearing a blouse or socks on consecutive days' in the particular language of high school girls in Kenya.[21] So, on the analogy of the regional dialects of KenE which the present study posited on the basis of loan expressions, social dialects can also be posited on the basis of added meanings.

---

[21] This information was provided by MA-in-Linguistics students Judith Mwikali and Dianah Nyabuto during a Sociolinguistics class in Sep-Dec 2017. Their list of words with in-group-language added meanings also contains the verbs *to hang* ('[for a student] to have a borderline mark, e.g. 49') and (for a student) *to float,* as in *I'm floating* ('I don't understand').

5.4 To what extent do the various KenE lexical features coexist with their StdIntE variants?

The idea of "coexistence of variants" was borrowed from Skandera (2003: 201–202), who remarks that "[...] the majority of the idiom characteristics of KenE must be regarded as merely acceptable (or less acceptable) variants that could be placed in a category of features that coexist with StdIntE variants [...]". He is of the opinion that "absolute features – that is, ones that do *not* coexist with StdIntE variants – must be assumed to be comparatively small because, in most cases, it is unlikely, and can hardly be proven, that a StdIntE variant is not still used by a sizable number of KenE-speakers" (Skandera 2003: 202). Skandera is specifically referring to idiomatic expressions. But what he said can be applied globally to the elements discussed under the three broad components of lexical and semantic aspects of KenE: loan expressions from indigenous Kenyan languages, coinages, and additional meanings.

To start with loan expressions, the issue is to know whether the same speaker of KenE uses both the indigenous expression and its English equivalent. No empirical evidence for this is available. But it can be claimed that while each loan expression was given an English translation (or equivalent) in the list in Table 5.1, not every definition/equivalent stands a chance of being used. Some words do have translations that can be used as the straightforward equivalents, that is, both denotatively and connotatively, of their original indigenous expressions. That is the case of e.g. *duka* ('shop'), *jembe* ('hoe'), *manamba* ('matatu tout'), *mandazi* ('doughnuts'), *panga* ('machete'), *shamba* ('farm'), and *uhuru* ('freedom', 'independence'). However, for some others, the use of the English translation would most likely not have the same connotation as that of the indigenous expression and, as a result, will hardly be used. For example, neither *the common man/woman* nor *the ordinary citizen* connotes the sense of patriotism associated with the Swahili word *mwananchi*. (Interestingly, in actual usage the English adjective *common* is used to premodify the noun *mwananchi*, making the expression *common mwananchi* the usual collocation.) Likewise, words such as *matatu* ('public service minibus'), *majimbo* ('federal states'), *mzee* ('old man', 'respectable man'), *ugali* ('boiled maize meal') are expected to be more frequently used than their English equivalents. For example, while *mzee* and *old ma*n have the same denotative meaning, the Kiswahili word connotes respect, while the English one is actually likely to offend the addressee if he is directly addressed as *old man*. For its part, the use of *respectable man* is likely to sound funny. And in relation to *ugali*, if someone went to a restaurant and ordered some *boiled maize meal*, the waiters would most likely wonder what it is was being ordered.

5.4 To what extent do the various KenE lexical features coexist — 169

Further, there are loan expressions whose English definitions are too long to be used smoothly (which would be the case of 'a stringed musical instrument popular in the Luo community', for *nyatiti)* or are simply ambiguous (which is the case of *busaa* 'a kind of homebrewed beer made from sorghum or finger millet', since there must be similar types of brew called something else in parts of Kenya other than its southwest). Examples of expressions whose meanings would be too long to be used are *kachumbari* ('a mixture of raw onions, tomatoes and pepper'), *kanzu* ('a flowing robe worn for religious purposes'), and *sufuria* ('a wide-bottomed-aluminium pot'). So, in all likelihood, only the words (e.g. *duka*) in the first group will have variants that are also used. But it can be equally assumed that for all the loan expressions, most KenE speakers are aware of both the indigenous word and its English translation.

With regard to the coinages of KenE, they can be divided into three groups: a) those that can be argued *not* to have StdIntE variants that coexist with them, b) those that do have such variants with the same denotative and connotative meanings, and c) those that do have such equivalents, but ones used with a different connotation. The first group contains the few expressions, such as *co-wife* and *wife-inheritance*, which refer to local Kenyan realities that have no equivalent in native English-speaking countries. In the second group can be placed all those expressions, like *to wreck havoc* ('to wreak havoc'), that were coined by simply using the "wrong" word. In the third group are those expressions which have a different connotation from their StdIntE equivalents. One such expression is *City in the Sun* ('Nairobi'), which was coined to connote how glorious the city was at the time. Another example is *to talk nicely*, which, as a euphemism, sounds "more acceptable" than its equivalent *to give a bribe*.

Beyond categorising the coinages of KenE into groups, evidence was sought of whether the KenE speakers are aware of the existence of StdIntE equivalents for the various coinages. The results show that the vast majority are probably not: in a preference questionnaire in which the present author asked University of Nairobi students (from several successive classes) to indicate which of the two structures they used (and gave them the option of ticking both of them in case they used both in their English), 80/94 (85%) of the respondents (62 postgraduate and 32 undergraduate students) indicated that they used only *to wreck havoc*, with 7/94 (12%) indicating that they used only *to wreak havoc*, and the remaining 3/94 (3%) indicating that they used both. And in a sentence completion task in which a sub-sample of 33 postgraduate linguistics students were asked to fill the gap in the sentence *The floods had – havoc in the area; rivers had burst their banks, flooding flat areas*, with the words which they thought could fit best in the gap, 9/33 (27%) of them inserted the verb *wrecked*, while only 1/33 (3%) inserted *wreaked*. Most of them inserted *caused*. In view of the very low percentage of those who said, on the preference task, that they used both *wreck* and *wreak*, and the very low percentage of those who, on the completion task, filled the gap with *wreaked*, it can be hypothesised that, as a general rule, the two variants of a given KenE coinage do not coexist in the linguistic competence of KenE speakers.

Turning now to the category of additional meanings, the issue is whether the added KenE meaning and the StdIntE one coexist in the linguistic competence of the same KenE speaker. An answer can be sought from the findings of a small-scale investigation into the issue by Atichi (2004) and by the present author in 2014. Atichi's (2004) study checked the extent to which 41 respondents were aware of "non-Kenyan-English" meanings of some select words. He reported that for *double-decker*, for example, only 1 (i.e. 2%) respondent was aware of its meaning of 'a sandwich made with three pieces of bread leaving two spaces that are filled with food' (2004: 77). In fact, for the eight words whose "unfamiliar definitions" (i.e. non-KenE ones) Atichi tested, the highest "familiarity rate" was 7%, which corresponds to only 3 out of the 41 respondents (2004: 77–78).

In the present author's own study, 24 postgraduate linguistics students were asked to give "all the definitions they knew" for sixteen words from the list of those said, in this chapter, to have acquired additional meanings in KenE. Here are the findings about some of the words: for *severally*, 19/24 (79%) of the respondents gave only the KenE meaning of 'several times' (though expressed variously), while only 1/24 (4%) gave the StdIntE meaning of 'separately'; the rest gave unrelated meanings, like 'furiously'. For *docket*, 19 (79%) gave only the KenE meaning of '(area of) responsibility' or 'government department', while only 1 (4%) gave this meaning and the StdIntE one of 'a document [...]'; the rest gave meanings like 'enclosed area'. In the case of *double-decker*, 11 (46%) gave the meaning of just 'a bed', 5 (21%) gave both meanings of 'a bed' and of 'a kind of a bus', 1 (4%) gave that of just 'a bus', while the rest either gave meanings unrelated to these three, or provided no meaning at all; none gave the meaning of 'sandwich'.

While the statistics reported for Atichi's (2004) study seem to suggest that an overwhelming majority of KenE speakers will be aware of just the KenE added meaning, those reported for the present author's study point to a smaller majority. In addition, the latter study produced unexpected results, as can be illustrated by two cases: the first concerns the verb *to enjoin*, for which only 2/24 (i.e. 8%) respondents gave a meaning that is close to that of 'to be made party to a legal case', which was claimed, earlier in this chapter, to be specific to KenE: one of them defined it as 'to make oneself part of a group', and the other as 'to come together'. All the remaining 22 (i.e. 92%) respondents defined it as 'to put/ join together'. This lack of awareness of the claimed KenE meaning can be attributed to the fact that this meaning belongs to the specialized register of law, a suggestion that will take us back to the idea of social dialect alluded to earlier.

The second case concerns the noun *exhibition*, which was defined in its KenE meaning as 'one of a group of stalls sheltered in a bigger shop partitioned into such smaller shops'. Only one respondent (who defined the word as 'a shopping mall with many small shops') offered a related meaning. All the other 23/24 (i.e. 96%) provided meanings that can be found in the dictionary. The most plausible way to explain this lack of awareness of the claimed KenE meaning is to argue that the word *exhibition* in its meaning of 'a kind of shop' is a feature of a regional, specifically urban, dialect of KenE. That is, while there are so many such "exhibitions" in a large town like Nairobi, there must be fewer of them in smaller towns, and they are definitely unknown in non-urban areas.

5.5 Formal vs. informal KenE vocabulary

As has been observed for all second language varieties, KenE has fewer levels of formality than native speaker varieties. Thus, typically KenE speakers have little awareness of what is formal and what is informal. On the one hand, some words that are said to be formal in international English dictionaries are virtually the only ones known and thus used in all contexts. That is the case of the verb *to alight (from a bus):* in KenE hardly anyone uses the verb *to get off*. On the other hand, some other words that are said to be informal are used in KenE even in very formal settings. For example, words like *cop* and *chopper* will be used as part of what is supposed to be the most official language. A sentence like *The top cop arrived in a military chopper* ('The top police officer arrived in a military helicopter') will be the natural way of saying things for a commentator on the occasion of a national day, for example. Here is an authentic illustration: while giving his state-of-the-nation address to the Kenyan Parliament on 28 March 2014, the president of the republic said this: *"Although this may be perceived as a temporary and painful **jab** [...]"*. Since he was alluding to the not-so-popular VAT increase proposed by his government, he must have borrowed the meaning of *jab* in its definition of an *informal* BrE word meaning 'an injection to help prevent you from catching a disease'.

In relation to the very lexical items under study, it can be assumed that where KenE speakers are aware of StdIntE alternatives, they can afford to use the KenE expressions in informal situations and reserve the StdIntE ones for formal ones. Thus, starting with the loan expressions into English, it can be easily envisaged that a given KenE speaker will have the option of using, in an informal context, those expressions, like *shamba* ('farm', 'plot of land'), that were argued (in the previous section) to have straightforward translation equivalents in English, and of reserving these latter for formal situations. However, expressions such as *ugali* ('boiled maize meal'), without straightforward translation equivalents, may not be avoided in formal situations. For the coinages of KenE, a few of them are clearly informal alternatives of formal ones. Examples are: the *City in the Sun* ('Nairobi') and *to grow horns* ('to be too proud', 'to be stubborn'). But it is hard to imagine how KenE speakers can avoid using, even in very formal situations, an expression like *to shift the goalposts* ('to move the goalposts'), as this is most likely the only one they know. As for StdIntE words which have been given additional meanings in KenE, since it is they that are either informal or formal and not their meanings per se, KenE speakers are expected to treat them the way they do English as an L2 variety in general, that is, with little distinction between levels of formality.

5.6 The influence of other varieties of English on KenE vocabulary

5.6.1 American English vs. British English vocabulary

As is the case with L2 varieties of English around the world, KenE vocabulary is expected to contain elements of at least the two most influential native varieties, American English and British English. This twin influence is easily observed in the higher education register. Words that are said (in the dictionary) to be specific to BrE and those said to be specific to AmE are both found used by the same university in Kenya, even though AmE terms are gradually replacing BrE ones. Thus, the AmE term *an academician* seems to be gradually replacing BrE *an academic*, while the AmE *higher learning* has all but replaced *higher education*, well beyond higher education circles. Similarly, universities in Kenya are replacing *postgraduate* (BrE) with *graduate* (AmE). For example, what was the University of Nairobi (UoN)'s *Board of Postgraduate Studies* has recently been "re-baptized" the *Graduate School*, and what was its *bookshop* is now its *bookstore*. And the word *faculty*, in its AmE meaning of 'all the teaching staff at a university, college, school, etc.' (according to the *CED*, 2009), is creeping into UoN vocabulary as well. Possibly in all Kenyan universities, the AmE (school/college) *term paper* is the typical name for a take-home written assignment. In many of them, the AmE *major* and *minor* are now in fashion. Surprisingly, though, when the two words came into KenE, they were not accompanied by *freshman* (instead of which *fresher* is sometimes used) or *sophomore, junior,* and *senior*. On the other hand, in the areas of primary and secondary education the terminology is still typically

British. For example, KenE uses *marks* instead of *grades* (except for *letter grades* A, B, C, etc.), *a class-1 pupil/student* instead of *a first-grader*, and *form*, instead of *grade*, to refer to any class/year in secondary school.

In the entertainment and media industries KenE tends to borrow more from AmE than BrE. Phrases like *news anchor, call-in (programme), take a listen,*[22] etc., are already frequent on television. In the banking, finance, and accounting registers, by and large KenE follows BrE: for example, the AmE term *checking account*, for 'current account', is unheard of. KenE also uses the noun *gratuity* ('a sum of money paid to an employee at the end of a period of employment') and the verb *ring-fence* ('guarantee that [funds allocated for a particular purpose] will not be spent on anything else'), two usages which, according to the *Oxford Dictionary of English*, specifically belong to BrE. But if there is one area where BrE is visibly more influential than AmE, it is that of the motor industry. The best illustration of this can be found in the vocabulary of the components of a car (see e.g. p. 20 of the illustrative insert in the *Cambridge Advanced Learner's Dictionary*, 3rd edn, 2008): of all the 18 components, e.g. *boot* (UK) vs. *trunk* (US), which are referred to differently in the UK and the US, only *side mirror* (US) is noticeably used in KenE instead of UK English *wing mirror*.[23]

Since, for historical reasons, one will naturally expect KenE vocabulary to be more of BrE than AmE, one way to establish this is to start from Crystal's (2003: 309) list of 183 lexical differences between AmE and BrE. They are arranged in pairs: opposite each AmE word, a BrE equivalent is given, and vice versa. So, the present author set out to determine whether for each of them KenE tended to use either the AmE equivalent or the BrE one. It was possible to make firm decisions for only 95 (i.e. 52%) of the words. It was thus decided that for 66 (i.e. 69%) of the 95 words, KenE typically used the BrE equivalent (e.g. *slip road* vs. *ramp* in AmE), that for 19 (20%) of them it used the AmE equivalent (e.g. *electric cord* vs. *flex* in BrE), that for 8 (8%) of them it used both the BrE and the AmE equivalents (e.g. both *holiday* and *vacation*), and that for 2 (2%) cases, it used neither. The latter two are *WC* (BrE) vs. *rest room* (AmE) on the one hand (KenE uses *the gents/the ladies,* and sometimes *bathroom*; seldom is *toilet* used), and *hall of residence* (BrE) vs. *dormitory* (AmE) on the other hand (KenE uses *hostel*). So, if Crystal's list is to be taken as a representative sample, one might say that KenE vocabulary tends to be BrE in about two-thirds of the cases. Over the years

---

[22] As in *take a listen* (AmE), for BrE *have a listen*, in several other expressions KenE tends to use the verb *take* rather than *have*: e.g., *to take a shower, to take lunch*, and *to take a siesta*.
[23] Note in passing that the AmE *parking lot* is gradually replacing the BrE *car park* in KenE.

this proportion is likely to decrease primarily due to the increasing number of AmE expressions in the English of the Kenyan youth.

Still based on Crystal's (2003) list, the following details will illustrate well how KenE vocabulary still draws more from BrE than from AmE. First, here is a list of 43 words which KenE *typically* uses and which are said by Crystal to be used *only* in BrE; their AmE equivalents are given in brackets: *chips (*vs. *French fries), current account* (vs. *checking account), dual carriageway* (vs. *divided highway), diversion* [as a road sign] (vs. *detour), dialling tone* (vs. *dial tone), driving licence* (vs. *driver's licence), goods train* (vs. *freight train), hire purchase* (vs. *instalment plan), interval* (vs. *intermission), jumble sale* (vs. *rummage sale), level crossing* (vs. *grade crossing), lift* (vs. *elevator), maize* (vs. *corn), mince [meat]* (vs. *ground/chopped meat), motorway* (vs. *freeway), nappy* (vs. *diaper), mudguard* (vs. *fender), newsagent* (vs. *news dealer), notice board* (vs. *bulletin board), number plate* (vs. *licence plate), pancake* (vs. *crepe), pavement* (vs. *sidewalk), petrol* (vs. *gasoline), post code* (vs. *zip code), puncture* (vs. *flat), queue* (vs. *line), racecourse* [for horses] (vs. *racetrack), removal van* (vs. *moving van), ring road* (vs. *beltway),* [a] *rise* [in wages] (vs. [a] *raise), roundabout* (vs. *traffic circle), shop assistant* (vs. *salesclerk), spanner* (vs. *wrench), sweets* (vs. *candy), terraced house* (vs. *row house), torch* (vs. *flashlight), trolley* (vs. *shopping cart), trouser suit* (vs. *pants suit), vest* (vs. *undershirt), waistcoat* (vs. *vest), wallet* (vs. *billfold),* and *whisky* (vs. *scotch).*[24]

Second, the following is a much shorter list of (only 11) words which KenE typically uses and which Crystal (2003) says are used *only* in AmE; their BrE equivalents are given brackets: *bathroom* (vs. *lavatory, toilet), billboard* (vs. *hoarding), building permit* (vs. *planning permission), can* (vs. *tin), electric cord* (vs. *flex), fire department* (vs. *fire brigade), garbage* (vs. *rubbish, refuse), kerosene* (vs. *paraffin), lawyer* (vs. *solicitor), molasses* (vs. *treacle),* and *public school* (vs. *state school).*

Beyond Crystal's list and words from specific registers, there are miscellaneous BrE expressions which KenE "prefers" over their AmE equivalents, and there appears to be a possibly even larger number of AmE expressions which KenE prefers over their BrE equivalents. From BrE, examples are *aerial* (vs. AmE *antenna), butchery* ('a butcher's shop', according to the *ODE*, 3rd edn, 2010), *don* ('a teacher at a university'), *sellotape* (vs. *Scotch tape), taxi* (vs. *cab), wardrobe* (vs. *closet), varsity* (for 'university'), and *white coffee/tea* (for 'coffee/tea with milk'). From AmE, first there is *sick* (vs. *ill),* in its

---

24 James Rumford, the present author's AmE informant, in comments on an earlier draft of this chapter, said that the following were also used in AmE: *chips* ("in *fish and chips"), puncture, queue, wallet, lavatory, toilet,* and *rubbish.*

predicative use, as in *John was absent because he was sick*. Hardly will KenE speakers say *because he was ill*. Then there are expressions such as *you guys* ('you people [of either sex]'), *one-on-one* (vs. *one-to-one*), plus, according to James Rumford (p.c., June 2014), all the following, most of which have been reported in previous sections of this chapter as being KenE: those mentioned by Bulili (2002) are *to beat a deadline, to give one a hand*; those mentioned by Atichi (2004) are *to be saved, to bring sb into the fold, to be cast in stone, to be in for a rude shock, to backslide, majorly,* and *to be pressed*; those mentioned by Skandera (2003) are *to mainstream* and *according to me*; those from the present author's own observations are *academy* ('private primary school'), *my baby* ('my child, who is no longer a baby'), *either* ('whether'), *leave alone* ('let alone'), *flyover* ('footbridge'), *semester* ('any division of the academic year'), *slippers* ('flip-flops/thongs'), *to ambush* ('to catch sb unprepared'), *to include* ('to be comprised of'), *to incubate (sb/an organization)* ('to give support to'), *to keep well* ('to be well', as in *I trust you are keeping well*), *to preach water and drink wine* ('to preach one thing but do sth different'), *to raise the red flag* (i.e. *to raise a red flag* in AmE, 'to raise the alarm'), *to school* ('to go to school'), *to up one's game* ('to redouble one's effort'), and *A journey of a thousand miles begins with one step*.[25]

5.6.2 What traces are there of other Englishes in KenE vocabulary?

The other variety of English whose influence can be noticed in the vocabulary of KenE is Indian English (IndE). Here are some IndE words, as defined by the *Oxford Advanced Learner's Dictionary,* 9th edn, 2015, which are frequently used in KenE: *godown* ('warehouse'), *incharge* ('the person who is officially responsible for a department, etc.'), *to ply a route* (for a *matatu*/bus 'to travel regularly along a particular route'), *chapatti* ('a type of flat round [South] Asian bread'), and some other foods (like *samosa*) or cooking ingredients (like *dhania*). It should also be noted that the following words, in their indicated meanings, were mentioned by Sailaja (2009: 68, 77) as being IndE usage: *hotel* ('restaurant'), *to shift* ('to move, especially house or office'), and *matchbox* ('a box of matches'). The same words are also mentioned in section 5.3 above among

---

[25] According to James Rumford (p.c., 2014), "Most Americans know this saying from Chinese *Qianli zhi xing shi yu zuxia*", translated as 'A journey of a thousand miles begins with **the first** step'.

those which have acquired additional meanings in KenE, the very meanings given by Sailaja.

The other two varieties that are expected to loan words to KenE are Nigerian English and (some variety of) South African English: first, Nigerian English because of the very many Nigerian films (from the series known as *Afrosinema* and *Africa Magic*) shown by Kenyan television stations. However, no examples are in hand at this stage of specific words that may have been borrowed already. Second, some vocabulary input is expected from the English spoken in South Africa because of the country's SuperSport channels that broadcast international sporting events and Kenyan football matches in Kenya. For example, the expression *bicycle kick* ('overhead kick') mentioned in Section 5.2 as a coinage of KenE might have come from South Africa; it is a common phrase in football commentaries on SuperSport channels.

5.7 Conclusion: the most visible features are *not* the most characteristic of KenE

The picture which this chapter offers of what is characteristic of KenE[26] in terms of its lexis and semantics can be summarised thus: some 60 loan expressions from Kenyan indigenous languages, some 170 expressions that were labelled as coinages of KenE, and a hundred odd expressions that already exist as entries in StdIntE dictionaries but which have acquired additional meanings in KenE.

The present author's claim is that it is not the lexical features that everybody can easily notice which form the backbone of the lexis and semantics of KenE but those that only language analysts can easily detect. Indeed, anybody who has been exposed to KenE will have noticed that a word like *mwananchi* ('citizen') is used almost in every politician's or civil society activist's speech. Such loan words are what anybody is likely to consider as representatives of KenE, perhaps because, to agree with Hancock and Angogo (1982: 317), "[p]ractically any local word can turn up in East African English". This is partly due to the normal code-mixing to be expected in bilingual speech, and partly to the

---

[26] Of course, one has to be aware of the fact, acknowledged by e.g. Schmied (1991a, 2004) and Skandera (2003), that many of the features are equally East African. For example, expressions such as *to avail, to bounce*, and *you are lost* were listed in the Ugandan English lexis by Fischer (2000: 59). Some of them may even be African: an online language analyst (consulted on 22 Dec 2017) has commented that he/she found the expression *all protocols observed* in the English used in Kenya, Nigeria, South Africa, and Uganda.

5.7 Conclusion: the most visible features are *not* the most characteristic of KenE

current trend, particularly by the communications and banking organizations in Kenya, to insert a local word, especially from Swahili and Sheng (its youth dialect), into the names of some of their products and services. (This trend will be looked at in detail in the next chapter on discourse features.)

Only linguists and those intellectuals really concerned about good usage are likely to notice that in terms of sheer numbers, KenE vocabulary is actually more characterized by its less visible features; "less visible" because almost all the words and phrases involved either sound like standard international English or do indeed exist in StdIntE but with additional meanings.

6 Discourse features

Schmied (1991a: 91) noted that the "features which occur at the discourse level" were "another important and rather neglected aspect of African English". More than two decades on, the same features are still neglected. Very little has been written about discourse features of e.g. Kenyan English. Schmied (1991a: 91) went on to specify that "By discourse we refer in this context to the use of more extended linguistic elements beyond single words or grammatical constructions, which are closely related to sociocultural usage and expectations in terms of the 'ethnography of speaking'". However, in the present study discourse features will be broadened to include even some grammatical aspects, specifically those concerning anaphora phenomena, on the inspiration of the following definition taken from Fromkin, Rodman and Hyams (2011: 167): "Discourse analysis is concerned with the broad speech units comprising multiple sentences. It involves questions of style, appropriateness, cohesiveness, rhetorical force, topic/subtopic structure, differences between written and spoken, as well as grammatical properties". In relation to this broad definition, the specific elements that can be argued to characterize KenE can be grouped into the following headings: anaphora phenomena (as part of grammatical properties and, to some extent, of aspects of style), polite requests and forms of address (as cultural appropriateness phenomena), code-mixing Swahili words into KenE discourse (as a rhetorical force device), and a reduced use of contracted verb forms in spoken KenE (thus making it look more of written than spoken).

6.1 Anaphora phenomena

There are three aspects of anaphoric reference that are of interest in this chapter: underuse of pronouns and other forms of anaphora, all-embracing and vague anaphoric reference, and reference to an unmentioned referent.

6.1.1 Underuse of pronouns and other forms of anaphoric reference

The nominal types of this underuse were somehow predicted by Schmied (1991a: 95), who said that "whereas demonstratives or other substitutes would be expected in native English the full noun would be mentioned repeatedly in African English". With specific reference to KenE, the traditional pronouns (i.e. pro-NPs) that seem to be most frequently affected by this underuse are the third personal pronoun *it* and the demonstrative pronoun *those*. But some other pro-forms tend to be underused as well, in particular the auxiliary (especially *do*) as a pro-VP (as in the Q-A sequence: *Do you like music? Yes, I **do***). Even rarer, if used at all, is the gap, usually used as a kind of pro-form in gapping constructions,[1] such as (a) *Mark the undergraduate papers and I will Ø the postgraduate one* – where the main verb is dropped altogether – and (b) *Things had to change, and change they did Ø*, where the main verb has been moved to a focus position clause-initially. Utterance segments such as *and I will Ø the postgraduate one* and *and change they did Ø* hardly occur in KenE. It is worth noting that the non-use of the auxiliary *do* as a pro-VP has been reported by Huber and Dako (2008: 371) in Ghanaian English as well. The authors comment that "*Yes, I did* [in response to a question like *You didn't find the book, did you?*] is rare", and that the response will tend to be *I found it*, instead of *Yes, I did*.

An illustration of the underuse of the pronoun *it* is example (1), which is typical of abstracts of postgraduate research papers in Kenya.

(1) **The study** *looks into the use of Swahili demonstrative syntactically and morphologically.* **The study** *focuses on the use of demonstratives in Nairobi. In carrying out* **the study***, judgmental sampling was used in the data collection such that only the relevant demonstratives were taken into account.* **The study** *also focussed on the noun classes that were in frequent use such that those that did not feature mostly were ignored.* **The study** *also involves the use of simple Swahili sentences as collected from the data.*
(from an MA research paper by J.P., Jan 2002)

Clearly, after using the noun phrase *the study* in the opening sentence, the author might as well have used the pronoun *it* to replace its four subsequent occurrences. Likewise, the author of the following example could have used the pronoun *it* to replace the subsequent occurrences of the word *mchongoano*.

(2) **Mchongoano** *is a verbal duelling game found in Kenya that is popular with the young but also appreciated by many adults for its humorous content.* **Mchongoano** *has been compared to the American dozens and sounds [...].* **Mchongoano** *fits in the understanding of a speech event and genre that is analysable within the ethnography of communication.* **Mchongoano** *is*

---

[1] Bernd Kortmann, while reviewing this chapter, commented that gapping was "a very odd construction in StE", anyway. So, perhaps there is little wonder if it is virtually non-existent in KenE as an L2 variety.

found to fit in the eight components of [Dell Hymes'] S-P-E-A-K-I-N-G mnemonic [acronym].
(from an abstract of a draft journal article by P.K., Dec 2013)

This example also illustrates the non-use of other expressions of anaphoric reference, e.g. the NP *this genre*, which could have been used to replace the same *mchongoano* and thus break the monotonous repetition of the latter.

Below is an example illustrating the non-pronominalisation of, or within, a prepositional phrase:

(3) *[This] part of the chapter focuses on the external and internal variations **of Ateso**. The genetic and typological classification **of Ateso** is discussed, before the two dialects **of Ateso** – as identified by the author – are introduced.*
(from a draft chapter of a PhD thesis by B.D., Sep 2015)

In this example, the second occurrence of the NP *Ateso* might as well have been replaced by an anaphoric expression like *the language*. As for its third occurrence, a reformulation replacing the PP *of Ateso* by its corresponding possessive determiner/pronoun *its*, so as to get the phrase *before its two dialects*, would have been stylistically more elegant. The underuse of the possessive determiner/pronoun is equally illustrated by example (4), in which the second and third NPs in bold type could have easily been replaced with the possessive *their*, so as to get *their context* and *their language*, respectively.

(4) *Information on **the Iteso people** is a useful step towards understanding the broader context of **the Iteso people**. It forms an advantaged starting point for the discussion of the language of **these speakers**.*
(from a draft chapter of a PhD thesis by B.D., Sep 2015)

Another rare structure is the demonstrative pronoun *those*,[2] particularly in its partitive use in the sequence *those of*. For example, it could have been easily used to replace the string *the results of* in the following example:

(5) *The first table **indicates the results of** the male pupils, table 2 **indicates the results of** the female pupils, and table 3 **indicates the results of** both male and female pupils.*
(from an MA research paper by F.U.S., Feb 2016)

---

[2] Regarding this rare occurrence of *those*, it will be remembered that section 4.15 discusses the use of the combination *those ones* for just *those*.

To put things into some perspective, frequency counts from the ICE-K sub-corpus show that *those of*, as used in the configuration *those of (you/us/them) who*, occurs much less frequently than *those who*: there are only 25 occurrences of the former in the written component of the ICE-K[3] and only 17 in its spoken counterpart, thus totalling 42; on the other hand, there are 187 occurrences of *those who* in the written component and 93 in the spoken, thus totalling 280. The ratio of occurrence (280/42) is therefore 6.7 for *those who* to 1 for *those of*.[4] The relatively low use of *those of* gets even more highlighted when it is related to the use of its singular counterpart, *that of*, which occurs much more frequently in the written ICE-K, with 73 hits, against only 23 for *those of*.

6.1.2 All-embracing and vague anaphoric reference or no referent at all

While some forms of anaphoric reference are underused in KenE, there are several others that tend to be overused, as they are given all-embracing and/or vague meanings, or have no referent at all. That is the case of *the same, whereby, this (is), is where, is when*, and *another*.

Here is illustration, from the ICE-K, of the use of *the same* as some kind of anaphor.

(6) a. *Enclosed, [...] is a self-addressed stamped envelope, through which you could return the completed [...] to ourselves, or alternatively, we could arrange to collect **the same** from your premises.*
   (W1B-BK30)
   b. *Service and Range: The services are 24 hours and the messages are received within 10 seconds. [...] The pager covers a radius of 60km within Nairobi. [...] We offer **the same** in Mombasa.*
   (W1B-BK26)
   c. *Kingozi-Interchange is a language and crosscultural trainers institute, trainers and consultants on **the same**.*
   (W1B-BK49)

---

[3] In this chapter the written component of the ICE-K will not include the "written-to-be-spoken" sub-component (100,606 words-long), as the main written sub-component (405,868 words-long) is already much longer than the spoken component (304,967 words-long).
[4] For the purposes of comparison with the ICE-GB (representing British English), even though in its written component *those of* occurs less frequently than *those who* (with 35 hits for the former against 79 for the latter), the ratio is much smaller than in its ICE-K counterpart; it is 2.2 to 1 (i.e. 79/35).

While it is easy to work out what the expression *the same* refers back to (i.e. envelope) in (6a), it is hard to tell what it does in (6b) and (6c). It seems that the "popularity" of *the same* in KenE stems from the fact that it can be used as an anaphoric reference to something which cannot be specified easily.

The word *whereby* is another all-embracing anaphor in KenE, as illustrated by the four uses of it, by the same person, in the following example.

(7) a. *Screening in special education is a kind of an examination **whereby** the children who have special needs are identified.*
 b. *[...] It can lead to wrong classification **whereby** the child is put in the wrong group or category.*
 c. *[...] It lowers self concept **whereby** these children feel that they are less or inferior to the others.*
 d. *[...] If [educational] policy matters on the needs of these children **whereby** they put them into consideration.*
 (W1A013K)

These examples show that even for the same writer/speaker *whereby* can mean 'in which' (in 7a), 'as a result of which' in (7b), 'which means that' (in 7c), and some meaning hard to determine in (7d). And, of course, *whereby* is also used to simply mean 'where' in KenE (as pointed out in chapter 5 on lexis and semantics), as the following example shows:

(8) *He will use correct grammatical sentences in his writing unlike in spoken record **whereby** we sometimes come across sentences that are not grammatical.*
 (W1A020K)

And it can also mean 'that is', as in the next example:

(9) *Thus, only four participants did poorly on this pair [of noun-class markers] **whereby** two [respondents] could not correct any single of the eleven instances.*
 (from an MA research paper by A.A., Mar 2011)

In addition to the all-embracing uses of *the same* and *whereby*, there is the vague reference that is frequently expressed by the demonstrative pronoun *this*, particularly in the sequence *this is*, as in (10):

(10) a. *Reinforcement should be done immediately after the response but not postponed to a later time. <#/>* **This is** *usually more effective because the learner will tend to correct himself right-away.*
   b. *The teacher must ensure that there is adequate lighting in the classroom. He must ensure that there is enough air circulation so that the room is not stuffy. <#/>* **This is** *by making sure that the room is clean and the windows can easily be opened to let air in.*
   (W1A021K)

The reference of the demonstrative *this* in (10a) and (10b) is vague because it does not refer to an entity/idea close to it: in fact, in (a) it does not seem to refer to the syntactically closer idea of "not being postponed to a later time", but, more plausibly, to the further one of "reinforcement". In (b), the reference of *this is* even more vague: it seems to refer to both ideas of ensuring that "there is enough air" and that of "the room not being stuffy".

Likewise, the expression *is where* is also frequently used in KenE with no clear anaphoric reference, as in (11):

(11) a. *We like to use the terminology visually impaired* **This is where** *uh we include those who are totally blind according to the legal definition*
   (S1B029K)
   b. *[…] in order to therefore deliver education effectively to this minority among fellow Kenyans uh there's need therefore to rectify if not to remove all these problems <#/>And* **this is where** *we're told the Kenya Institute of Special Education comes in […]*
   (S1BINT1K)

In both examples *where* is clearly used as a pro-form, but not as one which, as one would expect, replaces a locative noun phrase or a prepositional phrase indicating a place, a position, or an origin. Instead, in (11a) it is part of the definition of the non-locative NP *the terminology visually impaired*, while in (11b) it serves as a subject complement to the demonstrative pronoun *this*.

The sequence *is when* is equally used to refer back to expressions that are not those grammatically expected. Consider (12):

(12) *Gross addiction* **is when** *you are addicted to alcohol you are addicted to <-/>to drugs hard drugs you're addicted to everything*
   (S1B032K)

While, as an anaphoric reference, *when* is normally expected to refer back to temporal expressions, typically PPs, in (12) it is clearly used as the beginning of a predicate defining the subject noun phrase *gross addiction*.

The issue of referring to no referent at all concerns the determiner *another* (as in *another man*), which can be said to function as an indefinite article. But while in StdIntE the use of *another* in such a case presupposes that indeed another entity (of the same nature) has been mentioned before, in KenE it is not uncommon for speakers to use it without there being a second man already mentioned. For example, while narrating a story, a KenE speaker will say something like this: *We were walking along River Road when another thief snatched my mobile phone and ran away with it.* This will be said even if it is the very first thief the speaker will have encountered on that day. Here is an authentic example from the ICE-K:

(13) [A] *That's quite versatile eh [. . .] Whatever versatile means*
 [B] *That's like you know there is **another man** from Nyeri you give him fish he will never eat uh [. . .] You know that [. . .] Like [. . .]*
 (S1A012K)

Visibly, in this example *another* was used instead of an indefinite determiner like *a* or *some*, since there was no other man to contrast it with.

The singular form *another* has its plural counterpart, *others*, which too is used without referring to any previously mentioned entity, as in *Others were good, others were bad*, to mean 'Some were good, others were bad'. Mesthrie (2008c: 633) reports a similar usage in Black South African English: "BlSAfE has a construction that replaces '*some . . . other*' in parallel contrastive clauses by '*other . . . other*' (e.g. *Other people are nice, other people are not so nice*)".

6.2 Cultural appropriateness phenomena

Two broad phenomena where KenE is distinct from its ancestor, BrE, are relevant here: polite requests and forms of address.

6.2.1 Polite requests

In a pilot study of polite requests in KenE, Buregeya (2004: 104) observed that "the request structures used in Kenyan English [were] shorter and more limited in number than those in British English". The study concluded that "written Kenyan English tends to rely mainly on imperative structures of three forms:

the mere imperative [11%], the imperative mitigated by 'please' [25%], and the imperative mitigated by 'kindly' [11%]" (2004: 118). But it also observed that 18% of the requests involved the explicit use of the verb *request* (one of them being *"I herein request that you be my referee"*). All of these observations were based on a very limited number of (only) 28 requests made by university students to their lecturer between 1998 and 2003.

From late 2003 to late 2016, the same lecturer received another set of 83 requests mostly from his current and former students. An almost similar picture emerges from this new set of requests: 18% (15/83) of them were of the structure *please* + imperative verb, 16% (13/83) of *kindly* + imperative verb, while 16% (13/83) were various syntactic structures that all explicitly used the verb *request*. Another subset of structures that occurred with some non-negligible frequency, 13% (11/83), is that involving the mitigators *please* and *kindly* in various syntactic configurations, including both *kindly* and *please* together (*Kindly, please* + Verb). But this time round, and rather surprisingly, almost absent are the mere-imperative requests: only 1/83 was received.

The predominance of the three structures is also borne out by data from the ICE-K, as shown in Table 6.1.[5]

This table shows that the *please* + imperative verb structure is by far the most frequent one in both the spoken and written components, totalling about 30 (45%) of all the 66 structures.[6] And *please* was used in 14 (22%) other instances to complement modal verbs, the most frequent of which is *Could you please* + *verb*. This appears in 9 (i.e. 14%) of the total 66 request structures, but, quite interestingly, all the 9 appear only in the spoken component. The *kindly* + imperative verb structure also appears 9 times, but only in the written component – just the opposite of the *Could you, please* structure. As for the explicit use of the verb *request*, in total it appears in 8 (i.e. 12%) of the 66 requests, in 5 of which it is preceded by the mitigator *kindly*, suggesting that *I kindly request* is almost a collocation in KenE.

The observations reported in the preceding paragraphs by and large corroborate Buregeya's (2004: 104) conclusion that the request structures used in

---

[5] It might be that the corpus contains also some instances of mere imperatives (i.e. those composed only of verbs not mitigated by *please, kindly*, or a modal verb), but establishing this would have required checking the imperative form of each one of the hundreds (or thousands) of verbs effectively used.

[6] There are 115 hits of *please* + imperative in the written component (and 66 in the spoken), but most of them are not requests per se: they are orders (e.g. *Please attend without failure* [W1B-BK15]), instructions (e.g. *Please note the following* [W1B-BK95]), and advice (e.g. *Please do not hesitate to contact us* [W1B-BK24]).

Table 6.1: Polite request structures in the ICE-K sub-corpus.

	Request Structure	SPOKEN	WRITTEN	Total
1.	*Please* + imperative V	10	± 20	30
2.	*Kindly* + imperative V	0	9	9
3.	*Kindly, please* + imperative V	1	0	1
4.	*Could you please* + V	9	0	9
	Can you + verb + *please* + V	0	1	1
	Would you please + V	1	1	2
	Will you please + V	1	1	2
5.	*I/We kindly request you* + *to* V	0	5	5
	I/We request you + *to* V	0	1	1
	I/we wish to request you + *to* V	0	1	1
	I/we would request you + *to* V	0	1	1
6.	*Would you kindly* + V	0	1	1
	I/we kindly ask you + *to* V	0	1	1
7.	*I would/should be grateful if you...*	0	1	1
8.	*Do you mind* + *V-ing*	1	0	1
	Total	23	43	66

KenE are "shorter and more limited in number than those in British English". However, the support for the "shortness" of those requests does not seem to be strong. This is because a non-negligible number of long requests were also produced both in the student requests and those from the ICE-K. By "long requests" reference is here (subjectively) made to structures involving at least four elements: modal + subject + mitigator + verb (as in *Could you please let me know...*) or subject + (modal) + mitigator + request + object + verb (as in *I would kindly request you to resend the document*).

What is strongly corroborated by the data is the limited-in-number aspect: on the one hand, there is a predominance of just three words *please, kindly,* and *request,* while, on the other hand, there is a quasi-total absence of other structures such as *Do you mind* + *V-ing, Would you mind* + *V-ing, Could you possibly* + V, and *I was wondering whether/if you* + modal + V, which have been reported to be used e.g. in BrE and are basically the ones considered to be the "real polite requests". In relation to this, while recognising that *please* and *kindly* can be enough to make an imperative structure a polite request,[7] Quirk et al. (1985) hint at the fact that the requests based on these two mitigators are certainly a minority. The authors write:

> *Please* and (to a lesser extent) *kindly* [...] may be added to imperative sentences with the [...] force of a request to convey greater overt politeness [as in]: *Please eat up your dinner* [and] *Kindly move to the next seat.* Requests are often expressed by questions and statements, eg: *Will you shut the door, please?, Would you mind shutting the door?, Could you shut the door for me?, I wonder whether you would mind shutting the door.* (Quirk et al. 1985: 832)

And elsewhere two of Quirk's co-authors make it clear that "The word *please* has the sole function of indicating politeness when one is making a request. But it has little effect in itself: to give a really polite impression, *please* usually has to be combined with devices of indirectness, such as using a question, the hypothetical *could* or *would*, etc." (Leech and Svartvik 2002: 34). The two authors note that "there are many other indirect ways of making a polite request" and that "the following are listed roughly in order of least to most polite":

> I wouldn't mind a drink, if you have one.
> Would you mind starting over again?
> I wonder if you could put me on your mailing list, please.
> Would you be good/kind enough to let me know? <more formal>
> I would be (extremely) grateful if you would telephone me this afternoon.
> I wonder if you'd mind writing a reference for me.
> (Leech and Svartvik 2002: 176; the intonation markers in the original text have been left out)

They add that "these sentences are typical of <polite, spoken> English" (2002: 176). But it is worth pointing out that totally absent from these sentences are the mitigator *kindly* and the verb *request*, and that there is just a single occurrence of the mitigator *please*.

---

[7] For some other authors, the word *please* is simply not enough to make an utterance a request. Swan (2016: paragraph 310.2), for example, says the following:
Please makes an order or instruction a little more polite, but does not turn it into a request. The following structures can be used perfectly correctly to give orders, instructions or advice, but they are not polite ways of requesting people to do things.

> *Please answer by return of post.*
> *Please help me for a few minutes.*
> [...]
> *Carry this for me, please.* [...]

Leech and Svartvik's (2002) list above should be complemented with request structures involving "negative statements with question tags", such as the following:

(14) a. *You couldn't give me a light, could you?*
 b. *I don't suppose you could give me a light, could you?* (very polite)
 (Swan 2016: paragraph 310.4)
 c. *Nigel you couldn't give us a hand could you*
 (ICE-GB)

Swan (2016: paragraph 310.4) comments that such requests "are common in informal requests in British English". However, when it comes to KenE, one can safely hypothesize that they are "unheard-of", if not "unthinkable". Unfortunately, the ICE-GB corpus does not provide evidence to confirm that the structures being claimed here to be absent from or (at best) very rare in KenE are common in BrE. For example, against expectations, not a single instance of the structures *Would you mind* ..., *Would you be good/kind enough* ..., and *I would/should be ... grateful if* ... occurs in the entire spoken component of the ICE-GB. (And not a single one of them appears in the entire spoken component of the ICE-K either.) The written component of the ICE-GB is a little more informative, to the extent that it at least contains significant occurrences of *I would/should be ... grateful if ...*, which appears 23 times in it, against only 4 times in the ICE-K.

Notwithstanding the scantiness of corpus-based evidence, the literature offers us at least two reasons for naturally expecting a more limited range of request structures in KenE (a widely used L2 variety) than in BrE (a native variety). Firstly, a similar phenomenon has been reported in a comparable variety, GhE, about which Huber and Dako (2008: 370) write:

> A much lower rate of the politer modal forms than in BrE can be observed. Polite requests such as *could I/you, might I, would it be possible* and others are relatively rare. What is viewed as a polite request in Ghana is often what a native speaker of standard British English (StBrE) would consider an order with the addition of *please*. [The following structure], addressed to a lecturer in his office, illustrates this use: [...] *I want to borrow your pen, please.*

Secondly, and somehow to justify what is quoted above about GhE and can be said about KenE, the literature on second vs. foreign language learning and that on language and culture remind us that "for the second language situation, our sociolinguistic expectations [...] will conform to a different, *typically local* [emphasis mine], model with which learners are likely to identify" (Davies 1995: 148). And, as if to illustrate this quotation, Gupta (1999: 8) puts it clearly:

"When we learn a foreign language, we expect some cultural baggage to come with the language. [...] [But] the situation is very different in places where English is widely used. There we find a focus on *local* culture". She further adds that "It is inevitable that local standards develop wherever English is used for local culture" (1999: 9).[8]

What is quite intriguing, though, is that, with specific reference to the expression of polite requests, this "uncontested" local nature of KenE does not necessarily reflect the local culture embodied in the local languages of Kenya. The point is that the native languages of Kenya, which one would have expected to have influenced KenE, have the same structures as, or at least ones very similar to, the *indirect* and elaborate ways of expressing polite requests pointed out earlier in relation to native BrE. Take, for example, Swahili, the only indigenous language of Kenya serving as a lingua franca throughout the country (and the only language recognized in the country's Constitution as the national language). Below are some of the indirect ways which people use to express polite requests in Swahili:

(15) a. *Naomba unisaidie na shilingi elfu moja.*[9]
    'I beg that you help me with [i.e. lend me] one thousand shillings'
 b. *Sijui kama unaweza kunisadia na shilingi elfu moja.*
    'I don't know if you can help me with one thousand shillings'
 c. *Labda unaweza kunisaidia na shilingi elfu moja.*
    'Perhaps you can help me with one thousand shillings?'
 d. *Najiuliza kama unaweza kunisaidia na shilingi elfu moja.*
    'I am wondering whether you can help me with one thousand shillings'

---

8 It should be noted, though, that this idea of local culture influencing the nature of request formulas seems to apply even to native English, if we consider Leech, Cruickshank and Ivanič's (2001: 402) observation that "being polite is different in different countries", which they illustrate by saying that "'the *super* polite' request forms you hear in Britain are often felt to be too much polite in the U.S.A. and in other countries. One country tends to use politeness in one way, and another in another".

9 The structure *Naomba* ('I beg') + a complement clause (usually agglutinated into one verb form like *unisaidie* 'that you help me') is reportedly a typically Tanzanian Swahili expression but which is increasingly being used in Kenyan Swahili as well. Since the infinitive *kuomba* can mean 'to request' and 'to ask', in addition to 'to beg', the frequent explicit use of *I request* in KenE request structures can be argued to be an infelicitous translation of the Swahili *naomba*; "infelicitous" with reference to native English where the verb *request* is simply not polite enough to express polite requests. Notice that KenE seems to have avoided translating *naomba* by 'I beg [that]', because *I beg* would be demeaning in this context.

e. *Nilikua nataka kukuuliza kama unaweza kunisaidia na shilingi elfu moja.* 'I wanted to ask you/I was wondering if you could help me with one thousand shillings'

Since structures like those in (15) do exist in Swahili and other languages of Kenya, which are KenE speakers' L1s, and since similar structures exist in native English, the question that is hard to answer is why those indirect ways are rarely, if at all, used in KenE. It might be that KenE was influenced by Indian English in adopting the three main request structures prevalent in it. Writing about Indian English, Sailaja (2009: 93) points out ten "constructions that are unacceptable to native speakers of English in terms of appropriateness", among them the following three containing the key words *kindly, please* and *request (v): Kindly do the needful, We request you to please recommend ...*, and *Please arrange to do this at your earliest convenience ...*. In the absence of a clear answer, one should simply be contented with the conclusion that with regard to expressing polite requests, the local culture in KenE is only *partially* local, somewhere in-between the L1 culture and the native English culture.

6.2.2 Titles and forms of address

Wardhaugh (2010: 281) starts his section on "address terms" with a series of questions, including the following:

> How do you name or address another? By title (T), by first name (FN), by last name (LN), by nickname, by some combination of these, or by nothing at all, so deliberately avoiding the problem? What factors govern the choice you make? [...] All kinds of combinations are possible in English: *Dr Smith, John Smith, Smith, John, Johnnie, Doc, Sir, Mack,* and so on.

We know that the factors governing our choice have to do mainly with the addressee's social status and the level of familiarity and intimacy between them and us. So, as suggested in the quotation above, we should naturally expect "all kinds of combinations" even in KenE. However, some combinations are more common in it than e.g. in BrE because they are used in contexts where they would not be appropriate in native English.

These contexts are specified in the following quotation from Swan (2016: paragraph 326.2), in which the author describes and comments on the forms of address typically used in British (and American) English:

When we talk (or write) to people we generally name them in one of two ways.

[a] [By] first name

This is informal, used for example to relatives, friends and children.

[...]

[b] [By] title + surname

This is more formal or respectful.

[...]

Members of all-male groups sometimes address each other by their surnames alone (e.g. *'Hello, Smith'*), but this is **unusual in modern English**.

Mr, Mrs, and *Ms* are not generally used alone.

[...] *Excuse me. Can you tell me the time?* (NOT ~~Excuse me, Mr~~ or ~~Excuse me, Mrs~~.)

Doctor can be used alone to talk to medical doctors whom one is consulting, **but not usually in other cases**.

[...]

Sir and *madam* are used in Britain **mostly by people in service occupations** (e.g. shop assistants). **Some** employees call their male employers *sir*, and **some schoolchildren** call their teachers *sir* or *miss*. *Dear Sir* and *Dear Madam* are common ways of beginning letters to strangers [...] **In other situations *sir* and *madam* are unusual in British English**.

[Example:] *Excuse me. Can you tell me the time?* (NOT ~~Excuse me, sir~~ ...)

In American English, *sir* and *ma'am* are less formal than in British English, and are quite often used (especially in the South and West) when addressing people.

The words highlighted in bold type (emphasis mine) in the quotation encapsulate the key differences between KenE and BrE.

The quotation first suggests that for "all-male groups" to address each other "by their surnames alone" is "unusual in modern English". Leech and Svartvik (2002: 34) say more or less the same thing: "Interestingly, present-day English makes little use of the surname alone. Except in the third person reference (e.g. *Shakespeare, Bach, Bush*) to someone one does not know personally, but by repute, such as a famous author, composer or politician". However, whatever "modern English" and "present-day English" mean, this practice is definitely *not* unusual in KenE. In fact, it is very frequent, especially at the workplace, which is typically an urban setting where people from different tribes of Kenya and from other nationalities live. The practice is very frequent essentially because quite a number of educated Kenyans apparently do not want to make their first name known to the general public (instead they have it represented by just an initial or not at all), if by *first name* reference is made to the non-African name usually given through baptism. But since most Kenyans have at least two African names, one of them is the surname (i.e. the family name for most of them) and the other their "own" (i.e. given) name.[10] In many cases the latter is known to the public, but in some cases it is still kept represented by an initial. For those whose African names are known to their colleagues, one of them will, over time, be the regular one. It will then be used not only by male colleagues, but by their female ones as well. In academic circles the name will usually be preceded by the title, as will be seen below. Interestingly, for some reason female colleagues do definitely not like to be addressed by their surname alone. They seem to prefer their (non-African) first names or their (African) given names, even though they would not mind being addressed by their surname if this were preceded by a professional, especially academic, title. And, if they are married, they will generally not object to being addressed as *Mrs* + their husband's name (according to Dr Mrs Wambua, who read an earlier draft of this paper in Sept 2016).

The second key difference between KenE and BrE lies in the statement that "*Doctor* can be used alone to talk to medical doctors whom one is consulting, but not usually in other cases". Of course, KenE speakers use the word *doctor* to address medical doctors, but they also, and *characteristically*, use the term to address all other holders of a doctorate. It is the latter who actually demand it: most of them will remind the addressor that they are (now) *doctor* and, in some cases, if the addressor were to omit their title, he/she would be told that he/she must be mistaken about the identity of the addressee, who is no longer the same person without the omitted academic title. "Omitting the title *Dr* sounds disrespectful," commented Dr Wambua (personal communication, Sept 2016). Understandably, the same applies to *professor*, and even to *engineer*. Some addressees, notably from the Luo tribe, will even insist on being addressed by a combination of e.g. *doctor engineer*.

A significant detail in the use of *Dr* (and even *Mr* in this case) is that in KenE it can be accompanied by the first name as well, as in *Dr John* (or *Mr John*), obviously if that is the only name he is known by, but sometimes even when his surname is known to the addressor.

To digress a little more to *Mr*, this title is on many occasions replaced by its Swahili translation, *Bwana*, as in this example:

---

10 In some cases the surname will be easily recognizable if it is preceded by the morpheme meaning 'son of' in the various languages of Kenya. Thus, we can automatically tell that in *Ngugi wa Thiong'o* ('Ngugi son of Thiong'o) the surname is *Thiong'o*, because preceded by the prefix *wa* in Kikuyu, and that in *Daniel Toroitich arap Moi*, *Moi* is the surname, because of *arap* (in the Kalenjin language), etc.

(16) [...] ***Bwana*** *President, let's go ahead and close [them].*
(said by Kenya's Deputy President, on television news, 28 Mar 2014)

It is worth noting that *Bwana* appears 30 times (against 456 for *Mr*) in the spoken component of the ICE-K, even though in 8 of its occurrences (where, conveniently, it starts with a lower-case letter) it does not mean *Mr* as such, but is used as an interjection to address even female interlocutors, as in [...] *I mean it was hurting [...]* ***bwana*** (from S1A006K), where *bwana* means something like 'I tell you/I mean it'. In this latter case it usually occurs at the end of an utterance, where it syntactically occupies the position of the bigger *Bwana* and the three English titles *Mr*, *Mrs*, and *Ms*, which, according to Swan (2016: paragraph 326.2), "are not generally used alone".[11]

The third difference between KenE and BrE concerns the use of *sir* and *madam* (and *miss*), especially Swan's observation that "In other situations *sir* and *madam* are unusual in British English". To start with *sir*, in Kenya it is not a question of it being used by "some employees" – whether they are "in service occupations" or not – and by "some schoolchildren"; it is a question of *all* employees, including senior officials, being "on standby" to use *sir* to address their male superiors, especially when replying to the latter's phone call. The superiors would not feel that they were given enough respect if *sir* was missing from their juniors' reply utterances. *Sir* is also widely used in KenE to address "respected" customers (e.g. at banks), and strangers whom one feels are important personalities. In academic circles, people in leadership positions do not mind being addressed as *sir*, and some of them seem to prefer it to *Mr* + professional title (e.g. *Mr Dean*). Further, *sir* is frequently added to *Mr* + professional title (e.g. *Mr Chairman, sir)*, most likely on the influence of the routine formula *(Mr Speaker, sir)* used in parliament so frequently that occasionally members of parliament forget that *sir* refers to males only (like this MP, an assistant minister at the time, who, on 29 Jan 2009, at least three times addressed the interim speaker, a woman, as "***Madam*** *Speaker,* ***Sir***"!).

The situation is more complex, and rather intriguing, with the use of the term *mádam* (stressed on the first syllable, as in StdIntE). In public offices, in general, the junior staff are likely to use *mádam* to address their superiors, mostly prefixed to their professional title (e.g. *Mádam Director)*, who do not mind being called *mádam*. However, in academic circles, women lecturers do

---

[11] According to Zipporah Otiso (p.c., Sept 2016), in KenE *Mrs* tends to be used alone by students at schools where both husband and wife teach/work, to refer to the latter. Yet, the husband is rarely referred to as just *Mr*.

not like at all being called *mádam* by their students, and these in turn are well aware of that: they will do everything to avoid having to say *Mádam* + name, while they will not hesitate to address their male lecturers as *Mr* + name (in both cases if the lecturers concerned are not doctors or professors, of course).

Anecdotally, but very plausibly, women lecturers, and possibly women from some other professional categories as well, hate the term *mádam*[12] because of the "demeaning" connotations of the same term *madam*, but this time round pronounced with the stress placed on the second syllable (*madám*). It has been reported to the present author, by various classes of his postgraduate students, that this (second) *madám* referred to many things, including 'the [administrative] chief's wife', 'the local female primary school teacher', 'the female prison warder', and 'the terrible, feared woman/wife', all of which would be belittling for a university lecturer. However, and somewhat paradoxically, *madám* has at least one meaning which even female university lecturers are likely to find positive: that of 'professional woman', as pointed out by Atichi (2004). In this meaning, *madám* is used before the surname, usually instead of *Mrs*, for women of a high social status, like government ministers, as in (17) below.

(17) *My first question goes to Madám Wakhungu.*
(said by a female KBC TV journalist, R.M., at a press conference on 31 Mar 2014)

With Prof Judy Wakhungu being Kenya's Minister of the Environment (at the time), the word *madám* can only be construed to be positive in this example. And perhaps as another positive meaning, and according to University-of-Nairobi MA student, Dianah Nyabuto (p.c., Sept 2016), the expression *my madám* is used by some men to talk about their wives to someone, especially to introduce them, as in *this is my madám*.

A word should also be said about the use of *miss* and *ma'am* mentioned at the end of the quotation from Swan (2016). The term *ma'am* is rarely used. Zipporah Otiso (p.c., Sept 2016) pointed out that *ma'am* was used by students "especially in writing, to refer to lady lecturers/teachers whom they find motherly".

---

[12] The present author even heard, on 4 Sept 2016, a (young) female shopper address the saleswoman in the bakery section of a supermarket in the following way: "*Excuse me, Ms, make it four [packs of brown burger buns]*". The use of *Ms*, instead of the expected *mádam*, shows the extent to which the latter can and should be avoided by women. One explanation for this, provided by a young educated woman (Dianah Nyabuto, an MA student, p.c., Sept 2016), is that the title *mádam* connotes the idea of being "no longer young (in her 40's or older) and financially rich", and thus "deserving the respect which young females should not be entitled to".

The title *miss* is also rarely used, except in the case of beauty pageants, where phrases like *Miss Kenya* and *Miss Tourism* are very frequent. Otherwise, at school, children and older students are encouraged (by their teachers) to use *teacher*, a term which seems to be very much acceptable, even by some university lecturers. Actually, the Swahili word for *teacher*, *mwalimu*, is very popular among university lecturers, as a neutral form of address even in an otherwise conversational exchange in English, since it covers all Kenyan universities' academic titles, from *tutorial fellow* to *full professor*. It is a particularly convenient term when one of the interlocutors is not sure what the current title of the other is, and when one wants to avoid the use of *mádam* as well. *Daktari*, the Swahili word for *doctor*, is another such convenient term in informal conversations between lecturers. And *doc* is occasionally used in such conversations, too.

Another political title-cum-form of address is *Honourable/Hon* (together with its Swahili translation *Mheshimiwa*, which occasionally crops up in English discourse as well). Although not mentioned in the quotation from Swan (2016), it is one which cannot be ignored in the context of KenE, because of its frequency of use on a daily basis on both radio and television. The term is the professional title for members of the Kenyan Parliament (which, since the March 2013 elections, is composed of both the Senate and the National Assembly, following the promulgation of a new Constitution in 2010).[13] Linguistically, *Honourable* is mostly used before the surname, but sometimes before both the first/given name and the surname, though not before the former alone. It seems to be a very powerful title, presumably because of the political and economic power it connotes, powerful enough to stand on its own, without being combined with others, not even with the highly prized *Dr* and *Prof*. Thus, even MPs who are professors or PhD holders are usually addressed as *Honourable X*, and they seem to be quite satisfied with that.

What is more interesting from a linguistic point of view is that in KenE the title *Honourable* (with its abbreviated form *Hon.* being much more frequent in writing) is typically accompanied with either the name or the word *member* (usually in the recurrent question *Is the honourable member for Constituency X in order in saying that...?*). In contrast, in BrE, it collocates first and foremost with the word *friend*, but also with *gentleman* and *lady*, as in *my (right) honourable friend* and the *honourable gentleman/lady* – phrases not used in the KenE parliament.

---

13 The same Constitution created governors of counties, who, though elected as well, are not referred to as *Honourable*. They have actually laid claim to something bigger, *His Excellency*, the very title used for the country's president, a state of affairs which brought the National Assembly to pass legislation (in 2015) forbidding the governors to use the title, but to practically no success so far.

We can now check if the different claims made in the preceding paragraphs about the uses of the various titles and forms of address are reflected in their frequencies of occurrence in both the ICE-K and the ICE-GB. Table 6.2 provides the statistics about such occurrences.

Table 6.2: Occurrences of titles and forms of address in both the ICE-K and the ICE-GB.

Title/form of address	ICE-K: SPOKEN (304,967 words)	ICE-K: WRITTEN (405,868 words)	ICE-GB: SPOKEN (547,585 words)	ICE-GB: WRITTEN (466,405 words)
Mr	456 (= 1 in every 669 words)	506 (= 1 in every 802 words)	697 (= 1 in every 786 words)	335 (= 1 in every 1,392 words)
Mrs	49 (= 1/6,234)	27 (= 1/15,032)	89 (= 1/6153)	119 (1= 11,959)
Miss	8 (= 1/38,121)	2 (= 1/202,934)	26 (= 1/21,061)	12 (= 1/38,867)
Ms	1	20 (= 1/20,293)	0	2 (= 1/233,203)
Dr	106 (= 1/2,877)	130 (= 1/2,346)	50 (= 1/10,952)	39 (= 1/11,959)
Doc	0	0	0	0
Daktari	2	0	N/A	N/A
Mwalimu[a]	2	1	N/A	N/A
Professor[b]	55 (= 1/5,545)	62 (= 1/6,546)	43 (= 1/12,735)	49 (= 1/9,518)
Sir	14 (= 1/21,783)	73 (1= 5,560)	89 (= 1/6,153)	61 (= 1/7,646)
Madam(e)	5 (= 1/60,993)	23 (= 1/17,646)	6 (= 1/91,264)	2 (= 1/233,203)
Ma'am	0	0	0	0
Bwana	22 (= 1/13,862)	0	N/A	N/A
Honourable	2	7 (4 of which: Hon.)	219	1

[a] There are another three uses of *Mwalimu* which were not counted since they specifically refer to *Mwalimu Julius Nyerere* (the late and former president of Tanzania).
[b] Including its abbreviated form *Prof*, which, interestingly, appears a massive 30 times in the written ICE-K but only 3 times in the written ICE-GB.

If we refer to the ratios rather than the absolute figures, the table above visibly corroborates the more frequent use of the academic titles *Dr* and *Professor/Prof* in KenE than in BrE. It also indicates a slightly higher rate of use of *Mr*, which might be due, as already pointed out, to the use of *Mr* also with first names only in KenE. Regarding *Mrs*, the ratio figures suggest that while it appears more or less equally in the spoken components of BrE and KenE, it appears more frequently in written BrE than in written KenE. The lower frequency of *Mrs* in the written ICE-K may be related to the much higher use (20 times) of *Ms* in it than in the ICE-GB (only 2 times). But there are two surprising, unexpected observations from the table: first, there is the much higher frequency of occurrence of *sir* in the spoken ICE-GB (1 in every 6,152 words) than in the spoken ICE-K (only 1 in every 21,783 words), a higher frequency that might have to do with the very many uses (in the ICE-GB) of *sir* as a knighthood title, one which does not exist in Kenya. Second, there are the low frequencies of occurrence of *Honourable/Hon.* in both components of the ICE-K. However, this apparent deficit is compensated for in its written-to-be-spoken component (with a total of 100,606 words), not represented in the table: it contains a massive 384 hits of *Hon.* (and just 1 of *Honourable*).

It transpires from the preceding paragraphs that both the corpus-based and the present author's own sets of observations by and large corroborate each other. However, beyond this corroboration, an interesting question that can be asked is the extent to which the issue of local culture, which was earlier applied to the KenE expression of polite requests, is relevant to the KenE use of titles and address forms. A tentative answer is that, with regard to address forms, the issue is less intriguing. This is because some aspects of it (such as the fact that the surname can be used by itself in any context) seem to have been directly borrowed from the indigenous languages of Kenya, while other aspects do not really constitute an issue to the extent that in a language like Swahili there is only one term for the conflicting BrE ones: specifically, *Bwana* is used for both *sir*[14] and *Mr*, while *Bi*[15] is used for *Mrs, Miss, Ms,* and *Madam* (even

---

[14] However, while in KenE the replies *Yes, sir* and *No, sir*, are frequent and polite, their Swahili equivalents *Ndio, Bwana* and *La, Bwana,* respectively, would not be acceptable polite replies: *Ndio, Bwana* would connote the master-servant relationships of the colonial times, while *La, Bwana* would be an insolent reply. So, Swahili speakers will simply reply with *Ndio* or *La,* leaving out the titles.

[15] *Bi* seems to be a short form for *bibi*, which is the one discussed by Habwe (2010), about which he writes: "The honorific *bibi* 'lady' is also used widely in political circles to refer to women of higher ranking and women in general" (2010: 133), that is, the equivalent indeed of both *mádam* and *madám*.

though some Swahili dictionaries suggest that *Bi* means just 'Miss'). So, the potentially confusing choices encountered above about e.g. these female-gender markers are automatically dispelled. The only intriguing aspect about the use of titles and forms of address forms seems to be the origin of the pervasive use, in KenE but not in native English, of academic and professional titles (e.g. *Dr* and *Prof*): since they did not exist in native Kenyan languages in the first place, they came with English, but perhaps with another non-native variety of English, a plausible candidate being Nigerian English.[16]

6.3 A rhetorical-force device: code-mixing Swahili words into English

The idea that code-switching/code-mixing can be used as a rhetorical device to achieve some kind of rhetorical force has been applied to poetry and music.[17] But it has also been reported in sociolinguistic studies, as acknowledged in this statement: "Gumperz and others have also pointed out that code-switching can be used as a rhetorical device", quoted from the *International Encylopedia of Linguistics*, 2nd edn. (2003: 95).

The use of the Swahili interjection *bwana* discussed in the previous section seems to be one such rhetorical device which KenE speakers use to try to persuade their interlocutors. This type of codemixing clearly aimed at persuading the audience must have always been popular with politicians and is now becoming increasingly popular with commercial institutions, especially banks and telecommunications companies. The first set of examples below comes from politicians.

---

16 One could have thought of Indian English as another plausible source, since, as speculated in 6.2.1, it might have had an influence on the development of the three most common request structures. However, if what Sailaja (2009) says is true, then IndE has to be ruled out. The author writes: "Addressing a senior person directly – for example, *Professor Jagannath* said by a junior lecturer – is rare. Either *sir* is used or no address form at all. It is when two people are equals that they may be addressed with the titles *Mr, Mrs, Ms, Dr*" (2009: 87). This is an almost completely different situation from that which obtains in KenE.
17 The idea is suggested in the following two statements: a) "Below are analyses of code mixing and other rhetorical devices", quoted from Smith and Emezue (2015: 278); b) "Code-switching in the Andalusi kharjis [love songs] as a rhetorical device", which is the heading of a section in Zwartjes (1997: 277).

(18) a. *If your own elections, you being the cream of society, can be marked by ethnicity,* **jameni, tuko na shida** ['you people, we have a problem']
(said by the Kenyan president while addressing University-of-Nairobi students, 23 Aug 2016)
b. *[...] it is absolutely* **bure kabisa** ['it is absolutely totally useless']
(said by the then Kenyan president while addressing councillors, 14 May 2010)
c. *We now know.* **Kumbe** ['eh'], *it was not* **katiba** ['the constitution']. **Kumbe** ['eh'], *it is a continuation of people wanting to settle political scores.*
(said by the then Kenyan vice-president, 15 May 2010)

In these utterances, the switch to Swahili, a national language, must have been made to achieve emphasis. The next set of examples comes from institutions.

(19) a. **Kimbilia** *deal* **na** *Orange mania* [**'Rush**-for-deal-**with**- Orange mania']: *Pixi Dual SIM Smartphone at 5,799, Nokia 107 Dual SIM at Ksh 1,999 and much more. Only today and tomorrow at Orange shops".*
(An online advert from the Orange telecoms company, Aug 2014)
b. *"Open a* **zidisha** *bonus savings account"* ['Open a **multiplying** *bonus savings* account']
(A billboard advert from Barclays Bank of Kenya Ltd, seen in Aug 2014)
c. *"Beat* **Njaa***nuary* [the **hunger** of January] *by saving some extra cash! Get unbelievable discounts of up to 20% [...]"*
(An SMS from the Tuskys supermarket, 4 Jan 2019)

In these examples, the insertion of Swahili words was most likely not meant for emphasis, but to be a device used to fit in the current trend, on the part of commercial institutions, to use Sheng in their advertisements to appeal especially to the youth. (Sheng, a non-standard variety of Swahili, is an in-group language used by young people in Kenya, mostly those living in urban areas.) One of Sheng's key features is mixing vocabulary from the various languages of Kenya. In this context, although the Swahili words *kimbilia, na, zidisha*, and *njaa* ('hunger') in (19) are standard Swahili vocabulary, using them in the examples above might create the feeling that those utterances are actually in Sheng. Githiora (2016: 11–12) describes and illustrates "the popularity [which] Sheng now enjoys in all types of advertising by local small business, and multinational, corporate entities".[18]

---

18 There is even an advertising magazine in Nairobi called *PigiaMe* ('TelephoneMe').

6.3 A rhetorical-force device: code-mixing Swahili words into English

For its part, the ICE-K sub-corpus, particularly its spoken component, contains many instances of ordinary people's conversations in which there is a great deal of code-mixing Swahili words into English. Some of these are of the type of established loanwords (e.g. *baraza* 'public assembly' and *harambee* 'fundraising') identified in Chapter 5, but which are not of interest in the present case. Others are ad hoc loanwords that needed not be borrowed, and thus the code-mixing of which must have been designed to create some rhetorical effect.

Here are some examples illustrating the latter category, taken from university students' conversations:

(20) a. <$?> <#/>And even write a story about it [...]
   <$?> <#/>You know uh <#/>You had to know you had to [...] **jua** ['**know**']
   <$A> <#/>Yeah they are very interesting
   (S1A001K)

b. <$C> <#/> [...] Why should men cook
   <$?> <#/> [...] **Sasa we** ['**Now you**'] Jwan [...] **si** ['**why not**'] you ask us questions <#/>I think that time he was asking [...] **akina** ['people like'] Judy questions <#/> [...] **si** [...] **ndio** ['**isn't it?**']
   <$?> <#/>Yeah
   (S1A001K)

c. <#/>Because I mean <./>ho how did she know <#/>How <./>d <-/>How did they <#/>How did that [...] **kagirl** ['**little** girl'] know <#/>Maybe their mom told her [...] You know there are people who are so free
   (S1A011K)

In example (20a), the speaker did not have to borrow the Swahili verb *jua* ('know'), since he/she had just used its equivalent in English. Thus, the repetition of the same notion (of knowing) in Swahili must have been intended for emphasis. The use of the words *sasa* ('now'), *si* ('why not'), and *si ndio* ('isn't it') is a further illustration of the popular youth speech referred to two paragraphs earlier, even when the context (as in the case of the extracts in [20]) is not a typical Sheng one. The use of the diminutive prefix[19] *ka-* in *kagirl* ('little girl') is yet a further example of the Sheng-like speech and, even more relevant

---

[19] The diminutive prefix *ka-* is in fact not Standard Swahili (the standard one is *ki-*). Nonetheless, it is the one that is commonly used in Sheng and colloquial Swahili. *Ka-* must have been borrowed from most Bantu languages, which, unlike Swahili (a Bantu language itself), indeed use it as the standard diminutive prefix.

here, an illustration that the use of the full English word *little* would not have the same effect, that of stressing the fact that the girl was, from her physical appearance, 'too little to know'.

6.4 Written-English features in spoken KenE: contracted vs non-contracted forms

Non-contracted verb forms are expected to characterize formal, especially written, English, while their contracted counterparts are expected to characterize informal, especially spoken, English. Since spoken second language varieties have been observed to be more formal than their native variety counterparts, the working hypothesis is that there will be fewer contracted forms in spoken KenE (represented by SPOKEN ICE-K in Table 6.3) than in spoken BrE (represented by SPOKEN ICE-GB).

Table 6.3 shows that overall there are indeed fewer occurrences of the contracted forms (reflected in the higher denominators in the fractions in the table) and more of the non-contracted ones in spoken ICE-K than in spoken ICE-GB. To start with the contracted forms, for 38 (i.e. 95%) of the 40 in the table, there are proportionately fewer occurrences of them in ICE-K than in ICE-GB; the only two exceptions are *you'll* (with 1/3,315 in ICE-K vs 1/4,933 in ICE-GB) and *they'll* (with 1/5,980 in ICE-K vs 1/6,367 in ICE-GB). The two exceptions may principally have to do with the possibility that while *'ll* is normally the contracted version of *will*, in KenE it may also be that of *shall*, a modal verb which, as already pointed out in Chapter 4, tends to be overused. (Indeed, while there are 95 hits of *shall* in spoken ICE-K, there are only 89 of them in spoken ICE-GB, a much larger component, translating into a ratio of 1/3,210 for the former and 1/6,153 for the latter.) And for the specific case of *they'll* as an exception, some instances of it could actually be mere misspellings for *there'll*, in the ICE-K subcorpus, as is evident from the following example:

(21) *The most probable thing is that they'll be a re-channelling of efforts to other areas by the family*
(S1B035K).

It is worth noting that some contracted forms seem to be even non-existent in spoken KenE: in the entire spoken ICE-K, there is not a single occurrence of the following six forms: *could've, would've, should've, must've, shan't,* and *mightn't,* and there is just one occurrence of *mustn't* and *might've*. Further, the much lower ratios for the *'d* forms (*I'd, you'd, she'd, he'd, it'd, they'd*) cannot go

6.4 Written-English features in spoken KenE — 203

Table 6.3: Occurrences of contracted vs. non-contracted verb forms in SPOKEN ICE-K and SPOKEN ICE-GB.

Contracted form	ICE-K (304,967 words)	Ratio	ICE-GB (547,585 words)	Ratio	Non-contracted form	ICE-K (304,967 words)	Ratio	ICE-GB (547,585 words)	Ratio
	Hits	1/X[a]	Hits	1/X		Hits	1/X	Hits	1/X
I'd[b]	36	1/8,471	306	1/1,789	I would	207	1/1,473	233	1/2,350
					I had	45	1/6,777	127	1/4,312
you'd	35	1/8,713	145	1/3,776	you would	36	1/8,471	60	1/9,126
					you had	34	1/8,970	79	1/6,931
she'd	1	1/304,967	67	1/8,173	she would	9	1/33,885	21	1/26,075
					she had	7	1/43,567	46	1/11,904
he'd	4	1/76,241	145	1/3,776	he would	43	1/7,092	68	1/8,053
					he had	82	1/3,719	129	1/4,244
it'd	2	1/152,484	27	1/20,281	it would	48	1/6,353	194	1/2,823
					it had	23	1/13,259	44	1/12,445
they'd	6	1/50,529	80	1/6,845	they would	54	1/5,648	51	1/10,737
					they had	43	1/7,092	76	1/7,205
I'm	434	1/703	1,252	1/437	I am	77	1/3,961	127	1/4,312
you're	198	1/1,540	705	1/777	you are	533	1/572	95	1/5,764

(continued)

Table 6.3 (continued)

Contracted form	ICE-K (304,967 words)	Ratio	ICE-GB (547,585 words)	Ratio	Non-contracted form	ICE-K (304,967 words)	Ratio	ICE-GB (547,585 words)	Ratio
we're	127	1/2,401	360	1/1,521	we are	563	1/542	130	1/4,212
she's[c]	90	1/3,389	351	1/1,560	she is she has	66 49	1/4,621 1/6,224	38 43	1/14,410 1/12,735
he's	309	1/987	1,042	1/525	he is he has	205 96	1/1,488 1/3,177	131 62	1/4,180 1/8,832
it's	1,011	1/302	3,588	1/153	it is it has	702 78	1/434 1/3,910	567 99	1/966 1/5,531
they're	166	1/1,837	623	1/879	they are	487	1/626	182	1/3,009
could've	0	N/A	24	1/22,816	could have	32	1/9,530	59	1/9,281
might've	1	1/304,967	13	1/42,122	might have	14	1/21,783	45	1/12,169
would've	0	N/A	45	1/12,169	would have	42	1/7,261	143	1/3,829
should've	0	N/A	13	1/42,122	should have	26	1/11,730	55	1/9,956
must've	0	N/A	14	1/39,113	must have	28	1/10,892	38	1/14,410

aren't	10	1/30,497	130	1/4,212	are not	240	1/1,271	73	1/7,501
isn't	71	1/4,295	391	1/1,400	is not	297	1/1,027	158	1/3,466
can't	151	1/2,020	520	1/1,053	cannot	190	1/1,605	45	1/12,169
don't	716	1/426	1667	1/328	do not	111	1/2,747	49	1/11,175
doesn't	106	1/2,877	368	1/1,488	does not	93	1/3,279	29	1/18,882
didn't	106	1/2,877	552	1/992	did not	101	1/3,019	40	1/13,690
won't	24	1/12,710	149	1/3,675	will not	56	1/5,446	33	1/16,593
wouldn't	55	1/5,545	243	1/2,253	would not	44	1/6,931	30	1/18,253
couldn't	11	1/27,724	153	1/3,579	could not	25	1/12,199	17	1/32,211
haven't	14	1/21,783	264	1/2,074	have not	34	1/8,970	16	1/34,226
hasn't	8	1/38,121	75	1/7,301	has not	40	1/7,624	24	1/22,816
hadn't	8	1/38,121	62	1/8,832	had not	18	1/16,943	14	1/39,113
shouldn't	12	1/25,413	45	1/12,169	should not	54	1/5,648	19	1/28,820
mustn't	1	1/304,967	12	1/45,632	must not	9	1/33,885	4	1/136,896
shan't	0	N/A	3	1/182,528	shall not	5	1/60,993	2	1/273,793
mightn't	0	N/A	2	1/273,793	might not	19	1/16,050	20	1/27,379

(continued)

Table 6.3 (continued)

Contracted form	ICE-K (304,967 words)	Ratio	ICE-GB (547,585 words)	Ratio	Non-contracted form	ICE-K (304,967 words)	Ratio	ICE-GB (547,585 words)	Ratio
I'll	53	1/5,754	412	1/1,329	I will I shall	31 9	1/9,838 1/33,885	51 44	1/10,737 1/12,445
you'll	92	1/3,315	111	1/4,933	you will	80	1/3,812	54	1/10,140
she'll	9	1/33,885	22	1/24,890	she will	14	1/21,783	11	1/49,780
it'll	6	1/50,828	67	1/8,173	it will	82	1/719	83	1/6,597
we'll	50	1/6,099	132	1/4,148	we will we shall	30 65	1/10,166 1/4,692	39 17	1/14,733 1/32,211
they'll	51	1/5,980	86	1/6,367	they will	69	1/4,419	53	1/10,332

a 1/X: 1 in every X number of words.
b Here, and in subsequent 'd forms, 'd represents both *would* and *had*.
c Here, and in subsequent 's forms, 's represents both *is* and *has*.

unnoticed. Regarding the 16 forms involving the contraction of *not* attached to the auxiliary, even though in the two sub-corpora only 5 of them (*can't, isn't, doesn't, don't, didn't*) appear in any significant numbers, they do at much lower ratios in the ICE-K than in the ICE-GB.

Turning to the non-contracted forms, Table 6.3 shows that for each one of those involving the verb *be* (7 of them) and the negative *not* (16 of them), the ICE-K proportionately contains more of them than the ICE-GB. This observation, coupled with the inverse one that for each one of their contracted counterparts the ICE-K contains fewer of them than the ICE-GB, is a strong indication that spoken KenE sounds more of written than spoken, if comparison is made to a native variety.[20]

The statistics for the non-contracted forms *will* and *shall* also offer strong support for this: 7 out of the 8 in the table appear more frequently in the ICE-K than in the ICE-GB; the only exception is *I shall*. It is not clear why this appears less frequently in the ICE-K than in the ICE-GB while its plural counterpart, *we shall*, appears much more frequently. For their part, 3 of the 5 non-contracted forms involving *would* (*I would, you would, they would*) appear more frequently in the ICE-K than in the ICE-GB. It is not clear why only *she would* and *it would* appear less frequently.

The non-contracted forms involving the verb *have* present an untypical picture: 4 out of the 5 of them appear less frequently in the ICE-K than in the ICE-GB . The four are: *could have, would have, should have,* and *might have*; the only exception is *must have*. But at the same time no contracted counterparts of them appear in the ICE-K at all (except for just a single occurrence of *might've*). A plausible reason why the four forms appear less frequently in the ICE-K may have to do with the observation made earlier in 4.4.22 that in KenE the simple modals *could* and *would* (and possibly *should* and *might* as well) tend to be used also for their compound counterparts *could have* and *would have.*

6.5 Conclusion

The salient discourse features of KenE concern several aspects of anaphoric reference, aspects of cultural appropriateness related specifically to polite request structures and titles and forms of address, code-mixing Swahili words into

---

[20] Budohoska (2014: 79) used the contrast between contracted and non-contracted forms specifically involving *not* in the entire ICE-K to argue that KenE was more formal than BrE. She concluded that "The overall formality level on the basis of the analysed parameters was shown to be higher in the ICE-K" (2014: 87).

English to achieve some rhetorical effect, and a written-English feature (namely a limited use of contracted verb forms) which predominates in spoken KenE.

The anaphoric-reference-related features seem, on the face of it, contradictory: on the one hand, there are those that are underused (because less used than they ought to) and, on the other hand, those that are overused to the extent that they refer virtually to anything and sometimes to no referent at all. Regarding the former category this chapter discussed the underuse of the personal pronoun *it* and its possessive counterpart *its*, as well as the demonstrative pronoun *those*; concerning the latter category, the chapter discussed the pervasive use of *the same, whereby, this is, is where, is when*, and *another*.

Arguably, though, the quintessence of KenE discourse features is those reflecting its local culture; that is, structures used to express polite requests on the one hand, and titles and forms of address on the other. In relation to the former, KenE typically uses a limited range of request structures, basically three of them: a) *please* + imperative verb, b) *kindly* + imperative verb, and the explicit use of the verb *request + you*. None of the three is considered to be a typical polite request structure in British English, especially because they are direct. In particularly limited use in KenE are the requests based on indirect structures such as modal verbs, past tense forms, and questions, and characteristically absent from it are those based on even more indirect forms such as a negative statement + a question tag.

As concerns the other manifestation of local culture through KenE, that is in terms of how this variety uses gender-differentiation and professional titles and other forms of address, the key features to remember are the following: a) the fact that the last name tends to be used alone (while addressing or referring to male interlocutors), while at the same time the title *Mr* can be used even with the first name; b) the sacred and omnipresent nature of academic titles (particularly *Dr*); c) the dislike of the title *mádam* in academic circles, alongside the existence of another *madám* paradoxically used with both a pejorative connotation (to refer to women whose social status the speaker wants to belittle) and a positive one (to refer to professional women, such as government ministers); d) the pervasive use of *sir*; and e) the borrowing of the Swahili titles *Bwana* ('Mr'), *Daktari* ('Dr'), and *Mwalimu* ('teacher, professor').

In addition to manifestations of its local culture, KenE is also coloured by the codemixing into it of Swahili expressions – not just the title terms mentioned above – seemingly to achieve a rhetorical effect, whether to persuade the addressee or to relate to them (especially the youth). And, finally, spoken KenE sounds more of written than spoken, particularly in its overwhelming use of non-contracted verb forms.

7 Survey of previous work and annotated bibliography

This survey first summarises the general overviews which present KenE in at least two of its three broad (and most researched) areas of study, namely pronunciation, grammar, and lexis. Then it follows the order of the chapters of this book. The paucity of publications under some chapters, e.g. that on discourse features, suggests that indeed very little has been published so far on this particular aspect of KenE. Only publications that are publicly accessible, and are thus known even outside Kenya, will be included in this survey. In each section, the survey is arranged chronologically.

7.1 General overviews

Hancock and Angogo (1982), English in East Africa

After setting East African English within the larger context of English in Africa, this article describes some of its phonological, grammatical, and lexical features. Although the term *Kenyan English* is not used in the paper at all, "East Africa (Kenya)", "Kenyan [...] speech", and "English in Kenya" are. More relevantly, some of the phonological "ethnolectal features" discussed in the paper are related to a number of specific indigenous languages of Kenya (Kikuyu, Embu, Kamba, Meru, Luyia, and Dholuo), while a number of words used in East African English are attributed to borrowing from Kiswahili, the national language of both Kenya and Tanzania. Perhaps owing to the fact that this paper is one of the very first ones to have been written on KenE, it contains several uninformed claims (especially in its discussion of phonological features) which detract from its quality. One of those claims suggests that "Bantu tone or Kiswahili stress affects [...] the distribution of stress" (1982: 313) e.g. in words such as *mischievous, protestant,* and *surprise,* which tend to be stressed on the second syllable for the first two and on the first syllable for the third. This suggestion is quite misleading because, firstly, even those speakers of KenE whose first language is not Bantu tend to stress those words that way and, secondly, Kiswahili is not a stress-timed language.

https://doi.org/10.1515/9781614516255-007

Zuengler (1982), Kenyan English

This is the first publication to have taken the bold step to use the phrase *Kenyan English*, even though at the same time it admits that "There [were] no institutionalized varieties of English in Kenya [...]" and that "[...] the variety and its registers [were] possibly incipient [and] these [had] not been described yet [...]" (1982: 114). But since "[...] there [were] certain formal aspects of English which [distinguished] it from standard, native speaker varieties of English" which had been "nativized" (115), the paper discusses some lexical, semantic and syntactic features of what it expressly refers to as "the Kenyanness of English". It groups them into "direct lexical transfers", "semantic shifts", "syntactic shifts", "speech functions", "registers", and "stylistic devices". What makes the paper most interesting to read is that it illustrates with extracts from published literature, including that by the most popular Kenyan fiction writer, Ngugi wa Thiong'o.

Schmied (1991a), *English in Africa*

Schmied (1991a) is one of those publications (such as Hocking 1974) that should be among the first to be read before embarking on writing on KenE. It is the "first attempt to penetrate and systematize the network of English in Africa" (1991a: 3). Its chapter 3 ("Language forms") is an overview of what the components of African English (namely East African English, West African English, and Southern African English) have in common in comparison with their parent variety (Standard British English) and of how they differ in the areas of pronunciation, grammar, vocabulary, meaning, and discourse. In the area of vocabulary, for example, the book identifies quite a number of "lexical Africanisms in East African English", some of which are said to be used specifically in Kenya. Schmied (1991a) thus provides valuable information about KenE within the wider context of African varieties of English.

Mesthrie (ed.) (2008a), *Varieties of English 4: Africa, South and Southeast Asia*

Volume 4 of the Varieties of English series (published by Mouton de Gruyter) contains separate expert papers on the phonology, on the one hand, and on the morphology and syntax, on the other hand, of the varieties representing West

African English (Cameroon, Nigeria, Ghana, Liberia), East African English (Kenya, Uganda, Tanzania), and South African English. In the case of Cameroon, Nigeria, and Ghana, the papers are about both the educated variety of English and its pidgin counterpart. South African English gets the lion's share, as it is described under four of its sub-varieties: White South African English, Black South African English, Indian South African, and Cape Flats English. So, the volume is useful for linguists interested in comparing educated KenE with its counterparts spoken in West Africa and for those who may be interested in comparing White Kenyan English (which was studied by Hoffmann 2011a) and Indian Kenyan English (yet to be studied) with their South African counterparts.

Budohoska (2014), *English in Kenya or Kenyan English?*

This book, derived from a doctoral dissertation, is one of the (more recent) publications on KenE that are based on the Kenyan sub-corpus of the International Corpus of English (ICE-K), in addition to field data directly collected from Kenya. Besides the history and status of English in multilingual Kenya, it discusses individual morphological, syntactic, lexical, semantic, and stylistic features of KenE. It provides rich statistical information related to the frequencies of occurrence of specific words and phrases in the ICE-K sub-corpus. It should be noted, though, that the statistics provided in Budohoska (2014) about the ethnic groups and, hence, the indigenous languages of Kenya in the midst of which English is used in the country are rather misleading, as several of them contradict those from the 2009 Kenya National Population and Housing Census. The natural expectation from the inviting title *English in Kenya or Kenyan English* is that the author would have ended the book by being assertive about the existence of an established KenE variety. However, rather anticlimactically, the book ends inconclusively: "Even though this study confirms that it is too early to claim the existence of Kenyan English it has identified and described its characteristic features which indicate that such a variety might be in the process of emerging" (2014: 160). This is an echo of the beginning of the book, where the author refers to *Kenyan English*, the very expression used there, as "a hypothetical new variety of postcolonial English" (2014: 11). It is hoped that the data used in the present book will prove beyond doubt that KenE is clearly more than just "a hypothetical new variety".

7.2 History of the development of language policy in Kenya and of KenE

Gorman (1974), The development of language policy in Kenya with particular reference to the educational system

This dense book chapter contains a wealth of information about the "mixed fortunes" of the English language in Kenya from the colonial period to a decade after the country's independence. It transpires from the long chapter that the pre-independence period was one during which there was no enthusiasm from the British colonial authorities and ordinary settlers to promote English, with the limited teaching of it being done "almost entirely by the missionary orders" (1974: 403). (The period runs from the latter half of the 19th century – when the first British explorers, missionaries, and colonizers came to Kenya, to 1963 – when Kenya became independent.) For its part, the first decade of the post-independence period was that of language policies and constitutional amendments initiated, or approved, by the Kenyan government, all of which expressly promoted English. The post-independence period obviously runs to the present day and, equally obviously, of it Gorman (1974) covers only the decade from 1964 to 1974, one which saw the institutionalized dominance of English but with, at the same time, strong lobbying for greater "competition" from Kiswahili.

Mazrui and Mazrui (1996), A tale of two Englishes: the imperial language in post-colonial Kenya and Uganda

This article focuses on the post-independence period during which the successive language policies developed in Kenya were much more in favour of English than they had been before. It documents, from earlier sources (among which Gorman 1974), how English, the only official language of Kenya at the time, had to face the competition from Kiswahili, the only national language of the country then (and today). But this competition existed more in debates among the elite than in reality, the reality being that the influence of English was stronger than ever. This is how the authors themselves put it: "The sentiments of poets and politicians notwithstanding, however, there is little doubt that the social, economic and technological developments and dynamics in the region, as well as globally, are gradually leading to the consolidation of English in East African society, 'nativizing' it in the process while at the same time giving it a more global outlook" (1996: 296).

Skandera (2003), *Drawing a map of Africa: idiom in Kenyan English*

In its section "The linguistic history in Kenya in outline" (2003: 8–15), Skandera takes us back to the earliest possible contact of East Africa with the English language in the second half of the 19th century, when " [...] British missionaries, and with them the formal teaching of Standard English, came to eastern Africa [...]" even though "[they], and later expatriate language teachers, trained only a small African elite needed as administrators to carry out the British policy of indirect rule" (2003: 11). Then the book moves very quickly from this initial period to the long wait (detailed in Gorman 1974) which the English language had to endure before it could be spread as widely as possible throughout Kenya, by progressively (from about 1950) being allowed to replace Kiswahili as the language of instruction. In 1963 it was even entrenched in the Constitution of the Republic of Kenya, which "stated competence in English as the only language requirement for election into parliament, and [...] specified English as the sole parliamentary language" (2003: 14). However, like Mazrui and Mazrui (1996), Skandera at the same time acknowledges the stiff competition which English faced from Kiswahili, manifested, for example, in "an amendment to the constitution [which, in 1974] replaced English with Swahili as the sole language of parliament [...]". This replacement was very short-lived, though, since, "[i]n 1975, another amendment to the constitution repealed the previous one [...]" (2003: 14).

Schmied (2004a), East African English (Kenya, Uganda, Tanzania): phonology

This book chapter starts its "Historical background" by also reminding us that "English came late to East Africa" (2004a: 919). Then it begins its section on "Colonial language policies" by commenting that "[d]espite British colonial rule, colonial language policy was not simply pro-English [...]", a good illustration of this being the fact that "[e]ven the three British mission societies [...] did not use English in their evangelization" (2004a: 920). Furthermore, Schmied (2004a) informs us that "[t]he expansion of English down the social hierarchy began mainly at the end of colonial rule with the democratisation and expansion of education that was to prepare Africans for independence" (2004a: 921).

Schneider (2007), *Postcolonial English: varieties around the world*

Section 5.10 (pp. 189–197) of this book is devoted entirely to Kenya. It outlines the kind of very detailed historical account given in Gorman (1974) of why the spread of English in Kenya from the country's first contact with the language in the second half of the 19th to about the middle of the 20th century was limited. The section is also an excellent synthesis of previous accounts by Mazrui and Mazrui (1996), Skandera (2003), and several others, one structured to reflect the first three phases (foundation, exonormative stabilization, and nativization) of the five suggested in Schneider's (2003) Dynamic Model of the development of new Englishes. Phase 1 runs from the 1860s to 1920, Phase 2 from 1920 to the late 1940s, and Phase 3 from the late 1940s to the present. Towards the end, the section illustrates some KenE features with phonological, lexical, and syntactic examples used in some previous publications, but adds that while "[d]escriptive work on Kenyan English is increasingly done [...] codification cannot really be envisaged at this point" (2007: 197). This will explain why, for Schneider (2007), KenE has yet to reach the "endormative stabilization" phase. However, based on the data collected for the present book, it can be argued that it has definitely reached it.

Higgins (2009), *English as a local language: post-colonial identities and multilingual practices*

In its section "The impact of Swahili on the spread of English in Kenya and Tanzania" (pp. 21–28), Higgins (2009), like e.g. Gorman (1974) and Skandera (2003) before her, provides an account of how limited the use of English was in Kenya in the "colonial beginnings" (2009: 24). At the same time, the author offers a new analytical perspective by stating that during this period "[i]n Kenya the development of Swahili was quickly oppressed by the British when it became a unifying force politically" and "threatened their political authority" (2009: 25). She also introduces a somewhat new angle from which to look at the fortunes of English vs. those of Kiswahili in colonial Kenya by stating that "the eventual promotion of English in Kenya's education system developed as a result of linguistic and economic difficulties" (2009: 25). Both types of difficulties have to do with the impossibility of implementing a multilingual policy which would have included first languages (such as Kikuyu) and English, in addition to Swahili (meant to be promoted as a lingua franca). The author writes: "[...] a general inadequacy of educational facilities, teachers and materials stymied the development of multilingual primary education" (2009: 25). She adds: "[a]s a result of difficulties posed by a general lack of proficiency in Swahili and the use of four indigenous languages in primary school, the decision to focus on English became inevitable in Kenya" (2009: 26).

7.3 Geography and demography

For aspects of geography and demography described in the present book, the key reference is the four-volume report on the 2009 Kenya population and housing census published by the Kenya National Bureau of Statistics (KNBS) and the various publications derived from it. The comprehensive report was published in 2010, while the subsequent, shorter versions of it, in the form of "analytical reports" on specific aspects such as "population dynamics" and "population projections", were published in 2012. The present book draws mainly on the second volume of the report, which is dedicated to the "population and household distribution by socio-economic characteristics". With regard to the cultural aspects that must influence KenE usage, the present author was not able to find previous work dealing with the topic in any meaningful way.

7.4 Phonetics and phonology

Schmied (1991b), National and subnational features in Kenyan English

This is the first piece of writing to have been published on the pronunciation aspects of KenE. It is presented as "a micro-sociolinguistic study on the co-variation of pronunciation, social and contextual variables" (1991b: 420). It is based on the reading of a continuous text, a list of isolated words and word pairs by 43 teacher trainees (25 female and 18 male) (1991b: 421–422). The results of the study show that KenE pronunciation differs from RP mainly in the realization of vowels, the "most salient and consistent" of which being the realization of RP /ɜː/ as /a/ (1991b: 425). This is a national feature. The paper also identifies subnational features, that is those pronunciations that are heavily influenced by the phonology of the regional-cum-ethnic mother tongues of Kenya, which the paper groups into four groups: Central Bantu, Western Bantu, Kalenjin, and Luo. With regard to the "differences between the sexes", the study reports that "as in most comparable studies [...] women are more 'conservative', closer to the [RP] norm", and, by the same token, that "[t]he 'Africanisation' is, in all three [reading] styles, more noticeable with the men than with the women [...]" (1991b: 428). *Africanisation* is the term used throughout the paper, in lieu of *kenyanisation*, but without any explanation for the preference of the former to the latter. The chapter on phonetics and phonology in the present book naturally deemed Schmied (1991b) its most appropriate starting point.

Schmied (2004a), East African English (Kenya, Uganda, Tanzania): phonology

This book chapter widens the scope of Schmied (1991a) from just Kenya to its two neighbours (to the south and to the west) in East Africa. The bulk of its section on phonology proper is more or less a summary of the key findings of Schmied (1991a). With regard to the consonants, the author concludes that "even though phoneme mergers are clearly noticeable, they do not endanger the [standard English] consonant system as a whole" (2004a: 926). One pertinent detail he points out is that "at the subphonemic level", one consonantal feature common to the three EAfE varieties is that "[...] EAfE is non-rhotic" (2004a: 927). Regarding the vowels, he concludes that "the vowel system of EAfE" is, on the whole, characterized by three phenomena: "(a) Length differences in vowels are levelled and not used phonemically [...]", "(b) The central vowels of STRUT, NURSE and lettER [...] tend towards half-open or open positions of BATH [...]", "(c) Diphthongs tend [...] to be monophthongized" (2004a: 927). As a result, "East African varieties [of English] tend towards a basic five-vowel system [...]" (2004a: 928), namely /i/, /u/, /a/, /o/, and /e/. Concerning the eight RP diphthongs, the author suggests that six of them have been maintained, with the only two that have not being FACE and GOAT, which are realised as /e/ and /o/, respectively. Schmied (2004a) also briefly deals with "suprasegmental patterns", in relation to which he identifies three typical ones: "the avoidance of consonant clusters, the more regular word stress and the special rhythm" (2004a: 928). The short discussion (2004a: 929–930) of these three patterns contains claims that need a further look into them, which Chapter 3 of the present book offers.

Hoffmann (2011a), The Black Kenyan English vowel system: an acoustic phonetic analysis

This is the first acoustic analysis done specifically on KenE vowels. It was motivated by the need to complement previous auditory phonetics studies, such as Schmied (2004a). The paper begins its conclusion by reporting that "[t]he present study has confirmed several observations of earlier auditory phonetic studies on [Black Kenyan English]: the vowel system is characterised by a considerable number of qualitative as well as quantitative mergers". But it also adds this qualification: "Nevertheless, the resulting system is not necessarily a five vowel one" (2011: 164). More clearly, elsewhere it states that Black Kenyan English is characterised by "a trend towards a seven vowel system with two front and two back mid-vowels" (2011: 147). So, to the five /i, u, a, o, e/ identified in Schmied (2004a), Hoffmann adds /ɛ/ and /ɔ/.

Itumo (2018), *Acoustic features of the non-ethnically marked Kenyan English in the speech of selected university lecturers*

This is a comprehensive acoustic study of KenE, which deals with both its vowel and consonant segments. Since the study is cast within an "element theory" framework, its primary objective was to determine the internal element structure of KenE phonemes. Nonetheless, it came up with findings that are still comparable with those of Hoffmann (2011a): while the latter reports 7 monophthongs for KenE, Itumo (2018) reports 8, namely /i/, /e/, /a/, /a:/, /o/, /o:/, /u/, and /u:/. This difference in number arises from the fact that, for the latter study, there is still vowel length in KenE, except, rather surprisingly, for /i/. Regarding diphthongs (which Hoffmann 2011a does not analyse), Itumo (2018) agrees with Schmied (2004a) that six of the eight RP diphthongs appear in KenE as well, and that the two exceptions are those in FACE and GOAT. Concerning the consonants (which Hoffmann 2011a does not analyse either), Itumo (2018) has come up with several interesting findings showing "sub-phonemic" differences between RP and the KenE pronunciation (e.g. the absence of aspiration after voiceless stops), and with one phonemic difference, namely that KenE has only one interdental fricative for both /θ/ and /ð/ (some kind of a slightly devoiced /ð/), which brings the author to conclude that KenE has 23 consonants (compared to 24 in RP). Although the account of phonetics and phonology in Chapter 3 of the present book is not primarily based on acoustic measurements, it still relates its findings to those of both Hoffmann (2011a) and Itumo (2018).

7.5 Morphology and syntax

Hocking (1974), *All what I was taught and other mistakes: a handbook of common errors in English*

Hocking (1974) "deals almost exclusively with mistakes of syntax or grammar and does not attempt to cover the field of pronunciation errors" (1974: xiii). Nevertheless, it is *the* publication which anyone wishing to write about Kenyan English should read first, if anything because it is the very first one on the topic. And although its subtitle (in its 1984 republication) says that the book is "A handbook for East Africa", the "mistakes" discussed in it are undoubtedly typically Kenyan, if we go by the words of the author himself that "[a]ll the material has been developed and very extensively tested in the course of ten years of remedial teaching [...] eight [of them] at the Kenya Institute of Administration" (1974: xiv). The book is structured around individual words, phrases, and clauses which the author had observed to be recurrent mistakes or potential sources of mistakes. A major reason why anyone intending to write about KenE should read Hocking (1974) is that it constitutes perhaps the best evidence that however "unwanted" they might have been, systematic features of KenE have persisted for almost half a century after the author strongly and passionately advised his target readership – the teachers of English in Kenya – to get rid of those "mistakes" from their own English and that of their students. And the author himself did not rule out this (undesirable!) prospect, when he wrote: "It is possible that we may eventually develop a local, East African form of English ourselves, and if we ever do, it may be that some of the mistakes we are dealing with in this book will be part of it. However, that time has hardly come yet" (1974: 59–60). The present author's point of view is that not only has that time come, but it is also almost certain that the "mistakes" identified by Hocking have all "made it" into KenE.

Hudson-Ettle (1998), *Grammatical subordination strategies in differing text types in the English spoken and written in Kenya*

Hudson-Ettle (1998), a doctoral dissertation, is the first book-length work on KenE. Based on the ICE-K sub-corpus, it focuses on how various types of subordinate clauses are linked to the main clause, whether in a complementation relationship or in an adverbial one. Although Hudson-Ettle (1998) is clearly about the high-level aspects of syntax, having to do with clauses rather than phrases, and while the present book is essentially about the grammar of individual lexical items and phrases, the former proved to be a useful reference for the specific section in the latter book that deals with the pervasive use of the conjunction/complementiser *that* in KenE.

Buregeya (2001), *Simplifying the rules in the grammar of Kenyan English*

This article looks at the various morphological and syntactic phenomena that characterize KenE from the point of view of second language acquisition, as a result of which they are viewed as manifestations of the learners' inevitable psycholinguistic process of reducing the learning load of complex rules (and their exceptions) by simplifying them. The major specific rules discussed in the article and, for most of them, illustrated with authentic examples from the major Kenyan dailies and postgraduate students' papers are the following: the non-use of the apostrophe (in contracted verb forms and genitive structures), the (surprisingly) pervasive lack of number agreement between subject nouns and their verbs and between nouns and their determiners, the limited use of articles (especially the definite article), the regularisation of exceptions (e.g. the use of the progressive -*ing* on stative verbs, the use of the modal *shall* with second and third persons, the generalised pluralisation of the premodifying noun in a N+N sequence), and the avoidance of subject-auxiliary inversion in *yes-no* questions. All the morphosyntactic aspects discussed in Buregeya (2001) have been picked up in Chapter 4 of the present book.

Mwangi (2003), *Prepositions in Kenyan English*

Mwangi (2003) is the "third book-length and comprehensive investigation of a specific aspect of KenE" (2003: 54), after Hudson-Ettle (1998) and Skandera (2003). Like the latter two, it was derived from a doctoral dissertation. More relevantly, it is the "first book-length investigation of a specific aspect of KenE grammar carried out by a Kenyan" (2003: 55). Mainly based on the ICE-K sub-corpus, it compares the frequencies and patterns of usage of prepositions between KenE and BrE. Among the many key findings (excellently summarised in the conclusion) are the following: a) "There is evidence of an attempt to simplify the English prepositional system in KenE" (2003: 228); b) "[...] certain prepositions in KenE do not perform all the semantic functions which they perform in BrE" (2003: 229); c) "The functions not performed by these prepositions are 'transferred' to other prepositions" (2003: 229); d) "[Certain] semantic distinctions thus made in BrE are lost in KenE" (2003: 230); e) "[...] prepositions of location have a wider semantic range in KenE than in BrE" (2003: 235). The use of the preposition *in* can be used to illustrate all these points, as when it is used where *at* (e.g. *in a departmental meeting*) or *on* (e.g. *in the bus*) would be expected in BrE. The book even claims that some prepositions are disappearing from KenE, two specific cases mentioned being "*beneath* and *underneath*, whose functions are performed by the more general preposition *under*" (2003: 239). The present book, which devotes a long section (4.5) on various aspects of the use of prepositions in KenE, could not afford to ignore Mwangi (2003).

Schmied (2004b), East African English (Kenya, Uganda, Tanzania): morphology and syntax

One very familiar morphological feature discussed in this paper is the use of the plural morpheme -s on non-count nouns (e.g. *advices*), while a less familiar one is the use of adjectives as adverbs (e.g. "*Do it proper*", 2004b: 935). A key observation the paper makes about the syntax of East African English is that "[T]he basic interrogative word order is maintained in indirect speech and questions" (2004b: 936). The features discussed in the paper are illustrated with examples drawn mainly from the East African component of the International Corpus of English, ICE-EA. (It should be noted, though, that Ugandan English is not represented in it.) Schmied (2004b) was meant to be just "[a]n outline of grammatical features of East African English (EAfE)" – even though almost half of it is actually about discourse and lexis as well – and suggests that "deviations in grammar [in EAfE] occur in much lower frequencies [than those in phonology]" (2004b: 927). However, the very many grammatical features discussed in Chapter 4 of the present book constitute strong evidence against this suggestion, at least as concerns KenE.

Buregeya (2006), Grammatical features of Kenyan English and the extent of their acceptability

This article picks up some of the features of KenE discussed in Buregeya (2001) and many others (26 in total) and subjects them to acceptability judgements from more than ten dozen language-and-communication university students from eight successive classes. The results of this survey do not necessarily confirm what one would have expected in terms of which features were more acceptable than others and, hence, ones which would be claimed to be more entrenched in KenE usage. Quite revealingly, among the least acceptable (2006: 216) are those that are definitely very frequent in spoken KenE, including *Us we will contribute [up to] ten thousand shillings each* (which was the least acceptable of all), *If you do that [anyhow], you cannot be able to succeed*, and *The [equipment has] cost [a lot] of money, isn't it?* This reveals that the written-versus-spoken parameter is a key variable to take into account before claims can be made about which features are pervasive in KenE and which are not.

Buregeya (2012), Kenyan English

Written as part of the *Mouton World Atlas of Variation in English* (WAVE), this book chapter discusses a number of morphological and syntactic structures which it claims to be either frequent or rare in KenE. The frequent-features category distinguishes between the very frequent ones, labelled "pervasive" in the book (e.g. the dropping of the definite article *the* before unique elements like institutions) and the just frequent ones (e.g. the use of *us* + NP, as in *Us teachers work very hard*). The rare-features category includes the deletion of *to* before infinitives, as in *to enable somebody do something*. In its conclusion, the chapter notes that some of the very frequent features of KenE were not part of the 235 WAVE features that were investigated. One such feature is the use of the (semantically logical phrase) *(as) compared to* instead of *than* (as in *This chapter was easier to write compared to the preceding one*).

Buregeya (2013), Contextual variability in the acceptability of Kenyan English grammatical features

Using grammaticality judgements from more than two hundred educated KenE speakers, this article explores the contextual variability that was touched on in Buregeya (2001) and Buregeya (2006) and which seemed to characterize the acceptability and the use of various KenE features. It focuses on three linguistic contexts: the very lexical item that a given feature involves, the position of this feature within the sentence, and the type of the sentence itself (i.e. whether interrogative, negative, or positive in form). The article reports three observations: first, the features involving lexical items which are highly frequent in standard international English tend to be less acceptable than those involving less frequent ones; second, when the features in focus occur in salient (i.e. initial and final) positions in a sentence they tend to be less acceptable than when they appear in medial positions; third, certain features are less acceptable when they appear in statements (whether negative or positive, as in *I am/am not knowing anybody who has it?*) than in question constructions (*Might you be knowing somebody who has it?*). This issue of contextual variability permeates chapters 3 to 6 of the present book.

Aldrup (2014), The morphosyntax of Kenyan English

This undergraduate degree monograph is an excellent critique of Buregeya (2012) based mainly, but not only, on the ICE-K sub-corpus. It states clearly that its aim is to "try and ascertain whether Buregeya's ratings correspond to the linguistic reality in Kenya as captured in the ICE-K" (2014: 10). It opens its conclusion by reporting that "[t]he present study has shown that the morphosyntax of Kenyan English is characterized by a number of features that are clearly distinct from the British norm" (2014: 33), but closes it in a less assertive way: "Whether these features will stabilize and lead to the emergence of a new national standard remains to be seen" (2014: 35). What is more directly relevant to the comparison of the features identified in Buregeya (2012) is that Aldrup (2014) came to the conclusion that "it also became clear that none of the WAVE features could actually be rated highly pervasive in KenE [...]" (2014: 35). However, this conclusion was made after the author herself acknowledged that "the ICE-K has its shortcomings" and that "the WAVE [survey] has its weak points as well [...] such as the subjectivity of ratings and high level of abstraction [...]" (2014: 35). Both of these qualifications may justify, at least in part, the fact that Buregeya (2012) identified eleven "highly pervasive" features while for Aldrup (2014) not a single one qualifies to be in this category.

7.6 Lexis and semantics

Bulili (2002), *A lexico-semantic analysis of Kenyan English (KenE)*

This MPhil thesis is the first systematic survey and discussion of individual words and phrases that can be argued to be typical of KenE. It identifies a total of 93 items, grouped into four categories: 27 "borrowed words" (e.g. *mwananchi* 'citizen'), 29 "coinages" (e.g. *something small* 'bribe'), 7 "semantic modifications" (e.g. *severally* 'several times'), and 30 "special collocations" (e.g. *leave alone* 'let alone'). What is commendable about Bulili (2002) is that, although it does not draw upon the ICE-K, it illustrates (almost) every single one of the words and phrases under analysis with examples drawn from authentic, meticulously documented, written and spoken sources. This enables it to conclude that "there are vocabulary items in English usage in Kenya, which are lexically and semantically typical of KenE" (2002: 147), even though "[the] respondents [were] reluctant to have KenE introduced in the major domains of education, the media, government administration, commerce and industry" (2002: iv).

Skandera (2003), *Drawing a map of Africa: idiom in Kenyan English*

Derived from a doctoral dissertation, this book, on such an apparently narrow topic as idioms, is arguably the best documented publication on KenE. It contains eleven chapters, excluding the introduction, and it is not until Chapter 8 that it starts focusing on the idioms of KenE. However, every chapter of it, including the one on methodology (Chapter 3), contains rich (historical, cultural, and linguistic) information about KenE. Even the chapters 5 to 7 about "International English idioms" illustrate with specific examples from KenE. The author does not content himself with drawing illustrative examples only from the ICE-K; he draws many more from the data which he himself collected by means of a meticulous and varied methodology (preference, substitution, and completion tests, complemented by informant interviews), which allowed him to report detailed frequencies of use, although he deliberately avoided having recourse to "rigorous statistical analyses with respect to the significance of the results [...]" (2003: 70). Almost every paragraph in the book's 11–page "Conclusions" chapter is an invitation to further research on KenE beyond its semantic aspects. The present book was very much inspired by Skandera (2003).

Atichi (2004), *The semantic distinctiveness of Kenyan English*

This is an MA thesis inspired by Skandera (2003). It concentrates on the extent to which the KenE meanings of the lexical items under study are acceptable to KenE speakers. The informants in the research were university students and lecturers and secondary school teachers. The study found that the informants were much more familiar with the so-called KenE meanings than with the dictionary ones for the same words. The highest acceptability rate for any given meaning from the latter category was only 7%. Atichi (2004), like Bulili (2002), although using a different terminology to refer to them, groups the KenE meanings into four categories: "altered meanings" (e.g. *severally* 'several times'), "added meanings" (e.g. *upcoming* 'with a promising future'), "word-formation meanings" (e.g. *mob justice* 'punishment meted out to a criminal by a crowd of people'), and meanings of "words borrowed from indigenous Kenyan languages" (e.g. *panga* 'machete').

Buregeya (2007), Aspects of the vocabulary of Kenyan English

This paper is basically a discussion of an expanded list of lexical items whose forms (whether loan words from indigenous languages of Kenya or coinages of

KenE) and meanings were discussed in Skandera (2003) and Atichi (2004). And, in turn, it served as the starting point for Chapter 5 of the present book.

7.7 Discourse features

Schmied (2004b), East African English (Kenya, Uganda, Tanzania): morphology and syntax

Although Schmied (2004b) specifically refers to "morphology and syntax" in its title, it contains a short section on "Discourse" (see pp. 937–938). There the author briefly discusses three elements: a) emphasis, as expressed through "the stressed reflexive pronoun [...] placed in front and repeated as a personal pronoun afterwards"; b) culture-specific discourse, such as the use of elaborate greeting formulas and other circumlocutory discourse "before launching into a direct request" instead of "toning down direct requests with [e.g.] *Would you mind telling me*", and c) the code-mixing with some Swahili expressions to achieve politeness. The use of direct requests in making polite requests in KenE is discussed in more detail in the present book's section 6.2.1.

Schmied (2004c), Cultural discourse in the Corpus of East African English and beyond

This article "looks at culture-specific lexemes in East African English and compares [them] with the international reference varieties of English, British and American" (2004c: 251). It does this because "[...] for even the cursory observer of East African English the most obvious language level with strong cultural implications shining through is the lexicon". With specific reference to KenE, the article uses as examples political terms borrowed from Swahili, such as *Nyayo* (referring to former "President Moi's 'footsteps' policy following Kenyatta's heritage in Kenya") and *wananchi* ('ordinary citizens'), and socioeconomic terms such as *matatu* ('a minibus or a bus used for public transport') (2004c: 252).

Buregeya (2004), Written requests in Kenyan English: an illustration of L1 culture adaptation in L2 acquisition

This paper shows how the grammatical structures used to express polite requests are not only simpler in form (with the most elaborate of them typically consisting of just the mitigators *please* and *kindly* + an imperative verb) but are also more limited in range, consisting almost only of three structures: a) a bare imperative structure, b) a mitigator + imperative, and c) the express use of the verb *request* (as in *I request that you* + verb). The paper is relevant to the present book to the extent that it deals with polite requests as one aspect of what the latter calls "cultural appropriateness phenomena" (see section 6.2).

7.8 Survey of previous work

Skandera (1999), What do we *really* know about Kenyan English?

With its section 2 "Survey of relevant studies", this is the first survey of the work that had been written on KenE at the time. And while it acknowledges that "A detailed and comprehensive description of the characteristic features of any of the East African Englishes [...] is largely missing", it adds that "Nonetheless, [there are] eight studies [that] contain partial compilations of features considered typical of the Kenyan variety", even though "Only four of them deal expressly with KenE" (1999: 220). The eight studies span a two-decade period, with Hocking (1974) as the starting point.

Skandera (2003), *Drawing a map of Africa: idiom in Kenyan English*

Chapter 4 of this book is devoted to a "Review of related literature". It is an extended version of the "Survey of related studies" section in Skandera (1999), not only in that it includes more pieces of writing on the topic but also in that it gives more details on those previously reviewed. The chapter warns us, though, that "[...] 6 of the 13 studies [reviewed] are not readily available" (2003: 75), either because they are out of print or were "never distributed [...] commercially" (2003: 76).

Mwangi (2003), *Prepositions in Kenyan English*

Mwangi (2003) opens its survey by referring to the question posed in the very title of Skandera (1999), namely "What do we really know about Kenyan English?", and then sets out to summarise the existing literature at the time: first, the studies on grammatical aspects, chief among which is Hocking (1974); second, those on pronunciation features (which get the lion's share of coverage), chief among which is Schmied (1991b); third, those on lexical aspects, chief among which is Skandera (2003), even though this latter deals specifically with idiomatic phrases rather than individual lexical items proper. In relation to this third aspect, Mwangi (2003) makes it clear that at the time there was "no systematic study that [had] been carried out specifically on the lexical aspects of KenE" (2003: 50). Mwangi's (2003) survey of the existing literature is very useful because for almost each of the works surveyed it points out its strengths and limitations, with a greater emphasis being put on the latter, which it summarises in the following terms: "As we have noticed with most of the studies on KenE and EAfrE so far, the lack of empirical evidence is their major shortcoming" (2003: 54). Section 4.5 ("Aspects of the prepositional phrase") of the present book was much inspired by Mwangi (2003).

8 Sample texts

The written texts selected into this chapter represent careful written English, which, in most cases, will have been edited by more than one person. This kind of English is meant to reflect the educated KenE that the present book set out to describe. With the exception of 8.11 and 8.15, each text, however short it is, contains at least two features (be they lexical, morphological, syntactic, or discourse-related) discussed earlier in the book. The features in question are pointed out, as language points of interest, below each text. In each case, cross-reference is made to the specific section where they were discussed. The texts have been reproduced verbatim, except for the highlighting, in bold face, of the features under analysis. (The word *sic* has been added after some potentially misleading typographical mistakes in the original.)

8.1 An email (on 4 May 2018) from the Chairman of the CHUNA Board, University of Nairobi (ca. 735 words)

Dear Members
Re: Products Review/Rebranding and Loans Default
Allow me to first of all express my gratitude on behalf of Ø$_{art}$ CHUNA Board and Staff for your overwhelming support during this challenging period of our[1] Sacco. Your goodwill has kept the spirit of the Sacco alive.
I want to assure you that the challenge**s** the Society is currently facing, especially liquidity, **is** being addressed by the Board and very soon our operatio**ns** and core business **is** going to stabilize.
As you are aware, part of the Society's capital structure is made up of debt from Ø$_{art}$ Bank which the Society has been servicing at a rate of 14.5% p.a. (1.25 p.m.) on Ø$_{art}$ reducing balance method exclusive of other inherent costs, like insurance, appraisal fee, etc. However, our loans are issued at 12% p.a. (1 %p.m.) on Ø$_{art}$ reducing balance method. The two compared, that is, we borrow at 14.5% and loan out at 12% means we are making a loss margin of 2.5% p.a. This does not make business sense and therefore is unsustainable going forward. We cannot be in business to make deliberate loses, that simply means we see, hear and even understand the consequences but ignore Ø$_{compl}$ with impunity.
Based on the above facts and others we intend to articulate during our Education meetings, we have reviewed our rates upwards to at least allow the Society to Break-Even. We intend to operationalize the new rates as early as this month of May, 2018. This will affect the new

---

[1] CHUNA is the name of the University of Nairobi's employees' savings and cooperative society (SACCO).

loans which will be issued from that date going forward and not loans issued before that date. We shall communicate the actual effective date soon.

We have also fragmented the current products to give you more options and choices in accessing funds at the Society. Our aim is for the Society to live up to the mandate **to** which it was established, that is harness membe**rs** Savings and issue loans to meet member's [sic] financial needs. It is not right that a members [sic] visits the Society for financial assistance but cannot get **the same** because we have no product(s) which can accommodate his/her payslip or terms of repayment.

We also have Savings products which **shall** earn the Saver attractive returns in terms of interest and other incentives. By you taking up such products you will also be helping the Society to self-Finance instead of $\emptyset_{compl}$ relying on external expensive funding.

We are organizing decentralized Education meetings to enlighten you on this and other issues like amendments to our By-Laws as directed by the Commissioner for Co-operatives Development. **In** these meetings we shall provide soft drinks/tea but not payment of allowances for the participants. We therefore encourage you to engage with us on our (the Society) Social media platforms we are going to open soon, email and even one on one. We also encourage you to support th**is** critical initiative**s**.

Secondly, I wish to address our members who are on short-term employment contract terms of service. First of all we appreciate your continued support to CHUNA despite the many challenges with the contract renewal issues some of you might be facing. **In** CHUNA, members have equal rights whether employed on permanent terms, long-term or short-term contract terms. I wish to state the following;

1. For **those** who have ran [sic] out of contracts and **the same** are yet to be renewed and also have no loan at all with CHUNA but **has** guaranteed some loans, CHUNA will grant you a loan of $\emptyset_{art}$ 80% value of your deposits. The 20% $\emptyset_{compl}$ is to cover **for** some of the loans you have guaranteed.

2. In case your contract has been renewed, CHUNA will give you a loan, $\emptyset_{prep}$ an amount which you can qualify $\emptyset_{prep}$ or repay within the contract period $\emptyset_{prep}$ considering all the factors.

[...]

Last but not least, you mandated us to ensure cost reduction at the Society. On that basis we are in the process of acquiring legal expertise to review some of the contracts which have been used to swindle funds from the Society and find a way $\emptyset_{prep}$ how some of them can be renegotiated downwards and/or terminated forthwith. You will see during this month an advert in a local daily calling for pre-qualification of specific suppliers including legal services and any other category which has been used previously as $\emptyset_{art}$ means of siphoning $\emptyset_{art}$ society funds. This will **enable us dismantle** the culture of possible collusion**s** with suppliers on preferential selective tendering.

Yours faithfully,
[S. D. L.], Chairman **to** the Board

The following are the language points of interest from Text 8.1:
- lack of number agreement in the first two of the following phrases: a singular verb was used for a plural subject (see 4.1.1) in *the challenges [...] is, those who have [...] but has guaranteed*;

- lack of number agreement: a singular determiner was used for a plural noun (see 4.1.3) in *this critical initiatives*;
- omission of the article (see 4.3.1), whether definite or indefinite, in the places marked Ø$_{art}$;
- omission of the obligatory complement (see 4.4.7) *them* in *but ignore Ø with impunity* (Note also the omission of obligatory complements in *instead of Ø relying* and in *the 20% Ø is to cover*, but not after verbs, and, hence, not discussed earlier in the book);
- omission of prepositions (see 4.5.4) in the places marked Ø$_{prep}$;
- use of a different preposition (see 4.5.1): *in* instead of *at* in *in CHUNA*, *to* instead of *for* in *the mandate to which*, *in* instead of *at* in *in meetings*, and *to* instead of *of* in *Chairman to the Board*;
- use of the N + N sequence instead of the N's + N one (see 4.3.2) in *on our (the Society) Social media platforms* and in *society funds*;
- overuse of the modal *shall* (see 4.4.2), in *Savings products which shall earn*;
- omission of *to* after *to enable* (see 4.4.15) in *This will enable us dismantle the culture*;
- giving the verb a PP-object instead of an NP-one (see 4.4.9) in *to cover for some of the loans* instead of *to cover some of the loans*;
- use of the plural *-s* on a non-count noun (see 4.2.1), namely *collusion* in *the culture of possible collusions*; and
- use of *the same* as an all-embracing anaphor (see 6.1.2) in *for financial assistance but cannot get the same* and *for those who have ran out of contracts and the same are yet to be renewed*.

8.2 An email (on 8 Aug 2018) from the CEO of CHUNA, University of Nairobi (ca. 140 words)

Dear Esteemed member
It has come to my attention that **members** with Emergency and School Fess [sic] loans **have been deducted twice** for the month of July, 2018. I sincerely apologize for the inconvenience and embarrassment this has subjected you to. This arose **due to** the fact that the **University payroll office** gave us recovery codes after the deadline to submit deductions had elapsed and only accorded us a day to adjust **all the recoveries** done in June, 2018 and include Ø$_{art}$ loans granted in July, 2018. In the process the office failed, albeit unintentionally, to stop the June **recoveries** under one percent.
CHUNA **commits** Ø$_{compl}$ to fully refund those affected **due to** the above said change in codes. Attached, find the refund form, fill Ø$_{compl}$ and forward Ø$_{compl}$ to our office for immediate processing. Remember to attach the July, 2018 payslip.
[M. O.], Chief Executive Officer [of CHUNA]

The language points of interest are:
- violation of selection restrictions (see 4.4.11) in *members [...] have been deducted*;
- use of a different preposition (4.5.1): *due to* instead of *from* or *out of* in *this arose due to*, and *due to* instead of *by* in *affected due to*;
- use of the N + N structure instead of the genitive *-'s* structure (see 4.3.2) in *the University payroll office* instead of *the University's payroll office*;
- use of the plural *-s* on the non-count noun *recovery* (see 4.2.1) in *all the recoveries* and *June recoveries*;
- omission of the definite article in *include Ø loans granted in July*; and
- omission of obligatory complements (see 4.4.7) in the form of the reflexive pronoun *itself* in *CHUNA commits Ø to fully refund* and of the pronoun *it* in *fill Ø and forward Ø to our office*.

8.3 From draft "Regulations and Syllabus for Master of Medicine in Urology", a University-of-Nairobi syllabus presented in Oct 2013 (ca. 150 words)

3.0 CREDIT TRANSFER AND EXEMPTIONS

The applicant may, on Ø$_{art}$ recommendation of the School Board and approval by Ø$_{art}$ Senate, be allowed to transfer up to a maximum of one third of the non-clinical taught course units offered **in** the programme.
3.1 Ø$_{art}$ Applicant seeking Ø$_{art}$ course exemption shall send a formal application to the Director, Board of Postgraduate Studies through the Dean, School of Medicine. Justification **of** Ø$_{art}$ request Ø and evidence **of** credentials which would support such a request **shall** be attached to the application.
3.2 Ø$_{art}$ Applicant registered **in** any other surgical speciality training**s** offered in the Department of Surgery, may after Ø$_{art}$ successful completion of part one examinations transfer credits and register **in** the Urology course **at** Year 3.
3.3 Holders of Ø$_{art}$ MMed General Surgery degree **of** the University of Nairobi or any equivalent qualification recognised by Ø$_{art}$ Senate **shall** be exempted from Part one. Applications for exemptions **shall** be processed after payment of Ø$_{art}$ prescribed fee.

The language points of interest are:
- omission of articles (see 4.3.1) in the places marked Ø$_{art}$;
- overuse of *shall* with 3rd pers. subjects (4.4.2), namely *a request, Senate*, and *applications*;
- use of a different preposition (see 4.5.1) in the following phrases: *in* instead of *on* in *course units offered in the programme, of* instead of *for* in *justification of*

request, in instead of for after the verb register in registered in any other [...] trainings and in register in the Urology course at Year 3, at instead of in in the latter phrase, and of instead of from in degree of the University of Nairobi;
- use of the plural -s on a non-count noun (see 4.2.1) in in any other [...] trainings; and
- having one preposition shared by two conjuncts requiring different ones (see 4.5.3) in the phrase request and evidence of credentials, in which the noun request should have taken for as its own preposition.

8.4 From an article, by W.T. & M.M., on an election petition, in *The Standard* (25 Mar 2013, p. 1 & p. 4) (148 words)

[...]
   Today the court **shall** deal with preliminary and housekeeping matters before the actual hearing begins. The rules require that the hearing must start within two days after the pre-trial conference and will continue uninterrupted.
   The judges have in the past week been holding long private sittings with the Supreme Court Registrar, going through all the papers and other material filed in court since Saturday last week.
   "By the time the parties are coming to court for hearing, the judges **will be knowing** what kind of case they have," said Chief Registrar of the Judiciary [...] on Saturday.
   The court **shall** also formerly [sic] consolidate the three petitions and give directions on how they **shall** be heard and determined expeditiously.
   It **shall** frame the contested and uncontested issues in the petitions. Some of the parties have filed their questions, which they want the court to determine and make declarations on. [...]

The language points of interest are:
- the overuse of the modal *shall* with 3rd pers. subjects (see 4.4.2) and
- the use of the progressive on a stative verb (see 4.4.1) in *will be knowing*.

8.5 From "State to review public varsity fees", an article by A.O. in *The Standard* (12 Jun 2013, p. 7) (161 words)

[...]
   In addition, lecturers will have their pay reviewed depending on courses they teach starting October. This means that lecturers in the faculty of medicine, for example, are likely to draw higher salaries than their counterparts in the faculty of arts and social sciences.
   It also means that fees charged **on** science subjects are likely to be **higher compared to** Ø$_{rel}$ arts disciplines once the board for the fund is put in place. Currently, all lecturers

in the same category take home similar salaries regardless of programmes they teach **Ø**$_{\text{prep}}$.

Once implemented, there **shall** be clear disparities in pay for lecturers in public universities. Section 53 of the Universities Act establishes the fund that **shall** provide monies for financing universities.

The minister said that the board will be in place in three months' time. But the Universities Academic Staff Union (Uasu) immediately said that they would only appreciate the new concept once they **have** seen the pay proposal from the Salaries and Remuneration Commission.

The language points of interest are:
- overuse of *shall* with 3rd pers. subjects (see 4.4.2) in *there shall be* and *the fund that shall provide*;
- lack of backshift in indirect speech (see 4.4.6) in *have* (in *[the Union] said that they would only appreciate the new concept once they have seen the pay proposal*);
- use of *compared to* as the second element of the comparative (see 4.6) in *higher compared to arts disciplines*;
- use of the preposition *on* instead of *for* in *fees charged on science subjects* (see 4.5.1);
- omission of the preposition (see 4.5.4) *on* in *programmes they teach* Ø; and
- non-use of an anaphor (see 6.1.1) which was expected after *compared to*, for the phrase to read like this: *fees charged on science subjects are likely to be higher compared to [those charged for] arts disciplines*.

8.6 From "Fund Status Report as at 30th October 2009", a notice from the youth enterprise fund in *The Standard* (18 Nov 2009, p. 44) (ca. 150 words)

Youth Employment Scheme Abroad

The Fund is mandated to **facilitate young people** whose services are not engaged locally but are required abroad to secure temporary employment. In regard to this objective the Fund has:
- Established a Steering Committee on Youth Labour Export whose membership comprises key government ministries such as Labour, Foreign Affairs, Immigration and Ø$_{\text{art}}$ relevant private sector players.
- Is in the process of engaging three local Private Employment Agents to **source** and place Ø$_{\text{art}}$ **youth in** Ø$_{\text{art}}$ international labour market.
- Over 1,500 **youth have been facilitated** to secure employment abroad particularly in the Middle East. The **youth are facilitated** to secure necessary documentation**s** such passports and certificates of good conduct as well as in financing of air tickets as part of relocation cost.

– Ø$_{art}$ Cabinet Memorandum on Ø$_{art}$ Youth Labour Export Framework is now ready, and has been presented to the Cabinet Office for deliberation and approval.

The language points of interest are:
- violation of selection restrictions (see 4.4.11): human objects have been used, instead of non-human ones, in *to facilitate young people, the youth have been facilitated / the youth are facilitated*, and *to source [the] youth*;
- omission of the definite article (see 4.3.1) in the places marked Ø$_{art}$;
- use of a different preposition (see 4.5.1): *at* instead of *of* in *status report as at*, and *in* for *on* in *place youth in international labour market*;
- use of the plural *-s* on the non-count noun *documentation* in *to secure necessary documentations;* and
- omission of the genitive *'s* (see 4.3.2) after the noun *fund* in *Fund Status Report*, which should have been *"[the] Fund's Status Report"*

8.7 From "Setting the record straight on school heads", an article by J.K. in *The Standard* (24 Apr 2015, p. 13) (222 words)

[...]
　　The truth of the matter is that the regulations have not interfered with the power of the Teachers Service Commission (TSC) to appoint school heads and to exercise disciplinary control over them should circumstances **warrant** Ø$_{compl}$. The regulations acknowledge the Constitutional and legal mandate of the TSC. [...]
　　[...] It is only proper that the TSC identifies a replacement that the Cabinet Secretary can now **entrust** the management of school finances and other resources Ø$_{prep}$ –a power which in law is outside the purview of the TSC.
　　[...] Under Schedule Four (15) and (16) the Cabinet Secretary for Education is in charge of education policy [...] and [...] Universities, tertiary educational institutions and other institutions of research and **higher learning** and primary schools, special education, secondary schools and special education institutions. [...]
　　The ministry organised four consultative meetings [...]. **Except** Ø$_{prep}$ the 9/10/2014 meeting, all other meetings were covered by the media. There was **a give and take** Ø$_{compl}$ during many of these sessions and the substance of the Regulations was **interrogated** by the stakeholders. I believe the **substance** of the Regulations **are** well meant and if supported is likely to give Kenya a platform upon which it can deliver to her children the best education within its power, in terms of resources and the fund of knowledge, experience and wisdom all players in education have.

The language points of interest are:
- omission of an obligatory complement (see 4.4.7) in *should circumstances warrant* Ø;

- omission of the preposition *with*, which should go with the verb *entrust*, and of the preposition *for* after *except* (see 4.5.4);
- violation of selection restrictions (see 4.4.11) in *the Regulations were interrogated*, where the non-human subject *regulations* was used a human one;
- use of *higher learning* for *higher education* (see 5.6.1);
- lack of number agreement (see 4.1.2) in *the substance of the Regulations are well meant*, where a plural verb, *are*, was used for a singular subject, *substance*;
- omission of the genitive *'s* (see 4.3.2) after the noun *teachers* in the *Teachers Service Commission*

8.8 From an advertised pre-publication blurb of a book called *Handbook for data analysis using SPSS*, by O.M.J. (2002) (164 words)

This Handbook on Data Analysis using SPSS for Windows assumes no prior knowledge of SPSS and statistics. Data Analysis **skills is** a prerequisite for any body [sic] who wants to work at the decision making level of any result oriented institution. For research institutions the knowledge is paramount and mandatory. It provides a well-illustrated and simplified text to learners of data analysis-using SPSS for windows.

The Handbook is divided into three sections.

The Introductory Section introduces SPPS for windows and data analysis. Discover what data analysis and SPSS are, what SPSS can do for you.

The SPSS Procedures **Sections discusses** all the data analysis procedures available in SPSS for windows. This section provides detailed explanations of how the procedures are used and how to access them.

$Ø_{art}$ Statistics in Pure English Section provides $Ø_{art}$ very detailed discussion of the most commonly used statistics available in SPSS and other similar statistical programs. The author explores how similar statistical **programs handles** data and the types of output**s** they produce.

[...]

The language points of interest are:
- lack of number agreement (see 4.1.1) in *skills is a prerequisite, the [...] sections discusses,* and *programs handles data*
- omission of articles (see 4.3.1) in the places marked $Ø_{art}$; and
- use of the plural *-s* on a non-count noun, *output*, in *the types of outputs they produce* (see 4.2.1).

8.9 From "Knut to call nationwide strike from September 1", an article by E.M. in the *Sunday Nation* (5 Aug 2018, p. 2) (170 words)

Teachers insist that they will hold a nation-wide strike from September 1 and paralyse Ø$_{art}$ schools' opening for Ø$_{art}$ third term.

The Kenya National Union of Teachers (Knut) is demanding that the Teachers Service Commission scraps the performance appraisals policy and Ø$_{art}$ delocalisation of teachers.

Knut assistant secretary general Collins Oyuu said during the Mombasa Annual General Meeting that the teachers employer **has** introduced the policies without consulting teachers.

He said the union will order all teachers to camp at the TSC offices come September.

"If the TSC does not listen to us on August 21, 2018, we shall say enough is enough and down our tools come September 1. We will not open schools. We love industrial peace but Ø$_{art}$ TSC has remained adamant," he said.

He said delocalisation **has** affected the teachers and learners' performance in a number of schools. "Out of Ø$_{art}$ 70 schools that were affected by fires, 58 had new principals," said Mr Oyuu.

He said despite Ø$_{art}$ teachers furthering their studies, most of them remained stagnant in their job positions.

The language points of interest are:
- omission of the definite article (see 4.3.1) in the places marked Ø$_{art}$;
- lack of backshift in indirect speech (see 4.4.6) in *has introduced* and *has affected*;
- use of a different preposition (see 4.5.1) in *during the Mombasa Annual General Meeting*, where *during* was used instead of *at*; and
- omission of the genitive *'s* (see 4.3.2) after the noun *teachers* in *the teachers employer*

8.10 From a questionnaire by a University-of-Nairobi MA student, W.W.B. (Apr 2001) (87 words)

Basic questions in interviewing and elicitation
1. Are you a typical Bukusu?
2. Lubukusu and English are different languages. **Isn't it?** If yes, how different?
3. In a conversation or discussion with your fellow Lubukusu speakers who also know English, you supplement and complement Lubukusu with English often enough by switching from Lubukusu to English and mixing the two languages. **Isn't it?**
4. **You also bring in other languages you know like Kiswahili?**
5. Why don't you just stick to Lubukusu to say what you have to say?
[…]

The language points of interest are:
- the use of *isn't it?* as an invariant question tag (see 4.12); and
- no subject-auxiliary inversion (see 4.7) in the question *You also bring in other languages you know like Kiswahili?*

8.11 From a questionnaire by a University-of-Nairobi MA student, T.B. (May 2012) (80 words)

MA (Linguistics) Research Questionnaire Marking Scheme
[...]
    Instruction: Answer the questions as precisely as possible in the spaces provided. Fill in the blanks with a suitable word or phrase.
a) James is fatter **than/compared to/as compared to**. [Note:] **Any correct form of the comparative**.
b) Mary is less talkative **than/compared to/as compared to** Wairimu.
c) Compared to Joy, Tom is tall.
d) The bull, compared to the cow, is fat.
e) Her speech was better **than/compared to/as compared to** her mother's.

The language point of interest is:
- use of *compared to/as compared to* as alternative forms to *than* in the comparative structure (see 4.6)

8.12 From Daniel Nyaga's (1997) book *Customs and traditions of THE MERU* (304 words)

After all that had been done, the suitor's mother prepared a very big gourd of gruel and went to visit the girl's family. Afterwards, the mother of the engaged girl filled the same gourd with gruel and went to see the family into which her daughter would marry. This was followed by a team of women from **the suitor's side** who, carrying gourds of gruel, went to see **where** their son was **courting**. In turn, the women from **the girl's side** filled the same gourds with gruel and went to see **where** their daughter would **be married**. All this exchange of offerings, besides being marriage celebrations, was also meant to be a chance for the in-laws to get acquainted.

    When all this had been done, the mother of the boy mobilized the women of the whole village with offerings of gruel, and went to see **where** their son **was getting married**. At the same time, the suitor prepared himself to go and introduce himself to his in-laws and to offer some tobacco to his girlfriend. The engaged girl received that tobacco and took it to her "grandmother," the midwife. She **never snuffed Ø$_{prep}$** it nor it was snuffed by any other member of her family. Afterwards the girl's mother organized all the women of her village, and after filling with gruel the gourds that had been left by the women from **the suitor's side**, they went to see **where** their daughter would **be married**.

While taking offerings to **the suitor's home**, the women who were closely related to the girl did not simply enter **the suitor's home**. They refused to enter until they were given gifts. They even had cloaks spread on the way for them to step on, as they entered. This was done in honour of their daughter **that** she was a virgin. (p. 112)

The language points of interest are:
- use of *to be married somewhere* (and the additional *to court somewhere*) (section 5.2.1);
- use of *never* for *did not/would not* (section 4.4.23);
- omission of the preposition (section 4.5.4) *at* in *she never snuffed* O *it*;
- use of *side* for 'place where one lives' (see *those sides* in section 5.2.1) in *from the suitor's side* and *from the girl's side*;
- non-use of the pronoun *it* as an anaphor (section 6.1.1) in *the girl did not simply enter the suitor's home*; and
- ubiquitous use of *that* in *their daughter that she was a virgin* (see section 4.3.5; however, in this particular case *that* does not introduce a complement to the preceding noun but reads as a conjunction of the type of *because*).

8.13 From Meja Mwangi's (1974) novel *Carcase for hounds* (223 words)

The fear in his mind changed into complete emptiness. Then came understanding and hate. He had been **swindled** Ø$_{compl}$ and thrown to the dogs. He felt cheated and fooled. The hate boiled up and turned into murderous rage. Rage directed at the little general, the soldiers, the governor, everybody. Mixed with this hate was fear, an instinctive fear, the fear of a trapped beast. He had been tricked into a corner and had his back to the wall. He did not wish to be destroyed. The beast in him barred [sic] its fangs in a bid to fight its way to safety. His overloaded mind **whirled** Ø$_{prep}$ and nausea flowed **through** him in the brew of fear and hate. Fight his way out, fight his way out, fight his.... Out to where? To his home? To Ø$_{art}$ Pinewood Forest Station? Back to Simba and the D.C.? Never! He would fight his way to hell, to heaven, to the grave. Anywhere but the Forest Station. Yes, he would plough through his enemies. He would blast his way through everything.

The big red eyes cleared and in the place of the confused darkness he saw the face of the District Commissioner, tall, proud and white. White and hateful. D.C. Kingsley and his mascot Simba. The general's eyes bored into the two and **his hate was for them**. [...] (pp. 102–103)

The language points of interest are:
- omission of an obligatory prepositional phrase (see 4.5.4), namely *out of*, after *swindled* in *He had been swindled Ø and thrown to the dogs*;

- use of a different preposition (see 4.5.1), namely *through* instead of *inside* in *nausea flowed through him*;
- omission of an obligatory preposition (see 4.5.4), possibly *around*, after the verb *whirl* in *His overloaded mind whirled Ø*;
- omission of the definite article (see 4.3.1) in *To Ø Pinewood Forest Station?*; and
- transposition of a local language idiom into English (see 2.3) in *his hate was for them*.

8.14 From Ngugi wa Thiong'o's (1982) novel *Devil on the cross* (353 words)

[...] But my father neglected *family planning* of any kind. We, his children, were more numerous than his **lands** could support. I inherited only three things from my father: literacy, words of wisdom from his own mouth, and the letters he used to get from his European friends.

"I was educated at Maambere, Thogoto, in Kiambu district, and I completed *junior secondary*. I became a teacher and taught in the same school for about two years. Then I joined the High Court, Nairobi, as a *court clerk and interpreter*. Our saying is true: **the young of a goat steals like its mother**. I had returned to my father's origins.

'The State of Emergency found me in the law courts. My father was one of the elders who were used by the colonialists in the purges of the Mau Mau followers. But as for me, I didn't know which side I should support. I wasn't cold and I wasn't hot. I stayed like that, lukewarm, hiding in the law courts as an interpreter for those involved in murder cases.

"When **Uhuru** came, it found me in the same law courts, *marking time* with my meagre salary. I paused to check which way the Earth was spinning, the direction of the wind. Then I started a few petty businesses, shop- and **hotel**-keeping. But they were never profitable. In those days I had not yet mastered the holy commandments of a man-eat-man society.

"It was then that I recalled my father's words before he died of **the disease of overeating**. He had summoned me to his house, and he told me: 'You have to be wise to start a few shops and **hotels**. We have a saying that a pastoralist does not stay in one spot. On a journey, nobody carries food for anyone else; each traveller carries his own. A salary is nothing for a man with a family to **look up to**. But at the same time, we black people cannot manage petty trades that need patience. It's only Indians who have that kind of patience. My son, listen to your father's words of love. [...] (pp. 101–102)

The language points of interest are:
- use of the plural *-s* on the non-count noun *land* in *his lands* (see 4.2.1);

- transposition of a local language idiom into English (see 2.3) in *the young of a goat steals like its mother* (to mean something like 'like father like son') and in *he died of the disease of overeating* (for, simply, 'he died of overeating');
- use of the Swahili word *uhuru* to mean *'independence'* (see 5.1.1);
- use of the word *hotel* to mean 'eating place/restaurant' (see 5.3.1); and
- use of a different preposition in *a family to look up to* instead of *a family to look after*.

8.15 Picture of the name of a furniture-selling shop on Koinange Street, Nairobi

The language point of interest is the use of the plural *-s* on the non-count noun *furniture* (see 4.2.1).

8.16 The audio samples

The audio samples selected into this chapter consist of readings, by six informants, of the *Boy Who Cried Wolf* passage (mentioned in 3.1.1). Three of the informants are male (MHN, MLN, and MWB) and three are female (FLB, FLN1, and FLN2). The language point of interest in these readings is the realisation of the different vowels of English, as tested against Wells's (1982) lexical sets. (The informants FLB, FLN1, and FLN2 also read some words in isolation and the same words placed in a short text, targeting the existence or otherwise of the diphthong /eɪ/ and the schwa /ə/.)

9 Conclusion

Chapters 3 to 6 are very detailed descriptions of the phonological, morphological, syntactic, lexical, and discourse features of KenE. In relation to the phonetic and phonological aspects, the key observations made in Chapter 3 are the following: a) KenE has replaced the mid central vowels of RP with /a/, although the schwa seems to have survived in one or two phonological contexts; b) it has neutralised the distinction between short and long vowels, in most words; c) it has monophthongised the RP /əʊ/ (perhaps in every word concerned) and /eɪ/ in most words; d) in most words it has adopted a spelling-pronunciation involving all the five vowel letters (with <e> being the most involved and <u> the least involved); e) it has regularised the pronunciation of the letters <h> and <b> by phonetically realising them where they are silent in RP (except in the words *hour/hourly*, *debt* and *doubt*); e) it has neutralised aspiration where it is expected after voiceless stops in RP; f) it practically allows no assimilation, elision and *r*-linking; g) it has adopted a single stress-placement rule for (seemingly) all the verbs ending in <ate> and for most of those ending in <ise>; h) it has made the adjectival suffix *-ative* a stress-attracting one; i) it has significantly reduced the very many exceptions associated with stress placement in compound words by stressing the first element, as its general rule; at the same time, though, it has created its own exception to this rule: it stresses the second element if this is a letter or a number (e.g. *South ʹB* and *Form ʹFour*); j) it has created its own stress-placement contrasts between verbs and nouns (e.g. *a ʹrequest* vs. *to reʹquest*); l) in its intonation patterns, it has widened the scope of the level tone at the expense of the rising one.

Regarding morphological and syntactic features, Chapter 4 discusses close to sixty grammatical features that are pervasive in KenE, thus showing that KenE is as much a matter of grammar as it is of pronunciation and lexis, contrary to the suggestion made in earlier literature (e.g. Hancock and Angogo 1982, Hudson-Ettle and Schmied 1991, and Schmied 2004b), that it is "mainly" a matter of the latter two. It transpires from the chapter that the pervasiveness in question depends both on text type (whether written or spoken) and on the nature of the lexical item involved. With regard to text type, a few features are pervasive only in spoken KenE (e.g. the use of *can be able* and of the invariant tag *isn't it?*), while a few others (much fewer, though) are pervasive only in written KenE (*e.g.* the use of the infinitive for the modal *should* and the complementation with *as follows*). But the vast majority of features are pervasive in both speech and writing. Examples are the following eight, which are the most frequent in the sample texts in Chapter 8: a) the use of a different preposition from that expected in StdIntE, b) the omission of prepositions, c) the omission of the definite article,

d) the use of the plural -s on non-count nouns, e) the use of the modal *shall* with 3rd person subjects, f) the lack of tense backshift in indirect speech, g) the use of *compared to* instead of *than* in a comparative construction, and h) the omission of obligatory complements after verbs. Concerning the idea that the degree of pervasiveness depends on which lexical item is involved, and even on the linguistic context around it within a sentence/utterance, one example is the omission of the definite article systematically before the noun *majority* but not before other nouns; another one is the use of the progressive *-ing* with the stative verb *know*, which is more frequent when the progressive auxiliary *be* is preceded by a modal (*he may be knowing*) than when it is not (*he is knowing*). Chapter 4 also provides illustration of the fact that even the highly pervasive grammatical features of KenE still coexist with their StdIntE counterparts, as variants of the same structure. (This coexistence was not observed in the case of pronunciation aspects and seems to apply to only a few cases in relation to lexical and discourse aspects.)

With regard to the lexical and semantic aspects of KenE, Chapter 5 first discusses a list of some sixty loan words (e.g. *uhuru* 'independence') which KenE has borrowed from some indigenous languages of Kenya, mainly Swahili. It is such loanwords that are easily associated with KenE. Second, it discusses a much longer list of (some 170) expressions referred to as coinages of KenE, almost all of which are existing English words which, in most cases, were combined to form phrases and sentences whose meanings express local Kenyan practices, realities, beliefs, etc. (e.g. *to lie low like an envelope* 'to keep a low profile'). KenE speakers in general are not aware that those coinages are in fact not StdIntE expressions. Third, the chapter discusses another list of (a little over a hundred) expressions, mostly single words, which exist in StdIntE dictionaries, but to which KenE has assigned additional meanings not (yet) available in these dictionaries. An example is *double-decker*, used in KenE to mean also 'a bunk bed'. In terms of the coexistence of variants observed in the case of grammatical structures, most of the loanwords have translation equivalents, but most of these latter do not necessarily have the same connotations as the loanwords themselves and, thus, are usually not used as their variants. Some of the coinages (e.g. *to wreck havoc* 'to wreak havoc') have their StdIntE equivalents as their potential variants. In reality, though, no evidence is available that whoever uses *wreck havoc* also uses *wreak havoc*. Towards the end of Chapter 5, the focus shifts from the lexical items that are KenE proper to the preference, of KenE, for BrE words over their AmE equivalents or for AmE words over their BrE equivalents. The chapter reports, as one might have expected, that on the whole KenE (so far) uses more BrE expressions than their AmE counterparts. Finally, the chapter traces a few of KenE expressions and additional meanings to Indian English (e.g. the meaning of *a hotel* as 'a restaurant') and points to some future potential influence from Nigerian English (through cinema) and South African English (through sports).

As for the discourse aspects of KenE, Chapter 6 first focuses on anaphoric reference and highlights the fact that KenE makes little use of 3rd person pronouns and determiners (notably *it, its*, and the demonstrative pronoun *those*) while at the same time overusing the expressions *the same, whereby, this is, is where, is when*, and *another*. Then the chapter shifts to two areas of discourse that have to do with cultural appropriateness: polite requests, on the one hand, and titles and forms of address, on the other. The key observation made about the former is that KenE basically uses three request structures: *please* + verb, *kindly* + verb and *I am/was requesting you to* + verb. Rarely does it use the indirect structures involving modal verbs, past tense forms, question structures, and negative statements accompanied by a question tag. About titles and forms of address, a key observation is that KenE attaches much importance to *Dr*, both as a title and a form of address, and to *Sir*, as a form of address. A KenE peculiarity was also noted: the mixed "fortunes" of the address form *madam*. This word is much disliked when used (and stressed as *mádam)* to address an academic, and also when used (and stressed as *madám*) to belittle the social status of the addressee; on the other hand, it is well received when used to refer to professional women. The chapter ends by looking at two other, unrelated, markers of KenE discourse: one linguistic, namely the overwhelming use of non-contracted forms, which makes spoken KenE sound rather like written, and one sociolinguistic, namely the codemixing of Swahili words into English to achieve a rhetorical effect.

The paragraphs above offer a good synopsis of the panoply of markers of KenE, some of which are shared by other varieties of English in Africa and beyond. Future research into KenE is likely to unearth more features of it, like those related to types and functions of tones and to additional meanings assigned to StdIntE words. But further research is particularly needed to look deeper into the variability (related to spelling, to nature of lexical item, to position in a sentence, etc.) that is quite pervasive in KenE usage. In the meantime, though, it is hoped that this book will lead those linguists who still insist on using the phrase "English in Kenya", instead of "Kenyan English", thus sticking to the idea that the latter is still in its "nativization phase" and has not yet reached its "endonormative stabilization phase", to change their minds and confidently speak of *Kenyan English*. (The two phases correspond to stage 3 and stage 4, respectively, in E. Schneider's Dynamic Model of New Englishes; see e.g. Schneider 2003: 253.)

The present book may be seen as a major step in codifying KenE, whose features are so entrenched that most KenE speakers are not even aware of them (with the exception of some lexical items, notably the loanwords). And even when they are, they are equally aware that they cannot do away with them, even if they wanted to. This is particularly true of pronunciation features: teachers of English in Kenya are very much aware of the RP pronunciation of the word *word*, for example, but many of them cannot even imitate it. Equally, even when KenE speakers are told that both *chairman* and *chairmen* have exactly the same pronunciation, they simply do not want to accept this fact (the way L2 learners of French do not want to accept that both *Monsieur* and its plural *Messieurs* have exactly the same pronunciation). They somehow need to rely on a spelling-based pronunciation in order to distinguish between one chairman and more than one. It would equally be a waste of time (if not too much asking!) to ask KenE speakers to have a different pronunciation (as is the case in RP) for each one of the three <*o's*> in *protocol*. And, beyond the pronunciation of individual sounds, so would it be to ask them to stop using *isn't it?* where it is not grammatically correct in StdIntE. Similarly, most KenE speakers would not easily abandon saying *so that we can be able to succeed*. Nor would it be easy for them to insert an auxiliary and a direct object into the "direct" question *you get?*, uttered with a level tone – a question that tends to punctuate a conversation between KenE speakers. Therefore, unlike Sey (1972: 10), who said, while describing Ghanaian English, that "[t]he surest way to kill Ghanaian English, if it really exists, is to discover it and make it known", the present author is not worried at all that raising the KenE speakers' awareness to its features will kill these. The roots of KenE are now too deep to be uprooted. Hocking's (1974) very strong language warning against the grammatical "mistakes" he was describing then has had no tangible effect at all. Neither has the explicit provision – in the textbooks used in primary and secondary schools in Kenya – for teaching British English grammar rules and the Received Pronunciation model. Likewise, no description of KenE at this late stage can reverse its endonormative stabilization course.

References

Abdulaziz, Mohamed H. & Ken Osinde. 1997. Sheng and Engsh: Development of Mixed Codes among the Urban Youth in Kenya. *The International Journal of the Sociology of Language* 125(1). 43–63.
Aldrup, Marit. 2014. *The morphonsytax of Kenyan English*. Kiel: Christian-Albrechts-Universität zu Kiel Bachelor's degree thesis.
Alo, M. A. & Rajend Mesthrie. 2008. Nigerian English: Morphology and Syntax. In Rajend Mesthrie (ed.) 2008a. *Varieties of English 4: Africa, South and Southeast Asia*, 323–339. Berlin: Mouton de Gruyter.
Aoko, David. 1974. Language Use within the African Independent Churches of Nairobi. In Wilfred H. Whiteley (ed.), *Language in Kenya*, 253–262. Nairobi: Oxford University Press.
Atichi, Alati R. 2004. *The semantic distinctiveness of Kenyan English*. Nairobi: University of Nairobi thesis.
Bauer, Laurie. 1983. *English word-Formation*. Cambridge: Cambridge University Press.
Bhatt, Rakesh M. (2008). Indian English: Syntax. In Rajend Mesthrie (ed.) 2008a. *Varieties of English 4: Africa, South and Southeast Asia*, 546–562. Berlin: Mouton de Gruyter.
Biber, Douglas, Stig Johansson, Geoffrey Leech, Susan Conrad & Edward Finegan. 1999. *Longman grammar of spoken and written English*. London: Longman.
Bobda, Simo Augustin. 2008. *Cameroon English: Phonology*. In Rajend Mesthrie (ed.) 2008a. *Varieties of English 4: Africa, South and Southeast Asia*, 115–132. Berlin: Mouton de Gruyter.
Bokamba, Eyamba G. 1982. The Africanization of English. In Braj B. Kachru (ed.) *The Other Tongue: English across cultures*, 77–98. Urbana: University of Illinois Press.
Bosire, Moyaka. 2008. *Sheng: The phonological, morphological, and social profile of an urban vernacular*. New York: State University of New York at Albany dissertation.
Braber, Natalie & Jonnie Robinson. 2018. *East Midlands English*. Boston and Berlin: Mouton de Gruyter.
Brown, H. Douglas. 2000. *Principles of language learning and teaching*, 4th edn. New York: Longman.
Budohoska, Natalia. 2014. *English in Kenya or Kenyan English?* Frankfurt am Main: Peter Lang.
Bulili, L. Ethel. 2002. *A lexico-semantic analysis of Kenyan English (KenE)*. Eldoret: Moi University MPhil thesis.
Buregeya, Alfred. 2001. Simplifying the Rules in the Grammar of Kenyan English. *Occasional Papers in Language and Linguistics* 1. 1–23.
Buregeya, Alfred. 2004. Written Requests in Kenyan English: An Illustration of L1 Culture Adaptation in L2 Acquisition. *Occasional Papers in Language and Linguistics* 2. 104–123.
Buregeya, Alfred. 2006. Grammatical Features of Kenyan English and the Extent of Their Acceptability. *English World-Wide* 26(2). 199–216.
Buregeya, Alfred. 2007. Aspects of the Vocabulary of Kenyan English: An Overview. *Occasional Papers in Language and Linguistics* 3. 1–32.
Buregeya, Alfred. 2008. *CLE 102: English usage in Kenya*. Course materials written for the Centre for Open and Distance Learning. Nairobi: University of Nairobi.
Buregeya, Alfred. 2009. *Course notes for CLL 303: Introduction to Sociolinguistics*. Centre for Open and Distance Learning (CODL). Nairobi: University of Nairobi.

Buregeya, Alfred. 2012. Kenyan English. In Bernd Kortmann & Kerstin Lunkenheimer (eds.), *The Mouton world atlas of variation in English*, 466-474. Berlin: Mouton de Gruyter.

Buregeya, Alfred. 2013. Contextual Variability in the Acceptability of Kenyan English Grammatical Features. *The University of Nairobi Journal of Language and Linguistics* 3. 1–27.

Chomsky, Noam & Morris Halle. 1968. *The sound pattern of English*. New York: Harper & Row.

Constitution of Kenya 2010 (the). Nairobi: Government Printer.

Cruttenden, Alan. 2014. *Gimson's pronunciation of English*, 8th edn. London and New York: Routledge.

Crystal, David. 2003. *The Cambridge encyclopedia of the English language*, 2nd edn. Cambridge: Cambridge University Press.

Deuber, Dagmar, Carolin Biewer, Stephanie Hackert & Michaela Hilbert. 2012. Will and would in selected new Englishes: General and variety-specific tendencies. In Marianne Hundt & Ulrike (eds.). *Mapping unity and diversity world-wide: Corpus-based studies of New Englishes*, 77–102. Amsterdam and Philadelphia: John Benjamins.

Davies, Alan 1995. Proficiency or the Native Speaker: What are We Trying to Achieve in ELT? In Guy Cook & Barbara Seidlhofer (eds.), *Principle & Practice in Applied Linguistics*, 145–157. Oxford: Oxford University Press.

Fisher, Allestree E.C. 2000. Assessing the State of Ugandan English: An Account of the Nature and Key Features of an East African Variety. *English Today 61* 1 (1).57–61 and 110.

Fromkin, Victoria, Robert Rodman & Nina Hyams. 2011. *An Introduction to Language*, 9th edn. Wadsworth: Cengage Learning.

Githinji, Peter. 2006. *Sheng and variation: The construction and negotiation of layered identities*. Michigan: Michigan State University dissertation.

Githinji, Peter. 2008. Ambivalent Attitudes: Perception of Sheng and Its Speakers. *Nordic Journal of African Studies* 17(2). 113–136.

Githiora, Chege. 2002. *Sheng*: Peer Language, Swahili Dialect or Emerging Creole? *Journal of African Studies* 15(2). 159–181.

Githiora, Chege. 2016. Sheng: The Expanding Domains of an Urban Youth Vernacular. *Journal of African Cultural Studies*. Available online at: http://dx.doi.org/10.1080/13696815.2015.1117962. Accessed: 2 Sep 2016.

Gorman, Thomas P. 1974. The Development of Language Policy in Kenya with Particular Reference to the Educational System. In Wilfred H. Whiteley (ed.), *Language in Kenya*, 397–453. Nairobi: Oxford University Press.

Greenbaum, Sydney & Randolph Quirk. 1990. *A student's grammar of the English language*. London: Longman.

Gupta, Anthea Fraser. 1999. Standard Englishes, Contact Varieties and Singapore Englishes. In Claus Gnutzmann, (ed.) *Teaching and learning English as a global language: Native and non-native perspectives*, 59–72. Tübingen: Stauffenburg Verlag.

Gut, B. Ulrike. 2008. Nigerian English: Phonology. In Rajend Mesthrie (ed.) 2008a, *Varieties of English 4: Africa, South and Southeast Asia*, 35–54. Berlin: Mouton de Gruyter.

Gut, B. Ulrike. 2009. *Introduction to English phonetics and phonology*. Frankfurt am Main: Peter Lang.

Habwe, John. 2010. Politeness Phenomena: A Case of Kiswahili Honorifics. *Swahili Forum* 17. 126–142.

Habwe, John. 2016. *Pendo la karaha*. Nairobi: Moran (E.A.) Publishers.

Hancock, Ian F. & Rachel Angogo. 1982. English in East Africa. In Richard W. Bailey & Manfred Görlach (eds.), *English as a world language*, 306–323. Ann Arbor: University of Michigan Press.

Hewings, Martin. 2013. *Advanced grammar in use*, 3rd edn. Cambridge: Cambridge University Press.

Higgins, Christina. 2009. *English as a local language: Post-colonial identities and multilingual practices*. Bristol: Multilingual Matters.

Hilbert, Michaela & Manfred Krug. 2012. Progressives in Maltese English: A Comparison with Spoken and Written Text Types of British and American English. In Marianne Hundt & Ulrike Gut (eds.). *Mapping unity and diversity world-wide: Corpus-based studies of New Englishes*, 103–135. Amsterdam and Philadelphia: John Benjamins.

Hocking, Benjamin Dominic W. 1974/1984. *All what I was taught and other mistakes: A handbook of common errors in English*. Nairobi: Oxford University Press. [Republished in 1984 as *Common errors in English: A handbook for East Africa*).

Hoffmann, Thomas. 2010. White Kenyan English. In Daniel Schreier, Peter Trudgill, Edgar Schneider & Jeffrey P. Williams (eds.), *The lesser-known varieties of English*, 286–310. Cambridge: Cambridge University Press.

Hoffmann, Thomas. 2011a. The Black Kenyan English Vowel System: An Acoustic Phonetic Analysis. *English World-Wide* 32(2). 147–173.

Hoffmann, Thomas. 2011b. *Preposition placement in English: A usage-based approach*. (Studies in English Language). Cambridge: Cambridge University Press.

Huber, Magnus. 2008. Ghanaian English: Phonology. In Rajend Mesthrie (ed.), 2008a, *Varieties of English 4: Africa, South and Southeast Asia*, 67–92. Berlin: Mouton de Gruyter.

Huber, Magnus & Kari Dako. 2008. Ghanaian English: Morphology and Syntax. In Rajend Mesthrie (ed.), 2008a, *Varieties of English 4: Africa, South and Southeast Asia*, 368–380. Berlin: Mouton de Gruyter

Hudson-Ettle, Diana. 1998. *Grammatical subordination strategies in differing text types in the English spoken and written in Kenya*. Chemnitz: Technischen Universität Chemnitz PhD Dissertation.

Hudson-Ettle, Diana & Josef Schmied. 1991. Deviation and language awareness in Kenyan popular literature. In Josef Schmied (ed.), *English in East and Central Africa 2* [Bayreuth African Studies, Series 24]. 1–20.

Hudson-Ettle, Diana M. & Josef Schmied. 1999. *Manual to accompany the East African component of the International Corpus of English*. Chemnitz: Chemnitz University of Technology manuscript.

Hundt, Marianne & Katrin Vogel. 2011. Overuse of the Progressive in ESL and Learner Englishes – Fact of Fiction? In *Exploring second-language varieties <i> and Learner Englishes: Bridging the gap*. [Studies in Corpus Linguistics 44], Joybrato Mukerjee & Marianne Hundt (eds.), 145–165. Amsterdam: John Benjamins.

International Encyclopedia of Linguistics (the), 2nd edn., 2003. Oxford: Oxford University Press.

Itumo, Joshua. (2018). *Acoustic features of the non-ethnically marked Kenyan English in the speech of selected university lecturers*. Nairobi: Kenyatta University PhD thesis.

Jowitt, David. 1991. *Nigerian usage: An introduction*. Lagos: Longman Nigeria.

Kallen, Jeffrey L. 2013. *Irish English – Volume 2: The Republic of Ireland*. Berlin: Mouton de Gruyter.

Kenya Institute of Education. 1987. *Integrated English: A course for Kenya secondary schools - Students' book 1*. Nairobi: Jomo Kenyatta Foundation.

Kenya National Bureau of Statistics (KNBS). 2010a. *The 2009 Kenya Population and Housing Census, Vol. II: Population and Household Distribution by Socio-Economic Characteristics*. Available online (through: Downloads - Population and Housing Census 2009) at: www.knbs.or.ke/index.php?option..population-and-housing-census-2009. Accessed: 30 April 2017.

Kenya National Bureau of Statistics. 2010b. *The 2009 Kenya Population and Census Highlights*. See: www.knbs.or.ke/index.php?option..population-and-housing-census-2009. Accessed: 30 April 2017.

Kenya National Bureau of Statistics. 2012a. *The 2009 Kenya Population and Housing Census: Analytical Report on Population Atlas, Vol. XV*. See: www.knbs.or.ke/index.php?option..population-and-housing-census-2009. Accessed: 30 April 2017.

Kenya National Bureau of Statistics. 2012b. *The 2009 Kenya Population and Housing Census: Analytical Report on Population Dynamics, Vol. III*. See: www.knbs.or.ke/index.php?option..population-and-housing-census-2009. Accessed: 30 April 2017.

Kenya National Bureau of Statistics. 2012c. *The 2009 Kenya Population and Housing Census: Analytical Report on Population Projections, Vol. XIV*. See: www.knbs.or.ke/index.php?option..population-and-housing-census-2009. Accessed: 30 April 2017.

Kenya National Bureau of Statistics. 2012d. *The 2009 Kenya Population and Housing Census: Analytical Report on Population Projections, Vol. XIV*. See: www.knbs.or.ke/index.php?option..population-and-housing-census-2009. Accessed: 30 April 2017.

Kortmann, Bernd & Kerstin Lunkenheimer (eds.). 2012. *The Mouton world atlas of variation in English*. Berlin: Mouton de Gruyter.

Kortmann, Bernd & Kerstin Lunkenheimer (eds.). 2013. *The electronic world atlas of varieties of English. Leipzig: Max Planck Institute for Evolutionary Anthropology*. (Available online at http://ewave-atlas.org. Accessed: 20 July 2018)

Kramsch, Claire. 1998. *Language and Culture*. Oxford: Oxford University Press.

Labov, William. 1966. *The social stratification of English in New York City*. Washington, DC: Center for Applied Linguistics.

Leech, Geoffrey & Jan Svartvik. 2002. *A communicative grammar of English*, 3rd edn. New Delhi: Pearson Education.

Leech, Geoffrey, Benita Cruickshank & Roz Ivanič. 2001. *An A-Z of English grammar & usage*. New edition. London: Longman.

Lightbown, Patsy M. & Nina Spada. 2013. *How languages are learned*, 4th edn. Oxford: Oxford University Press.

Mazrui, Alamin. 1995. Slang and Code-Switching: The Case of *Sheng* in Kenya, *Afrikanistiche Arbeitspapiere* 42. 168–179.

Mazrui, Alamin M. & Ali A. Mazrui. 1996. A Tale of Two Englishes: The Imperial Language in Post-Colonial Kenya and Uganda. In Joshua A. Fishman, Andrew W. Conrad & Alma Rubal-Lopez (eds.), *Post-imperial English: Status change in former British and American colonies, 1940–1990*, 271–302. Berlin: Mouton de Gruyter.

Mbangwana, Paul. 2008. *Cameroon English: Morphology and syntax*. In Rajend Mesthrie (ed.), 2008a, *Varieties of English 4: Africa, South and Southeast Asia*, 416–427. Berlin: Mouton de Gruyter.

Mesthrie, Rajend (ed.) 2008a. *Varieties of English 4: Africa, South and Southeast Asia*. Berlin: Mouton de Gruyter.

Mesthrie, Rajend. 2008b. Synopsis: Morphological and Syntactic Variation in Africa and South and Southeast Asia. In Rajend Mesthrie (ed.), 2008a, *Varieties of English 4: Africa, South and Southeast Asia*, 624–635. Berlin: Mouton de Gruyter.

Mesthrie, Rajend. 2008c. Black South African English: Morphology and Syntax. In Rajend Mesthrie (ed.), 2008a, *Varieties of English 4: Africa, South and Southeast Asia*, 488–500. Berlin: Mouton de Gruyter.

Muthiora, John Mwangi. 2004. *The use of Engsh as a peer language among the youth in Nairobi*. Nairobi: University of Nairobi thesis.

Mwangi, Meja. 1974. *Carcase for hounds*. Nairobi: East African Educational Publishers.

Mwangi, Serah. 2003. *Prepositions in Kenyan English. A corpus-based study in lexical grammatical variation*. Aachen: Shaker Verlag.

Mwangi, Serah. 2004. Prepositions Vanishing in Kenya. *English Today 77* 20(1). 27–32.

Nyaga, Daniel. 1997. *Customs and traditions of THE MERU*. Nairobi: East African Educational Publishers.

Nyauncho, Osinde K. 1986. *Sheng: The social and structural aspects of an evolving language*. Nairobi: University of Nairobi Bachelor's degree thesis.

Nyutho, Ngure Edwin. 2015. *Evaluation of Kenyan film industry: Historical perspective*. Nairobi: University of Nairobi dissertation.

Oduor, A. N. Jane. 2010. A SWOT Analysis of the Language Policies in Education in Kenya and Ethiopia. *The University of Nairobi Journal of Language and Linguistics1*. 86–102.

Ogechi, Nathan. 2005. On Lexicalization in *Sheng*. *Nordic Journal of African Studies* 14 (3). 334–355.

Okombo, D. Okoth. 1987. *Study of English 1, Section C, Lecture 5: Kenyan English*. Nairobi: University of Nairobi Lecture Notes.

Plag, Ingo. 2003. *Word-formation in English*. Cambridge: Cambridge University Press.

Prabhakar Babu, B.A. 1971a. *Prosodic features in Indian English: Stress, rhythm and intonation*. Hyderabad: CIEFL postgraduate diploma research project.

Prabhakar Babu, B.A. 1971b. Prosodic features in Indian English: Stress, rhythm and intonation. *CIEFL Bulletin* 8. 33–39.

Quirk, Randolf, Sydney Geenbaum, Geoffrey Leech & Jan Svartvik. 1985. *A Comprehensive grammar of the English Language*. London: Longman.

Radford, Andrew. 1988. *Transformational grammar: A first course*. Cambridge: Cambridge University Press.

Roach, Peter. 2004. British English: Received Pronunciation. *Journal of the International Phonetic Association* 34(2). 238–245.

Roach, Peter. 2009. *English phonetics and phonology: A practical course*, 4th edn. Cambridge: Cambridge University Press.

Sailaja, Pingali. 2009. *Indian English*. Edinburgh: Edinburgh University Press.

Sala, Bonaventure. 2003. *Aspects of the Cameroon English sentence*. Yaoundé: University of Yaoundé dissertation.

Samper, David Arthur. 2002. *Talking Sheng: The role of a hybrid language in the construction of identity in youth culture in Nairobi, Kenya*. Pennsylvania: University of Pennsylvania dissertation.

Sand, Andrea. 2004. Shared Morpho-Syntactic Features in Contact Varieties of English: Article Use. *World Englishes* (23)2. 281–298.

Schmied, Josef. 1991a. *English in Africa*. London: Longman.

Schmied, Josef. 1991b. National and Subnational Features in Kenyan English. In J. Cheshire (ed.), *English around the World: Sociolinguistic properties*, 420–432. Cambridge: Cambridge University Press.

Schmied, Josef. 2004a. East African English (Kenya, Uganda, Tanzania): Phonology. In Edgar W. Schneider, Kate Burridge, Bernd Kortmann, Rajend Mesthrie & Clive Upton (eds.), *A handbook of varieties of English. Vol. 1: Phonology*, 918–930. Cambridge: Cambridge University Press.

Schmied, Josef. 2004b. East African English (Kenya, Uganda, Tanzania): Morphology and Syntax. In Edgar W. Schneider, Bernd Kortmann, Rajend Mesthrie & K. Burridge (eds.), *A handbook of varieties of English: A multimedia reference tool. Vol. 2: Morphology and syntax*, 929–947. Berlin and New York: Mouton de Gruyter.

Schmied, Josef. 2004c. Cultural Discourse in the Corpus of East African English and Beyond: Possibilities and Problems of Lexical and Collocational Research in One Million-Word Corpus. *World Englishes* 23(2). 251–260.

Schmied, Josef. 2007. Exploiting the Corpus of East-African English. In Roberta Facchinetti (ed.), *Corpus linguistics 25 years on*, 317–332. Amsterdam/New York: Rodopi.

Schmied, Josef. 2012. Tanzanian English. In Bernd Kortmann & Kerstin Lunkenheimer (eds.), *The Mouton world atlas of variation in English*, 454–465. Berlin: Mouton de Gruyter.

Schneider, Agnes J. 2015. *Ghanaian English: A corpus-based analysis of the progressive and the modal WILL*. Freiburg i.Br.: Albert-Ludwigs Universtät dissertation.

Schneider, Edgar W. 2003. The Dynamics of New Englishes: From Identity Construction to Dialect Birth. *Language* 79(2). 233–281.

Schneider, Edgar W. 2007. *Postcolonial English: Varieties around the world*. Cambridge: Cambridge University Press.

Sey, Kofi Abakah. 1972. *Ghanaian English: An exploratory survey*. London: Macmillan.

Skandera, Paul. 1999. What Do We *Really* Know about Kenyan English? A Pilot Study in Research Methodology. *English World-Wide* 20(2). 217–236.

Skandera, Paul. 2003. *Drawing a map of Africa: Idiom in Kenyan English*. Tübingen: Gunter Narr Verlag.

Smith, Charles & Gloria M. Emezue (eds.). 2015. *New Black and African Writing*, vol. 2. Lagos: Handel Books.

Ssempuuma, Jude. 2012. Ugandan English. In Bernd Kortmann & Kerstin Lunkenheimer (eds.), *The Mouton world atlas of variation in English*, 475–482. Berlin: Mouton de Gruyter.

Swan, Michael. 2016. *Practical English usage*, 4th edn. Oxford: Oxford University Press.

Trudgill, Peter. 1974. *The social differentiation of English in Norwich*. Cambridge: Cambridge University Press.

Trudgill, Peter. 2000. *Sociolinguistics: An introduction to language and society*, 4th edn. London: Penguin.

Upton, Clive. 2008. Received Pronunciation. In Bernd Kortmann & Clive Upton (eds.), *Varieties of English 1: The British Isles*, 237–252. Berlin: Mouton de Gruyter.

Wa Mberia, Kithaka. 2001. *Kifo kisimani*. Nairobi: Marimba Publications.

Wa Thiong'o, Ngugi. 1982. *Devil on the cross*. Nairobi: East African Educational Publishers.

Wardhaugh, Ronald. 2010. *An introduction to sociolinguistics*, 6th edn. Oxford: Wiley-Blackwell.

Wells, John C. 1982. *Accents of English, volume I: An introduction*. Cambridge: Cambridge University Press.

Wells, John C. 2014. *Sounds interesting: Observations on English and general phonetics.* Cambridge: Cambridge University Press.
Whiteley, Wilfred H. (ed.) 1974. *Language in Kenya.* Nairobi: Oxford University Press.
Zuengler, Jane E. 1982. Kenyan English. In Braj B. Kachru (ed.), *The other tongue: English across cultures*, 112–124. Urbana: University of Illinois Press.
Zwartjes, Otto. 1997. *Love songs from Al-Andalus: History, structure, and meaning of the kharja.* Leiden: Brill.

Index

accent-fixing suffix 48
accent-attracting suffix 48
(as) compared to used for *than* 111
accent-neutral suffix 47
additional meanings in KenE 159
– *(police) abstract, docket, double-decker, escort, flyover, hotel, (bus) stage, take-away, slippers, avail, enjoin, include, learn, overlap, record a statement, rewind, school, tried and tested, majorly, severally, by all means, cap., leave alone, where/when the rubber meets the road, wow,* etc. 159
– adjectives and APs 165
– adverbs and adverbials 165
– analogy 166
– in-group jargon 167
– literal, compositional formation 166
– logical derivation 167
– miscellaneous structures 166
– nouns and NPS 159
– phonetic similarity 167
– prepositions and PPs 165
– regional, urban dialects? 171
– semantic expansion 166
– semantic similarity 167
– social dialects? 167
– verbs and VPs 162
adjectives used as nouns 80
– *second born, secretarial, primary, secondary* 80
adoption of English names 26
African varieties of English 52, 63, 68, 88
– Black South African (BlSAfE) 68
– Cameroon English (CamE) 52
– Ghanaian English (GhE) 88
– Indian South African English (IndSAfE) 68
– Nigerian English 52
– Tanzanian English (TzE) 63
– Ugandan English (UgE) 63
Aldrup, Marit 83
all what for *all that* 127
all-embracing and vague anaphoric reference 182

– *the same, whereby, this (is), is where, is when* 182
AmE as *much as* for BrE *much as* 129
AmE vs BrE influence on KenE vocabulary 172
anaphora phenomena in KenE 179, 182
– all-embracing and vague anaphoric reference 182
– underuse of anaphoric reference forms 179
anaphoric phenomena in KenE 182
– no referent at all for *another* 182
Angogo, Rachel 63
appropriation of English 18
as such for *therefore* 126
aspects of connected speech in KenE 52
– Any assimilation, elision, and r-linking in KenE? 58
– Are there phonological styles in KenE? 57
– avoidance of rising intonation after tag questions 56
– frequent use of level tone 54
– infrequent use of rising tone 55
– intonation 53
– Is KenE rhythm syllable-timed or stress-timed? 52
– misplacement of the tonic stress 54
– rarity of complex tones 57
– rhythm 52
aspects of the noun phrase 71, 77
– noun+noun structure used for the genitive's structure 77
– omission of the definite article 71
aspects of the noun phrase in KenE 70
– adjectives used as nouns 79
– complementiser *that* used after nouns that do not require it 80
– pluralisation of the premodifying noun 79
– the N+N sequence 79
aspects of the prepositional phrase 105
– omission of prepositions and PPs 108
– one preposition shared by two conjuncts 108

- repetition of preposition at the end of arelative clause 107
- use of adifferent preposition 106
- Any "dead" or "vanishing" prepositions in KenE? 110

aspects of the verb phrase in KenE 81, 100, 101, 102, 103, 104, 105
- *as follows* instead of an object or a complement clause 96
- *be as a result of* for *be a result of* 97
- *can/could be able* for *can/could* 102
- continuous tenses after *This is the first time* 101
- *could* and *would* used for *should* 87
- *for*-introduced PP before direct object NP 92
- infinitive marker *to* for preposition *to* 105
- infinitive marker *to* omitted after *enable* + direct object 97
- infinitive used for *must* and *should* 100
- intransitive verbs used transitively 98
- lack of tense backshift 90
- *never* for *did not* 104
- NP complements instead of PP ones 94
- obligatory complements omitted 90
- overuse of modal *shall* 85
- past-tense forms equated with past-time meanings 103
- PP complements used instead of NP ones 93
- progressive *-ing* marked on stative verbs 82
- selection restrictions violated 94
- *shall* and *will* used after *if* and conjunctions of time 89
- *What you do ...* for *What you should do is ...* 100
- *who* used for *whom* 99
- *would* used for *will* and other modals 87

Atichi, Alati 140
audio samples 240

basing on used for *based on* 125
Bauer, Laurie 49
Biber et al. 81
Bobda, Simo Augustine 43

Bulili, Ethel 140

cinema 17
code-mixed set phrases 140
- *Jamhuri Day, Madaraka Day, Sheria House, Biashara Street*, etc. 140
codemixing 17
code-mixing Swahili words into English 199
- as a rhetorical-force device in KenE discourse 199
coexistence of KenE lexical features and their StdIntE variants 168
coinages of KenE 150, 152, 156, 158
- *academics, co-wife, failure to which, night runner, polite notice, shrubbing, sitting allowance, slay queen, add salt to injury, ashame sb, be cast in stone, be kidded, be married somewhere, be on sb's neck, lie low like en envelope, pick (a phone call), preach water and drink wine, raise the red flag, wreck havoc, second last, of which, all protocols observed, (last/next week) but one, don't count your chicks before they hatch, you can take it to the bank,* etc. 149
- adjectives and APs 156
- adverbs and adverbials 156
- compositional meaning 158
- ephemeral life 158
- figurative meaning 158
- miscellaneous structures 156
- nouns and NPs 150
- prepositional phrase 156
- verbs and VPs 152
colonial 3
commercial advertising 17
Commission 6, 8
- the Gachathi 8
- the Mackay 8
- the Ominde 6
complementiser *that* after verbs that do not require it 95
- *appeal, alert, cheat,* etc. 95
compound stress rule/Chomsky-Halle rule 49
consonant-related pronunciations 40
- absence of intrusive /r/ 41

Index — 255

- inserting avowel to split aconsonant cluster 43
- letter <g> 42
- little (or no) aspiration after voiceless plosives in KenE 44
- non-realisation of /l/ in the last syllable 43
- non-rhotic nature of KenE /r/ 41
- silent <l> in KenE 45n16
- substituting /dʒ/ for /ʒ/ in words of French origin 42
- substituting /gz/ for /ks/ 43
- substituting the voiceless /ʃ/ and /s/ for the voiced /ʒ/ and /z/ 41
- voiced plosives in KenE 45
- VOT values for plosives in KenE 44

Constitution of Kenya 6
contracted vs non-contracted forms 202
- as written-English features in spoken KenE 202
- some contracted forms seemingly non-existent in spoken KenE 202

contracted vs. non-contracted verb forms in SPOKEN ICE-K 203
Cruttenden, Alan 29
cultural factors 11

definite article in KenE 71, 72, 73, 74, 75
- addition before *Standard English* and *Almighty God* 75
- omission before abbreviations 71
- omission before *English language* 74
- omission before *majority of* 73
- omission before *Nairobi area* 74
- omission before *reason ...* 75
- omission before specific phrases 73
- omission before unique institutions 72
demography 11
digital 9
- migration 9
discourse features of KenE 179
- anaphora phenomena, polite requests and forms of address, code-mixing Swahili words into KenE discourse, contracted verb forms in spoken KenE 179
Dynamic Model 1

East African English (EAfE) 63
English in Kenya 1
English names as family names 17
Engsh 17
eWAVE survey 64

fiction 17
Fischer, Allestree 63n1
formal vs. informal KenE vocabulary 171

geography 11
Gorman, Thomas P. 1
Greenbaum, S and R Quirk 89
Gut, Ulrike 47

Habwe, John 198n15
Hancock, Ian 63
Higgins, Christina 1
high-flown English 17
Hilbert M and M Krug 82
Hocking, Benjamin DW 73
Hoffmann, Thomas 1
How is it called for *What is called*? 128
Huber, Magnus 45
Huber M and K Dako 119
Hudson-Ettle, Diana 63
Hundt M and K Vogel 82

indefinite article 76
- omission after *such* 76
indefinite article in KenE 76
- omission in set phrases/idiomatic phrases 76
indigenous 3
inflections in KenE 67
- addition of suffix *-ly* 69
- *furnitures, equipments*, etc. 68
- *oftenly, anyhowly, joblessly* 69
- omission of plural *-s* from fixed expressions and idioms 69
- plural *-s* added to non-count nouns and idiomatic expressions 67
International Corpus of English (ICE) 70
- Kenyan component (ICE-K) 70
intransitive verb used transitively 98
- *to be rained on* 98

isn't it as an invariant question tag 119
Itumo, Joshua 32

KenE 33, 35, 36
– acoustic studies 33
– "marginal schwa" 35
– vowels vis-à-vis Wells's lexical sets 36
Kenya 13, 15, 16
– cultural factors 16
– languages of 15
– population of 13
– religious affiliation 16
– tribes of 13
Kenya National Bureau of Statistics 11
– KNBS 11
Kenya Population and Housing Census 11
Kisumu 12
Kortmann, Bernd 64
Kramsch, Claire 16

lack of number agreement 64, 65, 66
– a plural verb used for a singular subject 66
– a singular verb used for a plural subject 64
– between a noun and its determiners/pronouns 66
– context-dependent 65
language of 20, 22, 23, 24
– audio-visual media 20
– cinema 23
– music 22
– religious preaching 24
language of urban youth 25
– Engsh 25
– Sheng 25
language policy in education 4
lexis and semantics of KenE 176
– the most visible features not the most characteristic 176
loan expressions in KenE 139
– a common-core list 139
– *askari, baraza, bodaboda, chang'aa, harambee, jembe, jua kali, Kamukunji, matatu, panga, shamba, sukumawiki, ugali, wananchi, Wanjiku*, etc. 141
– dictionary sources 140
loanwords 17

local vernaculars 6
Lunkenheimer, Kerstin 64
Luopean English 26

Mazrui, Alamin M. & Ali M. Mazrui 1
Mbangwana, Paul 109
Mesthrie, Rajend 70
Mombasa 12
morphological and syntactic features of KenE 63
– lack of number agreement 64
M-Pesa 17
music 17
Mwangi, Serah 106

N+N used for N's +N 78
– *women groups, women representatives, three years experience,* 78
newspaper 19
– *Daily Nation* 19
– *Taifa Leo* 19
– *The Standard* 19
Ngugi wa Thiong'o 20
no/not/none ... nor for *no/not/none ... or* 120
Non-use of *It is I who am* and *It is you who are* 121
non-use of subject auxiliary inversion 113
NP complements instead of PP ones 94
– *pick* for *pick up* 94
Nyutho, Ngure Edwin 23

obligatory complements omitted after 91
– *reach, appreciate*, etc. 91
Ochieng, Philip 94
Oduor, Jane 8
Ogolla, Margaret A 18
Okombo, Okoth 47
other repeated in the *other ... than* structure 125
Otiso, Zipporah 195
overgeneralised pronunciations 39, 40
– <ice> ending 40
– <mine> ending 39
– <ude> ending 39
– letter <u> 40
– letter <i> in *immigration* 39
– *national, rationing* 40

– past tense form <ew> 39
– *peasant* 40
– yod addition in KenE 39

past participial *gotten* vs. *got* 128
past-tense forms equated with past-time meanings 104
– *would* for *would have* and *could* for *could have* 104
period 1, 5
– post-independence 5
– pre-independence 1
pronoun (subj.) + pron. (obj.) sequence in subj. position 117
phase 1
– exonormative stabilization 1
– foundation 1
Plag, Ingo 49
plural *we* for singular *I* 119
polite request structures in KenE 185
– *please* + imperative, *kindly* + imperative, use of verb *request*, "*kindly, please*" + verb 185
polite request structures in the ICE-K 187
polite requests in KenE 191
– partially local culture 191
post-verbal adverbial *there* for dummy *there* 127
PP complements instead of NP ones 93
– *discuss about, research on, emphasise on,* etc. 93
president 7, 8, 13n2
– Daniel arap Moi 8
– Jomo Kenyatta 7
– Uhuru Kenyatta 13n2
print media 17
progressive *-ing* marked on stative verbs 83, 84
– *Could you be knowing ...?* 84
– lexically-conditioned 83
– variability based on linguistic context 83
pronoun (subj.) + pron. (obj.) sequence in subj. position 117
– *Me I ..., Us we ..., Them they ...* 117
pronunciation of Kene
– national features 31
pronunciation of KenE 33

– avoidance of central RP vowels 31
– devoicing fricative sounds 45
– FACE dipththong 35
– gender as a variable 43
– miscellaneous words 48
– phoneme mergers 40
– qualitative and quantitative mergers 34
– shortening of long RP vowels, monophthongisation of diphthongs 33
– subnational features 30
– substituting /a/ for the RP schwa /ə/ 32
– voicing the voiceless /ks/ 45
– vowel-related 31
– words ending in <age> 45

Quirk et al 91

radio 17
radio stations 21
relative determiner *whose* 115
religious preaching 17
resumptive pronouns 115
Rift Valley 12
Roach, Peter 29
Rumford, James 175

Safaricom 17
Sailaja, Pingali 53
Sand, Andrea 70
Schmied, Josef 1
Schneider, Agnes 88
Schneider, Edgar 1
schwa in KenE 32
selection restrictions violated 94
– *to facilitate sb, to interrogate sth,* etc. 94
Skandera, Paul 1
social media communication 20
spelling pronunciations 36, 37, 38, 45
– consonant-related 45
– definite article *the* 37
– letter <i> 38
– letter <o> 37
– letter <u> 38
– letter sequence <au> 36
– past tense forms *ran* and *had* 38
– pronouncing the silent <b> 45
– pronunciation of the letter <h> 45

- letter sequence <ia> 38
- letter sequence <ious> 38
- unstressed letter <e> 36
- vowel-letter-related 36

Ssempuuma, Jude 63n1

Standard International English (StdIntE) 71

summary of morphological and syntactic features of KenE 132

survey of previous work 209

Swahili 6, 7
- role for 6
- the national language 7

Swan, Michael 78

television 17

the much (I can do) 124

those ones for *those, these, they*, etc. 122

titles and forms of address in KenE 191
- first name, surname alone, *Mr, Dr, Dr + first name, professor, bwana, sir, madam, miss, ma'am, teacher, mwalimu, daktari, doc, honourable/ hon./, mheshimiwa* 191

titles and forms of address in the ICE-K 197

traces of other Englishes in KenE vocabulary 175
- Any trace of Nigerian English and South African English? 176
- Indian English 175

transposition of idioms 17

TV station 20, 21
- Inooro TV, Kameme TV, Kass TV, STN 21

- KBC, NTV, KTN, Citizen TV, K24 20

underuse of anaphoric reference forms
- personal pronoun *it*, demonstrative pronoun *those*, pro-VP "*do*", gapping 180

Upton, Clive 29

use of a different preposition 106
- *to admit sb at a hospital, to result to*, etc. 106

vowel-related overgeneralised pronunciations 39

Wells, John C. 29

word stress 47
- verbs ending in <ise>/<ise>, <ify> 47
- adjectives ending in <itive> 48
- adjectives ending in -*able* 47
- adjectives ending in -*ative* 48
- compound nouns stressed on the second element 50
- compound words 49
- miscellaneous cases 51
- names of months 47
- noun-verb contrasts 51
- nouns ending in -*ism* 48
- no stress shift in compounds 50
- verbs ending in <ate> 47
- words in which KenE stress placement is predictable 47

Zuengler, Jane 78

www.ingramcontent.com/pod-product-compliance
Lightning Source LLC
Chambersburg PA
CBHW060946230426

43665CB00015B/2088